W9-CLB-301

THE SOCIAL WELFARE INSTITUTION

The Social Welfare Institution

AN INTRODUCTION

Fourth Edition

Ronald C. Federico

Iona College and the
Westchester Social Work Education Consortium

CARNEGIE LIBRARY
LIVINGSTONE COLLEGE
SALISBURY, N. C. 28144

D.C. Heath and Company
Lexington, Massachusetts   Toronto

122119

PHOTO CREDITS

Cover: © 1983 Dick Luria

Author: Howard Studio, Inc., New Rochelle, New York

Chapter openers: 1. James Holland/Stock, Boston
2. Julie O'Neil/Stock, Boston
3. Courtesy, The Oakland Museum, Dorothea Lange Collection
4. Meri Houtchens-Kitchens/The Picture Cube
5. Evelyn Hofer/Archive Pictures, Inc.
6. Barbara Alper/Stock, Boston
7. Nick Sapieha/Stock, Boston

Copyright © 1984 by D. C. Heath and Company.
Previous editions copyright © 1980, 1976, and 1973 by D.C. Heath and Company

All rights reserved. No part of this publication may be reproduced or transmitted in any form or by any means, electronic or mechanical, including photocopy, recording, or any information storage or retrieval system, without permission in writing from the publisher.

Published simultaneously in Canada.

Printed in the United States of America.

International Standard Book Number: 0-669-06748-2

Library of Congress Catalog Card Number: 83-83271

TO Kathryne Wheatley

who helped to lay the foundation that has made this book possible

ABOUT THE AUTHOR

Ronald Federico received his Ph.D. in sociology from Northwestern University, where he studied under a fellowship from the National Institute of Mental Health. Prior to his doctoral studies, Dr. Federico earned his Master of Social Work degree at the University of Michigan in the program supported by the Russell Sage Foundation to combine social work education with study in the social sciences. He also graduated *magna cum laude* from Yale University with a Bachelor of Arts degree.

Dr. Federico has been at the forefront of social work education for the past decade. He has served on major bodies of the Council on Social Work Education, including the Board of Directors and special committees formed to study the future of the organization. He has also been active in the National Association of Social Workers at the local, state, and national levels. He is a member of the Academy of Certified Social Workers, and has been a frequent guest speaker and workshop leader for professional and educational groups. Dr. Federico has been an active consultant for social work educational programs, and has worked extensively as an on-site evaluator of social work programs seeking accreditation.

As Administrative Assistant to Dr. Betty L. Baer while she directed the nationally significant Undergraduate Social Work Curriculum Development Project, Dr. Federico was exposed to the thinking of social work educators around the country. This background, combined with his own experience as an educator, practitioner, and active participant in social work professional organizations, has enriched his writing. In addition to this book, Dr. Federico has written a number of books and articles in the fields of social work and sociology. He is currently on the faculty at Iona College, one of the schools participating in the innovative Westchester Social Work Education Consortium in Westchester County, New York.

During the life of this text, the structure of educational programs in social welfare has changed substantially. The increasing importance of social welfare in American society has led to the development of specialized professions, each meeting needs in particular areas of human behavior. Medicine is a good example. As medical technology has developed, so have medical specialties. Many doctors now specialize in heart surgery, respiratory problems, specific forms of cancer, kidney diseases, cataracts, and so forth. Support staff have also become increasingly specialized, so that teams of nurses work with surgeons performing specific kinds of surgery, technicians carry out specific types of treatment or therapy, and other kinds of specialists do the complex laboratory work to identify diseases. Specialization has also occurred in the other social welfare professions. The rapidly developing field of gerontology (work with the elderly) has people trained to work in nursing homes, to provide recreational services geared to the needs and abilities of the elderly, and to respond to the special needs of the elderly for physical care and proper nutrition. At the same time that specialization has been taking place, people in the helping professions have been becoming increasingly concerned with the needs of the whole person. Particular problems or needs have to be integrated, so that the person functions well in all areas of life. As a result, one hears about "holistic medicine" and self-help groups that seek to help people maintain their overall sense of well-being during specific kinds of crises, such as divorce or alcoholism. Sometimes it is difficult not to let our technology outstrip our ability to digest its meaningful contribution to our lives. As a result, maintaining a balance between the need for specialized and holistic treatment is often difficult.

These changes have profoundly affected career options in social welfare. The proliferation of social welfare professions, and the growth of specializations within specific professions, have created many exciting options for students thinking about a social welfare career. This fourth edition of *The Social Welfare Institution* consciously addresses this range of choices, to help students understand their options. At the same time, it continues to reinforce the perspective of previous editions that there is a base of knowledge about social welfare that anyone entering *any* of the social welfare professions must have. Understanding the structure of social welfare in our society is fundamental to understanding how any particular profession fits into social welfare as a whole. And because each profession contributes to the same overall goals, professionals in the many specific professions must know how to work together effectively.

This edition also responds to another development on college campuses. As higher education seeks to prepare its graduates to function effectively in a rapidly changing technological world, the need to understand social welfare has become apparent. No longer is social welfare relevant only for students wishing to enter one of the social welfare professions. Social welfare is increasingly responsible for ensuring an adequate quality of life for all members of our society. When change creates inevitable gaps and lags in people's ability to understand and cope with what is happening in their lives, it is the social welfare system that helps them to adapt. No longer is social welfare something that affects only a few; now it is a part of everyone's life throughout the entire life cycle. If social welfare is to continue to meet society's needs, and if people are to know how to use it most effectively, they need to learn about it. As a result, one of this book's goals is to provide the basic content that *everyone* should know in order to be an informed citizen.

Meeting both the needs of students exploring specific career choices and the general-education needs of all students may at first seem an almost impossible task, but further thought suggests that these two types of needs may not be all that different. Students considering a social welfare career need to carry on a dialogue with those who may have a healthy skepticism about specific social welfare programs or even about social welfare in general. Similarly, students who have never seriously considered a social welfare career need to hear from their peers why social welfare work is worthy of a lifetime's career commitment. Such dialogues can help to create social welfare professionals attuned to efficiently and effectively delivering services in ways that people can best use them. They can also educate an electorate that will understand and support a meaningful social welfare structure.

Objectives of This Edition

The Social Welfare Institution, Fourth Edition, has five major objectives:

1. *To help students understand social welfare as a social institution.* This perspective emphasizes the importance of the social welfare institution in the social structure and the way it reflects cultural values, existing knowledge, and political and economic processes. This approach provides the book's basic organization. Chapter 1 describes the functions of social welfare, whereas Chapters 2 and 3 focus on its structure. Chapters 4 and 5 examine the knowledge and value base of the social welfare institution. Chapter 6 helps readers relate the structural characteristics of social welfare to themselves, especially those considering a career in one of the helping professions. Chapter 7 integrates function, structure, and societal mandate by looking at contemporary issues facing our society and at how the social welfare institution can help address them.

2. *To help students examine their own value orientations, beliefs, behaviors, and potential for change.* Social welfare is heavily influenced by values at the individual, family, community, and societal levels. This book encourages students to explore how these levels of values differ, and how each influences social welfare. Their own personal values will strongly influence their behavior as social welfare professionals or as citizens who influence social welfare decision making.

3. *To help students develop logical, rational, knowledge-based approaches to analyzing social welfare.* This book encourages students to understand the interplay of knowledge and values. It will help them to think through their obligation, as educated people, to use knowledge in making decisions about their own behavior.

4. *To help students relate their knowledge about social welfare to that obtained in other courses and through life experiences.* This fourth edition focuses most directly on the knowledge foundations of social welfare derived from the biological, behavioral, and social sciences. It also explores the significance of social welfare within a broader, humanistic, liberal-arts perspective.

5. *To help students understand the demands and rewards of social welfare careers, including a reasonable estimate of future career opportunities.* A thorough analysis of all career opportunities is impossible, of course, but this book uses a diverse group of social welfare careers to illustrate the range of opportunities that exist.

Comparing this New Edition to the Previous One

This fourth edition adopts a more integrative view than did the third edition, focusing more clearly on social welfare as a social institution, the organizing framework for the book. Chapter 1 includes information about professions in social welfare other than social work, although the latter is still strongly represented. Chapter 2 uses a more systematic and systemic approach to understanding the structure of social welfare services, so that the implications for a range of social welfare professions can be more easily understood. Chapter 3 reorganizes the history of the development of social welfare to emphasize major trends, updated to include the significant changes that occurred during the 1970s and 1980s. Chapter 4 includes content on the helping process, referred to in previous editions as practice methods. It examines the common elements in helping and some of the ways that these are adapted in a number of specific helping professions. Chapter 5 further integrates knowledge foundations around the general categories of biological, psychological, social structural, and cultural knowledge. Chapter 6 considers a broader range of social welfare professions than previous editions, examines the nature of social welfare careers, and assesses future opportunities in these various areas. Chapter 7 continues to identify contemporary issues but now emphasizes the role of social welfare in addressing them.

Popular and useful teaching/learning tools have been retained and improved; these include end-of-chapter summaries, study questions, and recommended readings. The exhibits have also been retained, but they have been revised to provide a better balance between data about service delivery, descriptions of programs, and case material. They are now also grouped at the end of each chapter in sections called "Reflections on Social Welfare." The text refers to them by number, and their new location avoids interrupting the textual discussion. Most chapters now have tables, charts, and figures, providing illustrative data, in the body of the text. These are usually much briefer than exhibits.

This fourth edition retains an appendix, but it has been substantially modified. It consists of case material of several kinds, each of which is preceded by substantial discussion to help the reader relate the actual life events to conceptual content discussed in the body of the book. This new approach better integrates content about helping objectives, value systems, helping methods, and structural characteristics of the social welfare institution. The fourth edition also includes more photos, which were added for two reasons: They help to convey the substantive content of the book in a visual and affective manner, providing a valuable supplement to the conceptual and objective approach used in the text. They also help to make the book more visually interesting and attractive, inviting the reader into the text. Finally, the *Instructor's Guide* for the book has been completely rewritten to reflect the new organization and focus of the parent text.

My objective has always been to produce a book that students would find appealing, informative, and useful, and I believe that this edition is more effective in these respects than earlier ones. The text has been thoroughly revised to make the writing more lively and flow more smoothly. This is a basic textbook whose mission is to stimulate, help, and encourage. In this way students can understand as fully as possible the importance of the dynamic, but sometimes complex, social welfare system this nation has created. The book continues to be balanced and objective in its analysis of the social welfare institution, although the groundwork is laid for the further analysis of controversial issues through other assignments or other courses.

Acknowledgments

I hope that every educator and student will always feel free to tell me whether the book accomplishes its goals and to suggest ways for it to do so more effectively. This latest edition is certainly much richer because of such input in the past. It is the result of a process of growth and development that began more than ten years ago. Everyone who contributed to any of the earlier editions has influenced this one. I am particularly grateful to the instructors and students who, over the years, have taken the trouble to share with me their experiences in using one of the earlier editions of this book. Comments and suggestions by Dean Pierce, DSW, have also been of special help in my work on this revision. The enthusiasm and continued support of my publisher has also been significant in my having the opportunity to continue to improve the book. Nancy Osman, my current editor, has been especially helpful and supportive. In addition, the many people who have worked in various capacities during the actual production of this and earlier editions deserve my sincere gratitude for the many ways in which they have helped to make each book both attractive and accurate. I extend particular thanks to Bryan Woodhouse, production editor; Eve Mendelsohn, permissions; Sharon Donahue, photo researcher; and Mark Fowler, designer.

It would be nice to think that the various editions of this book have been mine exclusively. However, in spite of the work I have put into them, they are best understood as the joint product of many people, all working to help me produce instructional tools that will help improve the quality of this nation's social welfare system. To everyone who has participated in this process, thank you.

R.C.F.

CONTENTS

2   The Structure of Social Welfare   39

3   The Historical Development of Social Welfare   89

4 The Helping Process in Social Welfare   149

7   Social Welfare's Role in Shaping the Future   237

THE SOCIAL WELFARE INSTITUTION

Introduction

This book is about social welfare, a topic on which people frequently have strong opinions but little accurate knowledge. In the next chapter we will begin our formal analysis of what precisely social welfare means, but for now it will be helpful to look at some of the reasons it is important to you. Perhaps the most important reason for learning about social welfare is that it is a part of everyone's life. We are all enmeshed in a network of services and financial structures that affect what happens to us and our lives. Let's look at some examples:

- If we get sick, the kind of medical services available to us are determined by the structure of our social welfare system.
- The amount of income tax we have to pay each April is strongly influenced by our society's approach to social welfare.
- Whether or not we succeed in school is related to social welfare service-delivery structures.
- The availability of services like police and fire protection or public transportation is a function of social welfare.
- The availability of jobs and the quality of our work lives is affected by social welfare programs.
- When and how we die reflects decisions made about social welfare services.

1

We can see from these examples that the quality of our lives is very much influenced by what occurs in the social welfare system. As a result, the more we know about that system the more likely it is that we can use it effectively to improve the quality of our lives.

Understanding the Need for Social Welfare

It might seem that being concerned about what happens to us, however natural it might be, is narrow and even selfish. Actually, understanding social welfare helps us to see that this is not so. For one thing, ensuring that we have access to needed resources—such as adequate employment, for example—often requires establishing service-delivery structures that are useful for the many other people who are similar to us. For example, when you graduate from college you will want a job, just as most other college graduates do. To the degree that all groups in society realize that social welfare is a part of their lives, all are motivated to work for a service-delivery structure that effectively meets their needs. The result is likely to be an approach to social welfare that is universally useful. But looking out for ourselves helps create better services for others in another way, as well. Part of what makes our lives easier and more satisfying is knowing that our loved ones are well cared for. Seeing their children healthy and able to grow and develop is important to parents. Knowing that elderly parents will end their lives with adequate physical care and in socially rewarding environments is a concern held by all. Being able to share loving, mutually supportive relationships with whatever other adults we choose is also a universal goal. In these instances, all of which depend on the social welfare system in some way, meeting our own needs helps improve the quality of life for others.

One reason, then, for being concerned about social welfare is that it affects our own lives very directly. Another reason is that it seems to be in the news so much. We read in the newspapers about homeless people or alcoholism on the job, and we may even get impatient with the seemingly endless debates about how to deal with these problems. Racial and ethnic conflict seems to be never ending, in spite of numerous shocking incidents involving injury and death. Arguments go back and forth about income tax cuts, inflation rates, and unemployment, leaving us bewildered and anxious about our own financial security and future. And of course we all read about "welfare families" and "welfare cheats," perhaps getting angry at people who seem to exploit services beyond the legitimate need they might have for them. In addition to reading in the newpaper about these aspects of social welfare, or watching television reports about them, our friends and coworkers frequently discuss them. People often have strong feelings about social welfare, especially when values of independence, hard work, and self-sufficiency become involved. At times it seems as if feelings dominate, and that the facts are hard to locate. Learning about social welfare in this book will help to present the facts that can provide a context for discussions with friends, and that can make TV and newspaper accounts more understandable.

In addition to learning about social welfare because it affects you and your loved ones, and because it will help you to understand what you read and what you hear, there is perhaps the most important reason of all—because you are interested. Many people realize that they are fascinated by human behavior. They love to "people watch," and they can be deeply touched by the accounts of human accomplishments and human misery that fill books, movies, magazines, television, and newspapers. Some wonder whether they would like to work with people in a helping capacity, perhaps as a social worker, nurse, or teacher. Others know that their careers will be in other areas, like accounting, business management, or office work. Nevertheless, they are fascinated by people, even though they don't plan to pursue helping professions, and they realize that they have to get along with others, no matter what occupation they choose. For those interested in people, the study of social welfare will provide endless insights and delights. It will help to explain why people act as they do and how their behavior is influenced by the social welfare structures in which they are enmeshed.

Whether you study social welfare because you think you ought to, or because you simply want to, you will find it rewarding and useful. At times you may not find it fun, however. The study of social welfare often evokes strong feelings that spring from each person's distinctive value system. You may get angry because we do too much for people, or because we do too little. You may find yourself disgusted by what some people do, and you might even wonder whether we are capable of solving our human problems. At times you may shake your head in amazement at the decisions that are made about social welfare that seem to make little sense and that appear to be counterproductive. Whatever feelings emerge, keep looking for the reasons that underlie them and for the facts that will help you manage your feelings more effectively. In the study of social welfare, all feelings are equally valuable. Whatever your feelings are, as they emerge you will be learning about **yourself** as well as about social welfare—and what is more fascinating or more useful than learning more about ourselves?

The Nature of Social Welfare

By the end of 1982, the unemployment rate in the United States was 10.8 percent, a postwar record (King, 1982). One of the results of this economic problem has been the creation of an increasing tide of homeless Americans, people who have lost their jobs and homes and who crisscross the country seeking work. These people, sometimes called the "new poor" or "new homeless," are people who have generally been employed and stable, but who are now desperately searching for economic opportunities to replace those that have evaporated in their home communities due to the economic recession (Dusky, 1983; Peterson, 1982). As we will discover in Chapter 3, this phenomenon is not unlike what happened in the Great Depression of the 1930s.

What is very different about those forced out of work and even out of their homes and communities in 1982 compared to 1932 is the

Social change is constantly creating new needs. This homeless woman in Phoenix is one of a growing number of people who have been hurt financially and emotionally by the nation's recent economic problems. (Douglas Kirkland/Sygma)

societal response to their need. Whereas the Depression resulted in the passage of the Social Security Act, this society's most comprehensive effort to provide for the needs of its citizens, the "new poor" in 1982 encountered a very different societal response.

> Phoenix does not welcome transients. At one point it closed all its public shelters and only recently, under pressure, allowed one to open. The city also passed a law making it a misdemeanor to lie down in public. It has declared garbage public property, making it illegal to pick through it, and there have been proposals to spray the dumpsters with kerosene, making the refuse inedible, to discourage foraging (Peterson, 1982).

It is these differences in a society's approach to meeting the needs of its members that defines the nature of social welfare in that society.

Social welfare is a way of thinking. It is a society's collective image of its responsibility to its own members. This image can be very limited or very inclusive in terms of *what groups* will be helped, and *which of their needs* will be addressed. For example, people often see children as needing society's assistance because they are so vulnerable. Yet physically limited adults are less frequently helped in spite of their sometimes considerable vulnerability. Even children receive variable aid. Because the family has been assigned major responsibility for the care of its offspring, children raised in families with little income or little affection may be exposed to grave physical and emotional stresses. Yet society is reluctant to intervene, as illustrated by Veronica's sad story in Exhibit 1–1 in the "Reflections on Social Welfare" section at the end of the chapter.

Societies like our own are multicultural and characterized by substantial socioeconomic differences among various groups (called social classes). How, then, can we speak of a "collective image" about social welfare? Like any other aspect of societal decision making, social welfare decisions are made for the society as a whole by means of its political and economic structures. In a democratic society, all groups are thought to have representation in these structures through the voting process. This assumption has always represented more of an ideal than a reality. Racial and cultural minority groups and the poor have had less access to the political process, as a result of a complex interplay of many factors. These factors include exclusion from education, which makes it difficult to be aware of issues; language differences; laws that discriminated against certain groups (especially women and minorities of color) at the voting booth; economic manipulation of workers by employers, which is intended to influence voting; psychological terror tactics to intimidate voters; and the use of media to confuse and control people's votes.

As a result, decisions about social welfare do not always reflect accurately the needs of those who are most helpless. Bell (1983) is the most recent of a long line of scholars who have pointed out that social welfare can be used to help the well-to-do as well as (or instead of) the needy. The **manifest function** of social welfare is the one that is highly visible and intended by most people in society—to help the needy. However, there are also **latent functions** that are less visible and that serve the special needs of powerful groups that influence societal decision making. These functions include: substantial benefits for groups such as veterans to reward them for having done what they were told to do in spite of high risks; tax benefits to big businesses and wealthy individuals, to maintain the basic structure of capitalism; poverty-level benefits for the unemployed in order to pressure them into whatever jobs are available, even those with low and exploitative wages; and the maintenance of social welfare programs that provide minimal income rather than full employment, which would require more planning and cooperation by the business sector.

We can see, then, that social welfare is concerned with far more than the needy. It is integrated into the basic structure of society in ways that influence the lives of all groups—the rich and the poor, minorities and those in power. This point is explored more fully in Chapters 2 and 3. For now, we will return to the manifest function of social welfare— the primary focus of this book—because it allows us to describe and understand the structure of services that primarily address the needs of those who lack resources. The latent functions of social welfare are equally important, but they are best explored in courses that focus on social policy, organizational behavior, and political and economic deci- sion making. This book will mention these functions from time to time but will not attempt to address them in depth.

The Scope of Social Welfare

Social welfare's most obvious manifest function in society is to *help*. People may need help in many areas of their lives. Some are very obvious and dramatic—a person who has had a heart attack, someone who has been the victim of a violent crime, a person threatening to commit suicide, or a physically handicapped person who is having difficulty moving about because of obstacles like steps or unlighted areas. Sometimes people need help for problems in their lives that are less obvious to outsiders—women who live in beautiful suburban homes who have become alcoholic because of a sense of isolation and lack of importance; members of minority groups experiencing subtle discrimination, which prevents them from getting satisfying employ- ment; or children who are made to feel worthless by their families. There are many ways in which people can be in need, and social wel- fare services exist to help in these situations.

Social welfare services do not exist only for specific individuals, how- ever. Communities may also be having problems, such as deteriorated housing, the loss of jobs, inadequate roads or mass transportation, poor schools, and so on. People live in groups other than com- munities, too, and problems can exist in them, as well. Workers may feel exploited by their bosses, family members may experience severe tension because of problematic marital and parent-child relationships, residents of a home for the elderly may be abused by the staff, or renters in an apartment building may feel that services are inadequate.

In these cases, social welfare services are also appropriate, although they are focused toward *groups* of people rather than specific individuals. Naturally, individuals ultimately benefit from group-focused services. Nevertheless, providing services to groups is often more effective and efficient than providing them individual by individual. Exhibit 1–2 in the "Reflections on Social Welfare" section at the end of the chapter illustrates the interplay between the individual, group, community, and even societal levels in the creation of needs for which social welfare services are helpful.

Identifying Needs

We have already seen that some needs are more obvious than others. Yet a society can only attempt to meet those needs that it knows exist and that it has decided to address, so the question of how needs become identified is an important one. Specifically, identifying needs involves at least four elements:

What Needs Exist

Needs range from the very personal, to problems in interaction among people, to community and society needs. A commonly made distinction is between personal problems and public issues. If two people are getting a divorce, it is a personal problem, but if close to half of the marriages in society are ending in divorce, it is a public issue. In other words, the creation of a comprehensive social welfare system depends on a comprehensive definition of needs.

Who Has Needs

Different groups usually have different needs. This fact results from different groups having had different experiences in the societal structure, resulting in different goals, different resources, and different obstacles. All groups interact in one way or another, however, so a comprehensive social welfare system depends on the needs of all groups being identified. Although the needs of the coal miners of Appalachia may seem far removed from the needs of urban San Franciscans, their mutual dependence on adequate energy and social order creates a level of interdependence.

The Frequency, Severity, and Impact of Needs

Some needs result from rare unanticipated events, such as floods or earthquakes. Others are chronic, such as some types of physical limitations. Some create minor disruptions in behavior, such as those we experience when our car breaks down and we have no transportation. Others may prevent us from functioning at all, as is the case with severe mental illness. Here again, the point is that needs occur in many different forms, affect different people differently, and have varying impacts on people and situations. Our goal is to try to identify all of them and to build a social welfare structure that offers help in all cases.

Who Defines the Needs

Very often, persons who are actually experiencing needs are unable to interpret them to others. This may be because they lack the ability to effectively articulate their needs (children are an example), or because they are denied access to channels through which they can communicate with others. The poor, for example, are generally too powerless and fragmented to gain access to the mass media. As a result, the needs of one group are often interpreted and expressed by others— adults "know" what children need, and social researchers frequently define needs based on their research (Valle and Mendoza, 1978). Consequently, *who* defines needs is sometimes an important determinant of *what* needs are expressed and *how* they are expressed.

   Given the necessity of defining needs in order to create social welfare services, how might we go about this task in an orderly way? Two major strategies have been used:

Research

One strategy is to use highly codified and systematized methods of scientific research to study behavior and identify need. Two approaches are possible: objective and subjective (Zimbalist, 1977). An **objective research approach** uses systematically collected data to identify needs and levels of need. A good example is the concept of a poverty level. One way to try to decide whether poverty exists, and how severe the need is, is to set a base income level below which it is assumed that people will not have adequate financial resources to meet their minimal living needs. Such levels are calculated by the government on the basis of the percentage of their income that low-income people spend on food. In 1983, this official governmentally defined poverty level was $9,900 for a family of four or $4,860 for a person living alone (*Washington Social Legislation Bulletin,* 1983). One can then measure people's incomes and say that those whose income falls below the poverty line are living in poverty—regardless of whether these people actually feel poverty-stricken.

A second approach is more **subjective.** Instead of defining a fixed income level, one can ask people to define for themselves what they feel their needs are. Notice, however, that both approaches include the orderly, systematic collection and analysis of information. Even when asking people to evaluate their own situation and its meaning for them, this task is done systematically, and all the responses are analyzed using the same methods. In general, objective research methods have tended to be more popular. It tends to be easier to collect objective data and to apply set standards to all, especially when dealing with large numbers of people. Nevertheless, we know that this method ignores many of the subtle cultural and life-style differences that exist—and which are often very important (Fitzgerald, 1983). Unfortunately, some things are not easily objectified, and no matter how convenient the objective method may be, the subjective approach remains an important and useful alternative research strategy.

Practice Feedback

Another important source of information about needs is the daily practice of social welfare professionals. In the course of their work, they are exposed to people, structures, and situations. They have the opportunity to experience firsthand the realities of the lives of a wide range of people. They see where needs are not being adequately met or are being ignored entirely, or where services are being poorly delivered. Thus it is possible for professional helping people to systematically collect information from their own practice experiences and to organize such information so that it is helpful to those with decision-making reponsibility. Being a helping person is not just working with people in need—it is also helping to identify needs and to influence those with decision-making responsibility to be more aware of, and sensitive to, existing needs. Unless this task is accomplished, the daily interactions with people seeking help may be frustrated by inadequate resources.

In spite of increasingly sophisticated methods for obtaining informa-tion about needs, we know that many needs continue to be ignored. There are several reasons for this:

1. *Many needs are difficult to locate because they are invisible.* In-visibility may be of many kinds. Geographical isolation characterizes many rural areas, as well as many economically depressed areas in cities. As most people go about their daily affairs, they never have occasion to see the realities of urban slum life and never travel through the most economically depressed rural areas (modern high-speed ex-pressways have increased this type of avoidance). As a result, it is easy to forget that these areas exist, often with desperate needs within them. A second kind of invisibility lies in needs that are the result of interpersonal behaviors that occur in private. This factor contributes to making child-abuse needs so difficult to identify, for example. It usu-ally occurs in the home, where it is invisible to outsiders. Unless there are physical symptoms visible to people who see the child outside the home, it is difficult to detect. In addition, many forms of child abuse are mental rather than physical and may be even more difficult to spot.

A third factor making needs difficult to locate is that many personal problems are either not recognized or are denied by the person who has them. Several types of physical and physically related problems are not easily identified, even by health professionals. It is common for people to have such problems and never realize it, and thus they never have occasion to make their needs known. Other problems may be recognized but may be denied because of fear or embarrassment. A woman who is abused by her husband may be afraid to report her need for help because she fears her husband will abuse her even more. A person who is losing the ability to hear may be embarrassed to admit to others that this is happening. In either case, it is difficult for outsiders to spot the problem and identify the need to the appropriate people and agencies. A final difficulty in location results from many people with needs being inarticulate and disenfranchised. Poor people are often inadequately educated and unable to read about the availability of services or to manage to get to available resources. Minority people may be so intimidated that they are reluctant to make their needs known or to participate in service structures. If these needs are not visible to helping people in other ways, these people's inability to identify their needs to others may result in these needs not being identified and therefore ignored.

2. *Some needs are difficult to identify because people find them difficult to accept.* Many needs are unpleasant, and one way to deal

with them is to deny their existence. They may be messy or depressing, or they may violate societal values. The resulting response is frequently righteous indignation rather than attempts to carefully identify the need and then try to meet it. The elderly are often seen as depressing, or sometimes as scatterbrained, disheveled, and smelly. Rather than meet their needs for adequate stimulation, physical care, and social acceptance, they may be shunted off to minimal care homes where they can be ignored. An even more dramatic example is provided in Exhibit 1–1 in the "Reflections on Social Welfare" section at the end of the chapter. This tragic account of the life and death of a preteenage prostitute exemplifies the way in which a desperate but morally offensive need can be ignored and hidden.

3. *Many needs are not identified because it is impossible to gain agreement on how to define them.* Different groups frequently have different definitions of problematic behavior, which may result from value differences that affect perceptions about what is appropriate, acceptable, or important behavior. Minority groups may define confrontation as a necessary and legitimate way to deal with oppression and discrimination; nonminority group members may define such behavior as disruptive and illegal. Women may define consciousness raising as their first priority to insure their personal integrity; men may define child rearing as a higher priority for women than their development of a personal sense of well-being.

Another source of definitional differences can result from vested interests. Groups tend to define situations in ways that maximize their own self-interests and resist definitions that will result in their own loss of power or resources. Therefore, although corporations may define assembly lines as worthwhile contributors to economic progress for everyone, workers may see them as dehumanizing and demoralizing. As long as groups have the ability to resist each other's definitions of situations, it is unlikely that a consensus will be reached about needs. On the other hand, sometimes precisely this dissensus helps people to realize the diversity of needs that exist.

Meeting Needs Through Social Welfare

Social welfare scholars have developed various frameworks for understanding human needs. One of the best known is Charlotte Towle's concept of **common human needs** (1952) in which she noted that there are basic needs shared by all for food, shelter, affection, and productive activity. More recently, the Southern Regional Education Board

(SREB) developed a similar but more fully described perspective (McPheeters and Ryan, 1971). Obviously the perspective on needs adopted by social welfare professionals may vary in type or degree from that used by others. Business people might have different views about the desirability of financial security versus risk, and politicians might have their own definitions of what families or communities ought to look like. These differences reflect their own interests and are based on their own experiences. The view of social welfare scholars is not necessarily "better," but it does reflect data collected from a wide range of research projects and practice experiences. As a result, it is likely to more accurately reflect the real experiences of most people than data coming only from personal experience and filtered through self-interest. Let us now look at needs and the role for social welfare in meeting them as conceptualized by SREB.

Health

Physical and mental well-being is basic to the ability of people to function effectively. Good health is in part a developmental process that results from genetic inheritance and an environment that supports the attainment of genetic potential. Genetic inheritance is itself influenced by conditions during gestation, such as ingestion of alcohol and other drugs, cigarette smoking, adequate nutrition, and stress. After birth, many environmental conditions affect health, such as pollution, nutrition, stress, and exposure to life-threatening conditions like natural disasters, wars, and accidents. Social welfare is, therefore, concerned with factors that affect the environment as well as those that more directly provide services for people with physical or mental health needs. As a result, programs of the Environmental Protection Agency and the National Centers for Disease Control are as important as services provided by doctors, hospitals, mental hospitals, and therapists.

Financial Security

In a market economy such as our own, access to financial resources is basic to one's well-being. For most people, money is obtained by working. Social welfare programs, therefore, are often concerned with employment and training for employment. However, they also attempt to meet the needs of those who cannot work because of parenting responsibilities, infirmity, handicaps, lack of education, and so on.

Interpersonal Integrity

An individual's sense of well-being makes it possible to relate comfortably and effectively to others. Many factors—such as prejudice and discrimination, abusive treatment, lack of opportunities to develop, and genetically determined limitations—may impede a person's sense of self, however. Social welfare programs help individuals better understand themselves and the conditions under which they live, so that they can better use the resources available to them. Programs also exist to change social conditions that disadvantage people and destroy their sense of self-worth. Programs of the Civil Rights Commission are examples.

Family Integrity

The family has traditionally been the social unit of most immediate importance to individuals. Born into families, people depend on them for nurturance, physical care, and socialization. As adults, they create new families to provide for affection, emotional support, and child rearing. Increasingly, the concept of the family has been extended to include a wide range of committed relationships in which family-like interaction occurs, even though the people involved are not married or related through blood ties. Relationships among gay men or lesbian women are often of this sort, as are such patterns as single parenthood, communal living among the elderly, and group homes for runaways, battered spouses, and those with a history of mental illness, retardation, or crime. Because stable and nurturing social relationships are so important to the well-being of humans, families and family-like ties have generally been strongly supported in the social welfare system. A wide variety of economic programs, homemaker services, child-care arrangements, counseling resources, housing facilities, and health-care programs exist to support the family and family-like arrangements.

Community Integrity

Communities provide geographical units within which our social relationships occur. The structure of our government and economic system relies on communities for the provision of a wide range of resources and services in order to make them more accessible to community residents. Social welfare thus focuses many services—such as schooling, recreation, police services, economic programs, health care, and housing—in communities.

Needs and Services

Crisis Needs and Curative Services

In each of the areas just described, the level of service needed will vary by degree and type of need. Sometimes people are in **crisis,** a severe and often sudden period of need. Providing intensive services may resolve the crisis, after which few services are needed. A natural catastrophe, such as a flood or earthquake, or the sudden onset of an illness, are examples. Here social welfare services are **curative** in their focus, attempting to deal with an already-existing problem.

These Haitian refugees arriving near Miami Beach in 1981 are among the most recent of the many groups that have immigrated to this nation and that give it its unique culture. Throughout our history, immigrant groups have brought special needs, which the social welfare system has helped to identify and meet. (Randy Taylor/Sygma)

Rehabilitative Services

Needs may instead be chronic, whether severe or relatively minor. People living in economically depressed geographical areas, such as Appalachia or parts of the rural South, face a marginal existence every day. Social welfare services are needed on a regular basis to supplement their meager incomes and to help people cope with the debilitating effects of lack of opportunity and lack of hope. Ideally, such services attempt to be **rehabilitative** in that they seek to find long-term solutions to the problems. Community development programs, job-training programs, and parent-education programs are all examples of efforts to prepare people and communities to solve long-term problems.

Supportive Services

Some problems, however, are not completely solvable. People suffering from genetic brain damage, for example, will never be able to have that damage eliminated, at least not given our present level of knowledge about human physiology. In these cases, services can only be **supportive,** helping people to achieve the best possible life within the limitations they face.

Preventive Services

Perhaps the most efficient way of providing social welfare services is **preventive.** We know enough about the functioning of individuals, groups, and social structures to know what kinds of situations will create problems. For example, we know that war and economic chaos will produce migration, yet our immigration policy has been inconsistent and inadequate to handle people seeking refuge from events in Cuba, Haiti, and Central America. We know that physical abuse leads to psychological problems, yet we have not created adequate programs to prevent child and spouse abuse, to say nothing of the growing problems of "granny bashing," the abuse of the elderly. We also know that poverty is a physically and emotionally crippling condition for people and communities, yet we often continue to label it as a personal failing rather than a social problem. A preventive approach seeks to provide services that avoid the problems that otherwise have to be handled with either rehabilitative, curative, or supportive services (Prevention Report, 1982).

What Is Social Welfare?

Now we are ready to consider a definition of social welfare. William Robson (1976) wrote:

> The rights of citizens to the benefits of the welfare state must be accompanied by reciprocal duties. The need for complementary rights and obligations is particularly great in the fields of work, law and order, education, and the social services.

His statement expresses well the fact that society exists to meet the needs of its members as they are collectively defined and understood at any particular time, and recognizing that they change over time. It also emphasizes that a system of welfare services depends on the willingness of people to support it—to believe it is worthwhile, to contribute resources for it, to use its benefits in a responsible way, and to support public policy that makes a social welfare structure possible. Social welfare, therefore, seeks to balance the collective good with individual needs and desires. Finding the point at which this balance is best achieved is an ongoing activity in society since, as we have already seen, different groups have different ideas about where the balance should be.

Social welfare rests on societal definitions of the good and desirable, which in turn are embedded in societal values. These evolve over time and sometimes vary between groups in society. Keith-Lucas (1972) discusses three value bases commonly used in United States society: the capitalist-puritan, the humanist-positivist-utopian, and the Judeo-Christian. A summary of his analysis of the tenets of each and their implications for social-welfare beliefs and values is presented in Exhibit 1–3 in the "Reflections on Social Welfare" section at the end of the chapter. From these three value systems, a set of principles has emerged that are generally used in decision making about social welfare issues:

1. People should be free to choose (including the choice of failure).
2. Individuals matter, and their interests cannot be wholly subjected to those of the community.
3. People have neither the right nor the ability to judge others in terms of what they deserve.
4. Helping people find their own way is better than controlling them.
5. Feelings and personal relationships matter.
6. People should be treated like human beings, not as objects.

We have seen earlier, however, that various latent functions of social welfare may influence decision making in ways that violate some of these principles. For example, many social welfare programs *do* control people in order to create captive populations of workers, children, or the elderly. Access to such groups may be of great benefit to businesses as well as government bureaucracies.

What, then, is social welfare? It can be defined most succinctly as *improving social functioning and minimizing suffering through a system of socially approved financial and social services at all levels in the social structure.* This definition highlights three especially important characteristics of social welfare:

1. The phrase "improving social functioning and minimizing suffering" entails problem solving as well as developmental activities. As people seek to attain their life goals, they frequently confront obstacles that can be conceptualized as problems to be solved. However, the attainment of goals also involves using resources effectively. Therefore, social welfare focuses on helping people to better use their own and societal resources and does not deal only with situations in which problems exist.

2. Saying that social welfare rests on "a system of socially approved . . ." means that there can be no social welfare unless the society approves of such activities. Social groups exist and function because of agreed-upon types of interaction. In that sense, any group, small or large, is constantly renegotiating or reaffirming the collective decisions that created and maintain (or change) it. This process is also true of social welfare activities. They exist because they have been considered desirable, and their form is always dependent on the wishes of the groups of people involved, ranging from societal institutions to the smallest person-to-person interaction. As these wishes change, the mandate of social welfare changes. For example, public education for everyone is considered a basic part of our current social welfare institutional structure, but this was not true in the early history of this society.

3. The phrase "services at all levels in the social structure" suggests that social welfare activities are built into the fabric of society. Where and how they exist in society is very much part of the process of group definition and negotiation. Many social welfare activities are informally provided through such structures as the family and peer groups. Others are highly formalized, existing in structures specifically created for that purpose. But whether formal or informal, all are woven into the social structure.

It is these characteristics of social welfare—purpose, social mandate, and social structure—that enable us to talk about social welfare as a social institution. This enables us to understand social welfare as we would any other social institution: the family, education, religion, the economic institution, and the political institution. The institutional perspective will also provide a framework for the rest of the book. We will systematically examine the purposes of social welfare, its value and knowledge base, the way specific services and specific helping professions are organized around the purposes of social welfare, and the way social welfare interacts with other social institutions. In Chapter 2 we begin with service-delivery structures.

SUMMARY

This chapter has introduced you to the concept of social welfare. We have seen that it is society's response to human need. Through social welfare, society attempts to respond to needs that have been acknowledged as significant and for which society has some responsibility. Society sometimes accepts responsibility because it recognizes that people are suffering and need help. At other times, it responds because not to respond would risk social chaos. Whatever the reason for the response, social welfare entails a very wide range of services provided by many different helping professions. In the next chapter, we will look more closely at the way that social welfare services are organized.

REFLECTIONS ON SOCIAL WELFARE

The three exhibits in this section explore in more depth three aspects of social welfare raised in this chapter. The first addresses needs and how they get identified. The second also relates to needs, but looks at the differences in manifest and latent definitions of needs. The third exhibit goes into the value bases of social welfare in some depth.

EXHIBIT 1–1 The Difficulty of Identifying Needs

In the following account of the life and death of a 12-year-old prostitute, the struggle that people in and out of the social welfare system had in accepting and dealing with the needs being expressed by the young girl involved is evident. Equally evident is the girl's inability to articulate her needs and to find effective social welfare resources to meet them. In the labyrinth streets of Brooklyn and Manhattan—and many other cities—how many similar girls are hidden from view and from help?

The first time Veronica Brunson was arrested she was 11 years old. The charge was prostitution. Before another year passed, the police, unaware of her real age, arrested her 11 more times for prostitution.

At the age of 12 Veronica was dead—killed in a mysterious plunge last July from the 10th floor of a shabby midtown hotel frequented by pimps.

Veronica's death, which is being investigated as a possible murder, is one more grim crime statistic to the police. But Veronica's life, and her encounters with the city's social service and criminal justice systems in the last year, illustrate the problems and dangers confronting thousands of runaway girls and boys who turn to prostitution to survive alone on the streets of New York.

Six public and private agencies were partly aware of Veronica's difficulties and were supposedly providing aid. But none of the agencies knew her entire history and none intervened quickly enough to rescue her.

"The Brunson case is a classic example of how a kid can float through the entire system without getting any help," said Officer Warren McGinniss of the Police Department's Youth Aid Division, a specialist in runaways. "Even a

Source: Excerpted from "Veronica's short, sad life—prostitution at 11, death at 12," *The New York Times*, October 3, 1977, p. 1ff. © 1977 by the New York Times Company. Reprinted by permission.

baby-faced obvious child who claims she is 18 can parade through the entire process—arrest, fingerprinting, arraignment—without anyone asking any questions."

The six agencies—the Department of Social Services, the Board of Education, the Probation Department, the Corporation Counsel's Office, the police, and the Brooklyn Center for Psychotherapy—now cite bureaucratic barriers and communication breakdowns for their failure to act more effectively.

"You can't tell me appropriate intervention couldn't have saved her life," said the Rev. Bruce Ritter, director of Covenant House, a program assisting runaways. "The juvenile-justice and child-welfare systems in the city are chaotic. Programs just don't exist and everyone knows it."

Prostitution by 13-, 14- and 15-year-olds posing as older persons is no longer rare, but arrest for prostitution at the age of 11 is believed by vice squad detectives to be the youngest recorded here in decades.

In the summer of 1976, Veronica Brunson was 11, living in a fatherless home with her mother, Emma, who is now 34, and her brothers, Carson, 17, Douglas, 18, and Willie, 19.

Mrs. Brunson, unable to find work in her home state of North Carolina, had moved to Brooklyn when Veronica was 2. The family lived in a neatly kept, three-bedroom apartment in the Housing Authority's Marlboro Houses in Bensonhurst. In addition to their rent, the family received $318 monthly from welfare.

No Sign of Delinquency

By 1976 each of the Brunson boys had been arrested several times and had been in the juvenile courts. In contrast, Veronica, her mother, teachers and friends agreed, was well behaved, with no sign of delinquency. . . .

Pinched for money, Mrs. Brunson said she had made most of Veronica's clothing herself. "I tried to give her everything a little girl could want—clothing, food and some pocket money," Mrs. Brunson said in an interview. "She was a good little girl and if I told her to be home by six, she always was."

The Trouble Begins

At school, Veronica was a poor student. She had been left back once in the elementary grades, and in 1975 she was transferred to a special program for slow learners at Public School 253 in the Brighton Beach section. Her first year in the program went reasonably well, according to her teachers, and she was promoted to the sixth grade in June 1976.

Veronica's runaway problem suddenly began in midsummer of 1976, Mrs. Brunson said.

"One evening she came home with an older girl whose name was Diana who she met at Coney Island," Mrs. Brunson recalled. "Diana said she was 18 and wanted Veronica to spend a few days with her over the bridge (in Manhattan). I said no because I didn't think that girl Diana would be a good influence."

Several days later, Mrs. Brunson continued, Veronica disappeared for the first time, staying away from home for three days. On her return, Veronica told her mother she had stayed with her new friend Diana in Manhattan.

That July, Veronica continued to leave home for two- or three-day periods. Mrs. Brunson said that she had failed to report her daughter to the police as a missing person because Veronica would occasionally telephone her.

When the new school year began in September of 1976, Veronica failed to appear at P.S. 253. Checking into Veronica's absence, Bernard Lew, her guidance counselor, said he was told by her mother that she had been missing for more than a month. Mr. Lew said he urged Mrs. Brunson to contact the police.

First Arrested Last Fall

Police records show that Veronica was reported missing for the first time on September 19, 1976, after the school term had begun, and that her family said she had been missing for six weeks.

One day after the missing person report was filed, Veronica was arrested on a prostitution charge. A plainclothes officer said she had solicited him on West 42nd Street. The 11-year-old gave the police her real age and identity, and she was released in Mrs. Brunson's custody, pending action by the Family Court, which hears all criminal matters involving children up to the age of 16.

When Veronica returned to P.S. 253 in the autumn of 1976 her teachers and counselors were unaware of the arrest. Nevertheless, all of them said they noticed significant changes in her.

The year before she had dressed inconspicuously, almost shabbily. Now she used facial makeup and wore expensive looking, color-coordinated clothing, jewelry, high-heeled shoes and nylon stockings . . . .

The teachers, who were ignorant of her arrest, were most concerned about her chronic absenteeism, which eventually reached 121 of 180 school days that year.

Mr. Lew said that numerous telephone inquiries by staff members had been made about Veronica's absences. Her mother or brothers usually replied that the girl was ill, the teachers said.

Case Kept Out of Court

In the aftermath of the first arrest, Veronica and her mother were interviewed on October 8 by a Manhattan Family Court probation department officer. At that time, the officer decided that the matter should be kept out of the court, where Veronica could have been declared a "person in need of supervision," and possibly taken from her mother.

Instead, the probation officer, after consulting with child-welfare officials in the Social Services Department, decided that the case could be "adjusted" by sending Veronica for outpatient counseling at the Brooklyn Center for Psychotherapy, a private institution.

Under a policy of "diversion," the Probation Department tries to help youngsters without exposing them to formal court hearings before a judge.

Last autumn, the department, having made no inquiries at Veronica's school, had no inkling of her increasing truancy, her unorthodox dress or conversations with teachers about being recruited by pimps. Satisfied that the girl was getting adequate attention from the Social Services Department and the private psychotherapy center, the department closed her case in December. . . .

"She Was Still a Child"

Mr. Knepper said that Veronica had made one of her infrequent visits to his classroom on her 12th birthday, December 5, because she knew he was planning a party for her.

"She wanted that kind of attention and affection," the teacher said. "Despite all of her supposed sophistication it was obvious that she was still a child who wanted someone to help her." . . .

With Veronica no longer attending school, Mrs. Brunson and her son, Douglas, said that they were unable to prevent her running from home for brief periods. Mrs. Brunson acknowledged that she "sometimes" failed to report her daughter missing because she was confident of ultimately persuading her to return home and to school.

By May, Veronica was a familiar figure on the "Minnesota strip," a seedy part of Eighth Avenue from 40th to 50th Streets that is favored by street walkers. On the strip, Veronica, now five feet, two inches tall and weighing 110 pounds was known to other prostitutes as "Shortie" and by her childhood nickname, "Bay-Bay."

Police and court records show that between May 7 and July 18 Veronica was arrested 11 times in the midtown area. Usually she was charged with loitering for the purpose of prostitution, the most common misdemeanor used by the police to harass and temporarily remove prostitutes from the street.

Used Fictitious Names

Either through coaching from a pimp or older prostitutes, Veronica carried no identification and gave the police a fictitious name and address and said she was 18 when arrested. Two of her aliases were Vanessa Brown and Paula Brunson.

She always pleaded guilty in Criminal Court and often was released after being held overnight at a police station. But for two convictions she was sentenced to a total of 12 days, which she served among adult prisoners in the Women's House of Detention.

Only once during this series of arrests did Veronica reveal her real identity and age. Police Officer David Olenchalk, who arrested Veronica on May 12 on Eighth Avenue and 46th Street, said she wore a shoulder-length black wig and "easily passed for 18 or 19." While being booked at the Midtown North stationhouse, Veronica abruptly acknowledged her age and asked the police to call her mother.

Released in the custody of her mother, Veronica was referred for a second time to the Family Court. At an interview with a Probation Department Officer on May 20, Veronica disclosed that she had been arrested several times and had been in jail on Rikers Island.

Gerald Hecht, the city's Probation Director, said department files indicated that at the May 20 meeting, Mrs. Brunson "exhibited ambivalence about placement" of Veronica in an institution or a foster home and another interview was scheduled for a month later.

Crucial Postponement

Several hours after the May 20 interview, Veronica, once more using an alias, was arrested on a prostitution charge.

Dr. Judianne Densen-Gerber, a psychiatrist who is president of the Odyssey Institute, a group of private treatment centers for emotionally disturbed children, said that the month-long postponement by the Probation Department may have been crucial for Veronica.

"By admitting she was 12 years old, this child was clearly saying 'Help me, do something for me now.'" Dr. Densen-Gerber asserted, "Time is a critical factor for these children. They can't tolerate delay. It's like telling a person who's just had a heart attack to come back to the hospital in a month or two."

Veronica failed to appear for her scheduled interview at the Probation Department on June 29. Yet none of the three agencies—Probation, the Corporation Counsel or the Social Services Department—would petition the Family Court to have her picked up as a "person in need of supervision". . . .

With the Family Court proceedings in legal limbo, Veronica remained on the "Minnesota strip," occasionally getting arrested. Her last known arrest occurred on July 18 when she gave her age as 18. Pleading in Criminal Court to a charge of prostitution, she jumped bail rather than serve a 15-day sentence. . . .

"There are two stories on the street about her death," said Lieut. James Gallagher, the commander of the prostitution squad in Manhattan South area. "One that she was thrown out by a pimp and the other that she was having a fight with her pimp and fell out the window while sitting on the ledge."

"It's not unbelievable that a pimp would throw a girl out a window," he continued. "They brutalize girls if they hold back money, get fresh or try to get away from them."

Even in death, Veronica remained forgotten. It took the police nine days to identify her. Her fingerprints, taken in her "adult" arrests, linked her to fictitious names and addresses. Since no fingerprints are taken of children under the age of 16 there was no way of identifying her through Family Court records.

Neither Veronica's family nor any of the agencies reported her missing even after she failed to appear in Family Court. Detectives traced her after learning from Times Square prostitutes that she came from a Brooklyn Housing project and that her family name might be Brunson. . . .

EXHIBIT 1–2   Hurting by Helping

American society has traditionally been protective of women in the sense of defining female roles as primarily homebound and subservient to men. The women's movement has successfully shown the latent functions of these role definitions—preserving male dominance, limiting opportunities for women, and reducing the self-esteem of many women. These are problems that cross-cut many levels of behavior. Many women experience personal difficulties; relationships between family members are affected; the workplace is influenced; and the whole spectrum of women's activities in the social structure is shaken. This exhibit describes social welfare's response to several of these levels. It also illustrates how closely social welfare is tied to the other major institutions of society, such as the family, the political system, the economic structure, and so on.

Many people assume that as women increasingly abandon their traditional roles, previously male domains such as burglary, larceny, and auto theft are among those infiltrated by women. Thus they connect women's rights with a rise in the number of female criminals.

In fact, the relationship of sex roles to crime is much more complicated. For example, drug offenses account for the most precipitous rise in arrests of young women, having increased 5,375 percent between 1960 and 1975. A study of police handling of suspected drug users showed that women who cried, blamed their boyfriends, and otherwise acted in stereotypic ways during raids frequently convinced the police not to arrest them. Those young women who displayed "male" traits of hostility and aggression, however, were often arrested and processed.

Thus, the increase in women charged with crimes may reflect increased criminal activity, or it may result from more aggressive behavior on the part of women apprehended—or both.

These ambiguities, however, do not plague the juvenile justice system. There, young women and girls come in contact with police and the courts for a variety of reasons, and, sooner or later, their sex counts against them.

Three broad categories of youths find themselves involved in the juvenile justice system. Some are judged delinquent; some are deemed to be improperly cared for at home, or have no homes; and some are charged with "status offenses"—acts that, if performed by adults, would not be considered crimes. The word substituted for "conviction" in juvenile cases is "adjudication."

Between 70 and 85 percent of adjudicated girls in detention are status offenders, compared to a detention rate for boys charged with "children's crimes" of less than 20 percent.

Source: Excerpted from Paz Cohen, "A double standard of justice," *Civil Rights Digest,* Spring 1978, pp. 10–18.

Status offenses range from school truancy and running away to refusal to do household chores, use of "vile language," and promiscuity. An informal survey of child advocates throughout the country yielded only one instance of a boy institutionalized for sexual promiscuity, while sexuality appeared to be the underlying cause of most female referrals, even where not directly cited.

Undesirable boyfriends, staying out after curfew, wanting to get married and "incorrigibility" were among the complaints parents take to the courts along with their daughters. Pregnancy, fornication, or an abortion without parental consent falls more obviously under the category of promiscuity, but "truancy and incorrigibility," according to Mary Kaaren Jolly, staff director of the Senate Subcommittee on the Constitution, "are often nothing but buffer charges for promiscuity in girls—or the court's fear of future promiscuity." At home, in school, and throughout the many stages of the juvenile justice system, female sexuality evokes patronizing and/or biased treatment.

The Double Standard Revisited

Carol, 13, is now enrolled in a feminist counseling program. She was institutionalized due to her parents' double standard for male and female sexuality. "Boys do have it better," she says, "comparing my life to my brother's. I got sent up to an institution because I was messing around. He went out and got some girl pregnant. He was only 17 and he never got into any kind of trouble for it. She did, but he didn't."

When she has children of her own, Carol hopes they are boys:

It's just a hassle to raise girls because you've got to worry if they get caught having sex, then of course it's the girl that gets arrested on an unlawful morals charge. What do they do to the guy? Nothing.

It's just like in the family. If a man's daughter comes home and her hair's all messed up and her shirt's unbuttoned, he calls her a little slut. But if a boy comes home and tells his dad he made it with someone tonight, he says, "Oh, that's good. That's my son." That's just how it is.

Treatment of the crime of incest provides another example of the double standard. Most often, it is the girl—the victim—who is sent to a foster home while the father stays behind. And children's-rights advocate Kenneth Wooden estimates that 40 percent of the girls and young women in city and county jails who were picked up as runaways left home after being sexually molested.

Seventeen-year-old Dominica was sexually assaulted by one of her mother's four husbands. She ran away from home. Picked up by the police, she was placed on probation and returned home. Dominica left again, and was charged with violating probation. Thus she became a full-fledged delinquent.

For the young woman who engages in sexual intercourse of her own volition, school hardly offers a more understanding environment than home, should she become pregnant. Many schools suspend pregnant students or encourage them to "voluntarily" withdraw.

For the overwhelmingly male-dominated juvenile justice hierarchy, young women's sexuality is "offensive," as spelled out in the following statement made in 1975 by Hunter Hurst, Director of the Juvenile Justice Division of the National Council of Juvenile Court Judges:

The issue is that status offenses are offenses against our values. Girls are seemingly overrepresented as status offenders because we have a strong heritage of being protective towards females in this country. It offends our sensibility and our values to have a 14-year-old girl engage in sexually promiscuous activity. It's not the way we like to think about females in this country.

As long as it offends our values, be sure that the police, or the church or vigilante groups, or somebody is going to do something about it. For me, I would rather that something occur in the court where the rights of the parties can be protected.

"We play big daddy," confessed another judge.

Carol Zimmerman, Executive Director of the Arizona-based New Directors for Young Women, which compiled the foregoing comments, sees girls caught in a double bind: If they remain in school, they are molded along lines that limit their futures, and if they cut classes or stop going altogether, they can wind up in jail.

A great many young women out of school drop out because school isn't meeting their needs; because they aren't getting any encouragement, because the attitude is "you don't really need to learn a career, you don't really need to go on and work, you're going to be taken care of, you're going to marry."

They find no reason to stay in school, to attend classes. They drop out—and become part of the juvenile justice system. The courts say, "You're a truant, you're a dropout, I remand you to this-and-this facility."

"Sexism," adds Shirley McKuen of the Research Center on Sex Roles in Education, "is clearly a part of the curriculum in all educational agencies and institutions.". . . .

One important factor in the disproportionate detention rate for girls is that many times their parents refuse to take them home. When it comes time for a court hearing, this parental attitude can prejudice the female youth's chances, as Chesney-Lind points out.

"Children charged with crimes have natural allies in their parents at every step in the judicial process," she writes. But, "Parents of young people charged with status offenses are, themselves, the complainants, and they not only impugn the moral character of their children but frequently refuse to take them home in an attempt to force the court official to retain jurisdiction. Since the determination of good moral character is pivotal in the determination of guilt or innocence in the juvenile justice system, this parental orientation is significant."

A parental attitude toward young female offenders and minors in general is reflected in the 1967 U.S. Supreme Court decision awarding children some rights of due process, but not the same ones from which adults benefit. In re

Gault, the Court wrote that "The right of the State, as parens patriae, to deny to the child procedural rights available to his elders was elaborated by the assertions that a child, unlike an adult, has a right not to liberty but to custody."

State intervention is warranted, the Justices voted, when "parents default in effectively performing their custodial functions." When the State does inject itself in a child's life, they continued, "it does not deprive the child of any rights, because he has none."

Two years ago, adults receiving a jury trial stood a 48 percent chance of conviction; adults facing only a judge were convicted 65 percent of the time. In juvenile court, the "conviction" rate is a staggering 89 percent, according to Wally Mlyniec, Director of the Juvenile Justice Clinic of the Georgetown University Law Center in Washington, D. C.

Where young women are concerned, this conviction rate, combined with the "protective" or paternal attitude, portends a high probability for confinement.

Author Kenneth Wooden asserts that female juveniles receive longer sentences than male juveniles, although the girls' crimes are usually less serious. The average term of incarceration for a young man is 9 months, Wooden says, on charges ranging from truancy to rape, while the average period of confinement for young women offenders is one year—33 percent longer.

"The alleged justifications (for incarceration in secure facilities) may be diverse and not always apparent," Jolly offers, "but the subcommittee has discovered that the application and results are clearly discriminatory."

"The fact that . . . sexist community norms exist," adds Chesney-Lind, "is no justification for involving agencies of the law in their enforcement, any more than community prejudices would justify judicial racism."

For Judge Lisa Richette of the Court of Common Pleas in Philadelphia, "The offense of most of the young women going before the courts was nonconformity to a social model of what is accepted behavior for young girls. The juvenile courts should no longer act as a legal chastity belt placed around the waists of young women."

EXHIBIT 1–3   Value Systems Underlying Social Welfare's Societal Mandate

The following discussion of major value systems underlying society's approach to social welfare illustrates the complexity of societal values as well as the difficulty encountered in trying to define a coherent social welfare system based on such opposing values. Yet Keith-Lucas makes it clear that whatever the problems, values form the base upon which our social welfare institution

Source: Excerpted from Alan Keith-Lucas, *Giving and Taking Help* (Chapel Hill: University of North Carolina Press, 1972), pp. 138–43. Used by permission.

is built. The use of he *rather than less gender-specific terminology is in the original and has not been altered in this excerpt.*

There are in our culture three . . . more or less logical [value] systems. There are variations on these, . . . but for the purposes of this discussion these three may be sufficient.

The first such system, and possibly the most powerful among people as a whole, might be called capitalist-puritan or CP for short. Its basic assumptions might be summarized as follows:

1. Man is responsible for his own success or failure.
2. Human nature is basically evil, but can be overcome by an act of will.
3. Man's primary purpose is the acquisition of material prosperity, which he achieves through hard work.
4. The primary purpose of society is the maintenance of law and order in which this acquisition is possible.
5. The unsuccessful, or deviant, person is not deserving of help, although efforts should be made, up to a point, to rehabilitate him or to spur him to greater efforts on his own behalf.
6. The primary incentives to change are to be found in economic or physical rewards and punishments.

The prevalence of these assumptions needs no emphasis at this time. . . . the creed popularly thought of as "American" or even common sense, and as such is part of the heritage of most of us. . . .

So closely have God's favor and worldly success become identified that the successful are thought of as "good" and the unsuccessful as "bad" or inferior. Man takes over what was originally God's prerogatives of judgment and chastisement and those who do not exercise sufficient ambition or will are shamed, exhorted, punished, or left to the workings of the economic system.

Where the CP system of beliefs is associated with certain other religious values it has strong ethical content, in which success and failure to achieve certain ethical goals is thought of in almost exactly the same way as are material achievement and its opposite. The two systems meet in the matter of work, which has both a material and an ethical value, and in statements applying ethical standards to business enterprise, such as the statement, "Honesty is the best policy," or emphasis on the "service" motive in business. . . .

Almost diametrically opposed to this system is the one that can be called humanist-positivist-utopian, or HPU for short. This is the belief of most social scientists and many liberals, but is also held to some degree by people who profess CP views and by many religious people, despite some inherent contradiction. Summarized, its basic assumptions can be presented as follows:

1. The primary purpose of society is to fulfill man's needs both material and emotional.
2. If man's needs were fulfilled, then he would attain a state that is variously described, according to the vocabulary used by the specific HPU system, as that of goodness, maturity, adjustment, or productivity, in which most of his and society's problems would be solved.

3. What hampers him from attaining this state is external circumstance, not in general under his individual control. This, in various HPU systems, has been ascribed to lack of education, economic circumstance, his childhood relationships, and his social environment.
4. These circumstances are subject to manipulation by those possessed of sufficient technical and scientific knowledge, using, in general, what is known as "the scientific method," and consequently
5. Man, and society, are ultimately perfectible.

HPU-ism is perhaps difficult to see as a unitary theory, since many of its devotees have relied on a single specific for creating the utopia it envisages. Dewey, for instance, a strong HPU-ist, saw education as the answer; Marx, reform of the economic system; and Freud, the early Freud at least, the removal of repressions. . . .

The sources of this system are to be found in the Enlightenment and its first prophets were Rousseau and Comte. Today . . . many of its assumptions are inherent in modern materialism, at which point it joins hands with and lives somewhat uneasily with CP thought.

Behind, and yet parallel with these two systems is a third, for which it is harder to find a name. Perhaps the best that can be devised is the familiar "Judeo-Christian" tradition. . . .

Yet the system is essentially the system of assumptions about man and the universe that are inherent in the Jewish and Christian Scriptures, and is accepted, at least officially, although not always acted upon by the mainstream religious bodies, Catholic, Protestant, and Jewish.

Summarizing its basic assumptions in the same way as we have done for the CP and HPU systems, these might be presented as follows:

1. Man is a created being one of whose major problems is that he acts as if he were not and tries to be autonomous.
2. Man is fallible, but at the same time capable of acts of great courage or unselfishness.
3. The difference between men, in terms of good and bad, is insignificant compared with the standard demanded by their creator, and, as a consequence, man cannot judge his fellow in such terms.
4. Man's greatest good lies in terms of his relationship with his fellows and with his creator.
5. Man is capable of choice, in the "active and willing" sense, but may need help in making his choice.
6. Love is always the ultimate victor over force.

The position of this ethic vis-à-vis the others is a complicated one. In one sense it lies parallel to them and is a viable alternative, or a middle ground, especially in item 2, its recognition of man's simultaneous fallibility and potential. In another, it lies behind them and makes both of them possible. . . .

Probably most people are influenced to some extent by all three of these sets of assumptions. All have some value and it is not so much a matter of saying that one is good and another bad as it is of taking a position nearer or further from one or another extreme. Yet we do need to explore which set of assumptions is more likely to preserve the kind of values we see as important in helping, and which is most compatible with what we can observe in the process of helping as we know it.

Quite obviously the CP position is in general the least likely to lead to help. If man is totally responsible for his own actions, if he can better his condition by an act of will, if he can be induced to change by punishment or reward, then helping becomes a simple matter of us arranging the appropriate rewards and punishments. There is no room for relationships, or concern for another, except in a highly condescending and judgmental way.

This is the view of man that created the workhouse and the pauper's oath, which demands of children in Children's Homes or welfare clients that they work harder and behave better than other people, and which is terrified of any welfare measure that would make the receipt of relief in any way bearable or dignified. It assumes without question that welfare clients will "naturally" lie, cheat, or steal if given the chance, prefer laziness to work, and feign sickness in order to shirk working. And typically it is much more concerned to punish the few who may do such things than help the many who do not.

Yet it is not without some positive features. It does at least recognize that it is the person in trouble who must bear the final responsibility for his own betterment, and as such it has moderated some of the extreme implications of the HPU set of assumptions which, for many helping people, have appeared to supersede it.

In its initial impact on helping theory and practice HPU thought produced a tremendous outpouring of love and understanding. The helped person was freed from the total responsibility he had borne up till then for his own condition. He was no longer a second-class citizen, judged by his fellows. He was valued for his own sake. The particular social science which became the model for helping in the 1930s—analytical psychology—also stressed certain things which, if not strictly HPU—and indeed I shall argue that they are basically Judeo-Christian and not HPU at all—were at least acceptable to those who claimed to be humanists and utopians. These were in general:

1. A sense of man's common vulnerability. There were, and this is one of Freud's greatest contributions to helping, no longer "sick" and "well" people, but people who were in greater or less difficulty with problems that trouble us all.
2. A habit of looking at problems from the point of view of the helped person rather than from the outside, that is, treating him as subject rather than as object.
3. An emphasis on relationship as the principal means of help.
4. At least in the earlier stages a degree of awe in the face of new knowledge of a somewhat mysterious nature. . . .

One of the most important insights of the Judeo-Christian tradition is the nature of man himself. He is neither the evil being of capitalist-puritan belief, nor is he as good as many HPU-ists believe. But it is not so much a matter of steering between an over- and an underestimation of his nature as it is of recognizing two different factors in his makeup. The first is his fallibility and the second his ability, in certain circumstances, to work out for himself something somewhat better than his fallibility would suggest. This is far from saying that he has in him a potential which needs only some triggering, or some favorable circumstance, to tap. It means rather that with help, or where he is put to it, or from the depths of despair, he can sometimes transcend his own fallibility. Moreover this ability is found in the most unlikely places. It is often demonstrated by those whom objectively one would be forced to believe are unequipped or incapable. This is the constant surprise one comes up against in helping. Not infrequently it tends to have the air of the miraculous about it.

STUDY QUESTIONS

1. Identify as many social welfare services as you can in the community in which you live or go to school. You can try looking in the telephone book; what are you going to look under? Many communities also have special directories of social-welfare agencies; where do you think you could check to see if your community has one? After you have put together your list, study it and try to figure out how many kinds of needs are dealt with by these agencies. Can you also determine how many of the agencies are supported through public funds, and how many are supported through private funds (fees and contributions)?

2. From the list you put together in the preceding exercise, select an agency that interests you. Visit it and record your impressions. What kind of professionals work there, and who goes there for service? What does the agency look like? Do you consider it attractive? modern? welcoming? Does it seem well run? How do you think you would feel if you needed to use its services? Do you think others would be likely to feel as you do?

3. Try writing down your personal value system. How much freedom and responsibility do you think each individual should have? What rights and responsibility do you think each individual should have? What rights and responsibility do you think society has? Try to project the kind of social-welfare system that would result if it were created on the basis of your values.

4. What kinds of needs have you encountered in your own life—health needs, financial needs, counseling needs, and so on? How were your needs met? Were any not met? How did you find out about resources available to help you meet your needs? Were you satisfied with the help you got?

5. All of us have needs. Sometimes they are painful needs that we consider very serious, as when we get sick or hurt or lose our jobs. Other times they are fairly routine, like trying to get a bus schedule or getting our car repaired properly and economically. How does it feel to be in need? How comfortable are you in asking for help? Does your degree of comfort vary according to the type of need? Why do you think this is so?

SELECTED READINGS

Dusky, Lorraine (1983). Detroit's sad voices. *The New York Times Magazine.* June 12, 1983.

Auletta, Ken (1981). The underclass. A three-part series in the November 16, 23, and 30, 1981, issues of *The New Yorker* magazine.

Perspectives: *The Civil Rights Quarterly.* Published quarterly by the U. S. Commission on Civil Rights, 1121 Vermont Avenue NW, Washington, D. C. 20425.

Robson, William (1976). *Welfare State and Welfare Society.* London: George Allen and Unwin.

Weinberger, Paul, ed. (1974). *Perspectives on Social Welfare.* New York: Macmillan.

CHAPTER 2

The Structure of
Social Welfare

Social welfare as a concept is only as good as its implementation. The concept is fundamental to the creation of a service-delivery system, yet the way in which services are structured has an enormous impact on their effectiveness. In this chapter we will look at the structure of social welfare as well as some of its major programs. In the next chapter we will look at the historical factors that helped to create the social welfare structure we have today.

Social Welfare as a Social Institution

We saw in the last chapter that social welfare entails a commitment by society to help its members meet their needs. We also saw that this occurs according to values that define who deserves what kind of help. And finally, we noted that help is provided through structures created for that purpose and staffed by people whose job is to provide helping services. It is these characteristics of social welfare—social purpose, a normative value base, and an organized structure of activities—that define social welfare as a **social institution** (see Chart 2–1).

CHART 2–1   Social Welfare as a Social Institution

Social welfare as a social institution has the following characteristics:

Purposes

Manifest purposes (those that are explicit and agreed upon by most groups in society):

Helping people function more effectively

Helping people attain their life goals

Preventing individual and social breakdown

Strengthening other social institutions

Latent purposes (those that are not necessarily perceived and agreed upon by most groups in society):

Controlling people's behavior, especially the poor and minorities, by making them dependent upon services provided at a minimal level

Maintaining a capitalistic economic system by minimally interfering with the operation of the free market

Maintaining the autonomy of professions by limiting the power and choices available to users of the service

Normative Value Base

Human life is valuable.

People have some degree of responsibility for each other.

People should be as self-sufficient as possible.

Helpless and especially vulnerable groups deserve special care.

Professional helping should be provided efficiently and effectively.

People have the right to self-determination as long as they don't hurt others.

Organized Structure of Activities

The Helping Professions

Medicine, social work, teaching, human services, psychiatry, clinical psychology, and others.

Helping Professionals (Roles)

Doctors, nurses, psychiatrists, anesthesiologists, social workers, marriage counselors, police officers, community planners, and others.

Helping Organizations (Agencies)

Hospitals, nursing homes, community centers, schools, day-care centers, family-service agencies, prisons, and others.

You are already familiar with the other major social institutions of society—the family, education, religion, and the political and economic institutions. Let's look at the family, for example. The family performs several societal purposes, including providing and socializing new members of society, as well as meeting their emotional and economic needs. Families generally function according to societal norms and values, so most married people have only one spouse, and most children are not abused. And, of course, families are structured; wives and husbands, children and parents, siblings and relatives—all have particular parts to play in maintaining family life. In short, the family is a social institution.

The family also exemplifies another characteristic of social institutions: it interacts with other institutions. Families prepare children for school; school prepares them to work and to vote. Religion helps families to cope with tragedies, such as death, and to celebrate important life events, such as marriage and the birth of a child. Indeed, it is the interlocking of social institutions that enables a society to function day by day. The Watergate scandal during Richard Nixon's presidency was so devastating because the political institution seemed to be undermining the values and behaviors taught in school, church, and the family. Basic commitments of the society were suddenly called into question, with a resulting period of loss of societal direction and purpose. The noticeable rise in vagrancy and crime rates resulting from economic need caused by the worst excesses of Reaganomics had a similarly disturbing effect on other social institutions (Anderson, 1982).

Universal Social Welfare Services

When analyzing social welfare as a social institution, issues of residual versus universal social welfare become significant (Wilensky and Lebeaux, 1958). A **universal social welfare service** is available to all as a regular part of the social environment. Such services are considered **rights** of all the members of a society. For example, police protection, a safe water system, and public education are intended to be available to everyone regardless of their age, income level, ethnicity, or other characteristics. Sometimes universal services are called **public social utilities** or **institutionalized services,** alternative ways of expressing the idea of certain services as rights, or **entitlements,** of citizenship. Sometimes universal services exist for the use of one group. Public education is a good example. Most free education exists only through high school, so for the most part, it serves the population aged five to eighteen. Nevertheless, it is considered universal service because *all* youngsters in this age group have access to free public schooling.

Residual Social Welfare Services

Residual services are the opposite of universal services. Whereas the latter serve everyone who needs the service, residual services are intended to be restrictive. They are available only to those who can prove the existence of a specific need and who can also prove that they meet specified qualifications.

ELIGIBILITY.   Proving need and qualifications is called establishing **eligibility.** Aid to Families with Dependent Children (AFDC) is an example of a residual service. People can receive this financial-aid service only if a parent has minor children, has income below a specified amount, and also lacks other resources. In many states, AFDC is limited to one-parent families, and many parents are required to seek employment or undertake job training. We can easily see, then, that AFDC is a highly selective program (residual) in contrast to public education, which is intended to serve everyone (universal).

Informal and Formal Social Welfare Services

Social welfare services are provided through informal and formal structures. This book will emphasize formal helping structures, but the bond between informal and formal helping is a close one.

Informal Helping Structures

These social mechanisms help people to meet their needs without using professional helping people (doctors, psychiatrists, social workers, and so on). Friends usually try to help each other by giving advice, lending a friendly ear, perhaps lending money, running errands for each other, and exchanging services like babysitting. Friends are usually not formally trained to provide these services, nor do they usually get paid for them. Nevertheless, the services are important.

All of these services are also available through formal helping structures. Psychologists, psychiatrists, social workers, nurses, and doctors often give advice and are good listeners. Social workers help people apply for financial-aid programs, as well as arrange for transportation, homemaker, and child-care services. Indeed, these people are specifically trained to provide such services, and may do so with more expertise than friends or family members. Yet sometimes the informal system is more effective than the formal one. There are a number of reasons why (Landy, 1965).

1. **Access.** The informal helping system is part of the everyday life of most people. It is immediately available, and most people feel comfortable using it.
2. **Lack of obstacles.** Besides being readily available, the informal helping network has few barriers associated with it. There are no application procedures, few travel or child-care problems, and, most of all, no stigma. Admitting a problem to a friend is usually considerably easier than admitting that professional help is needed (Nelson, 1982).
3. **Knowledge.** Many people don't know what services are available in the formal helping network. One of the ways they find out is

by talking to people in their informal helping system, who then may also give them the emotional support they need to actually use the formal services.

Formal Helping Networks

In spite of the valuable contribution that informal helping makes to the total social welfare structure, it is the formal structure that carries the major responsibility for implementing society's social welfare commitments. It is the formal structure that is **accountable** for the type and quality of services provided, and that trains and uses people with special expertise in helping others. Indeed, sometimes informal helping networks break down and are unable to help people meet their needs. The family is a good example. High divorce rates and child and spouse abuse make the family more of a problem than a helping structure for some people. We will see in the next chapter that a major impetus for the growth of formal social welfare structures has been the inability of informal helping networks to meet many of the needs people have. There are two important characteristics of formal helping structures in social welfare: professions and bureaucracies. We will examine both.

THE PROFESSIONAL MODEL OF ORGANIZATION.   Hall (1978) identifies the following six characteristics of professions:

1. the use of the professional organization as a major reference
2. a belief in service to the public
3. belief in self-regulation
4. a sense of calling to the field and
5. professional autonomy.
6. specialized knowledge base

Examples of social welfare organizations organized along professional lines are the National Association of Social Workers, the American Medical Association, and the National Organization of Human Services. They usually have local chapters that offer their members a full range of services and activities, including meetings to exchange information and plan professional activities, professional publications, certification, and professional-liability insurance. It is through such mechanisms that the professional's identity is reinforced and maintained.

The helping person's identification with the profession combines with a belief in service to the public to make the specific organization

in which professionals work less important than their professional mis-
sions. Dunbar and Jackson (1972), talking about social workers working
in free clinics, express the ideal of professional commitment: "Accomplishing a job and delivering a service are more important to them than
hours, pay, professional status, recognition, or conventional agency
procedures." So, although a specific agency concentrates on procedures to help it most efficiently attain its objectives, professionals emphasize meeting human needs within the framework of professional
values. The two are not always compatible, as we will see later in the
chapter.

A belief in self-regulation and professional autonomy results from
the specialized knowledge bases and socialization procedures that
characterize professions. For example, physical therapists have specialized knowledge of the human anatomy and technical skills derived
from this knowledge. Both are learned through a well-documented
socialization process (Becker, 1961). Professionals maintain that nonprofessionals are not equipped to evaluate their competence, because
the nonprofessional has not mastered the specialized knowledge base.
It follows that professionals must be trusted to evaluate each other,
and impose necessary sanctions when appropriate. This in turn makes
it difficult for the user to influence the professional. However, professional organizations are sometimes too weak to be effective regulating
bodies. In some rare instances, gross incompetence may be overlooked to protect the professional image from potentially intrusive
legal action. In these unusual situations, professional autonomy may
actually interfere with service delivery.

A belief in service to the public and a calling to the field are important in creating a professional value system. Such values are often
codified by the professional organization and thus set the standard for
professional behavior. In the helping professions, such values usually
emphasize the value of human life and personal integrity, the
significance of knowledge, judgment, and self-awareness to help
others in a professional way, and the equal accessibility of service to all
who need it. For example, medicine has its Hippocratic Oath, and
social work values emphasize user self-determination, confidentiality,
and treating users with dignity and respect. Having looked at the characteristics of a profession, let us now explore the other feature of most
formal helping—its bureaucratic structure.

THE BUREAUCRATIC MODEL OF ORGANIZATION.   The bureaucracy is
a way to formally organize a variety of people and activities into "a

system of control based on rational rules" (Mouzelis, 1968:39). When organizational goals and means can be specified, when tasks can be broken into their component parts and rationally organized, and when tasks can be organized into hierarchical spheres of control, a bureaucracy can be an extremely effective form of social organization. For example, the calculation and payment of Social Security benefits is relatively straightforward, and is generally conceded to be effectively accomplished by the Social Security Administration bureaucracy. Because the bureaucratic form of organization is the major one in contemporary American society, its pervasiveness encourages its use in all organizational contexts. Its appropriateness in social welfare contexts, however, depends on the nature of the social welfare tasks to be performed and their suitability for the organizational characteristics of bureaucracies.

The formal characteristics of bureaucracies may be summarized as follows:

1. a high degree of specialization
2. hierarchical authority structure with specified areas of command and responsibility
3. impersonal relations between members
4. recruitment of members on the basis of ability and
5. differentiation of personal and official resources (Ibid.:39).

In the ideal bureaucracy, rational rules govern behavior, and individuals are expected to interact as organizational role occupants rather than as unique individuals. Given the above characteristics, a bureaucracy has several potential advantages: efficiency in the performance of set tasks in set ways by trained bureaucrats; predictable behavior; behavior that stresses competence more than personal feelings; and the possibility of rapid goal attainment, given the trained personnel and routinized activity.

On the other hand, the bureaucracy has several potential disadvantages. It can become quite inefficient when its highly formalized structure must be changed. It can be inhuman in responding to the human needs of those within it, which can seriously affect the motivation of workers and in turn impair both the quantity and quality of productivity. Workers can become so highly specialized that they may be unable to adapt to new working conditions and tasks (trained incapacity), and they may lose sight of goals by focusing so intensively on the means (technicism). Finally, in an attempt to gain personal satisfaction and power from the basically impersonal, rational structure, various types of informal organization may arise (Ibid.:99). Such organization may either supplement the formal organization and increase productivity (Ibid.:102–3) or it may conflict with the formal organization and disrupt or restrict productivity. Exhibit 2–3 in the "Reflections on Social Welfare" section at the end of the chapter illustrates the complexity and formal structure of the typical social welfare bureaucracy.

There are several problems that emerge from the bureaucratization of professional behavior. One is the need for bureaucratic structure versus the need for professional autonomy. A bureaucracy attempts to structure its positions in such a way that authority and responsibility are clearly specified. In this way, the organization has control over the behavior of its members, and intervention points are specified in the event that something goes wrong. This kind of structure automatically creates differences between participants in the organization. Since some have more power than others, there is an implicit or explicit assertion that some are more knowledgeable and skilled than others. This type of structure makes it very difficult to have the sharing among equals that a profession assumes. A profession recognizes that some of its members are more skilled than others, but also assumes that all are at least minimally skilled, and that a continual process of member communication will serve to increase the skills of all. When professionals are forced to work in a superior-inferior relationship, as happens in many agencies using a supervisor-worker system, there is a real danger that there will be a loss of motivation in workers who have been trained to think autonomously. Barriers to innovation may also be created. This problem often surfaces in settings where one professional group is a minority in relationship to one or more others. John Wax's article exploring social work's power in a medical organization is an excellent example of this issue (Wax, 1968).

A second problem is the need for bureaucratic structure versus the need for professional flexibility. The use of the profession as a major reference, belief in service to the public, and a sense of calling, all demand a commitment to helping others on the basis of their need. Bureaucracies are concerned with specifying who is to receive service and under what circumstances—hours of work, forms to fill out, location of offices, qualifications of staff, allocation of resources, and so on. Stanton's study of the Pangloss Mental Health Association illustrates this problem when it describes a Christmas party for mental hospital inmates that meets bureaucratic needs and rules much more than client needs or desires (Stanton, 1970). The confrontation of bureaucratic rules and professional values creates some special problems in social welfare:

1. *Gaps in service.* An agency sometimes offers only part of the services needed by a client, such as a Catholic Social Service agency that refuses to provide family planning information.
2. *Dividing the client.* In this situation, an agency divides up a client's problems into specialized parts, assigning different workers to deal with each part. Dividing the client and gaps in service can both be handled by referring clients to needed resources. This requires follow-up to make sure that the referral has been successful, something that often does not happen.
3. *Competition for resources.* Each organization seeks to preserve itself, and competes with other agencies for resources. Since each organization is accountable only for its own functioning, there is little encouragement for agencies to cooperate, although outside forces may require that they do so (United Fund drives or legislation mandating such cooperation, for example).

Exhibit 2–4 in the "Reflections on Social Welfare" section provides examples of some of these problems.

A third consideration is the effects of bureaucratic functioning on the provision of adequate services. It was noted above that bureaucracies tend to develop certain characteristics, many of which can interfere with the provision of services. For example, technicism, trained incapacity and informal organization can all impede bureaucratic functioning under some circumstances. Besides these potential problems, the very structure of a bureaucracy can be a problem:

> Youths trying to get help from an agency encountered multiple barriers, intended or otherwise. Rigid eligibility requirements that involved filling out long application forms prevented many from starting the process, caused some to give up in the middle, and turned many others away who were determined to be ineligible for service. Being minors away from home prevented many from receiving medical treatment. Being drug-users prevented many from receiving help without risking arrest. Other obstacles blocking agencies' service to street people were the long waits for service, entailing waiting lists and appointments at a future date instead of the date of contact, the extensive records, including extremely personal and sometimes socially damaging information . . . and the . . . cold atmosphere and middle-class appearance of the agency setting (Dunbar and Jackson, 1972:28).

Structure is vital to bureaucratic functioning—it provides durability and organization. Yet it can also create inflexibility that becomes a barrier between it and those who use it. With certain client groups or in certain types of emergency or sensitive situations, bureaucratic structure can prevent or distort service.

It should be evident that there are some built-in tensions between professions·and bureaucracies. Informal helping structures and the use of volunteers in bureaucracies help to reduce some of these problems. We will return to the issue of increasing professional effectiveness in formal bureaucratically organized social welfare structures in the last chapter of the book, since it is an on-going concern for the future. For now, however, we can summarize the preceding discussion by looking at the interplay between formal and informal helping structures in Exhibit 2–5 in the "Reflections on Social Welfare" section.

THE VOLUNTEER CONNECTION.   Many formal social welfare services make use of **volunteers,** nonprofessionals who voluntarily contribute their time to help formal structures operate more effectively. Volunteers bring many of the advantages of informal helping into formal structures. They usually relate to the people seeking help as peers rather than professionals, and they are more likely to have the time to be a friendly listener or help accomplish a personal task. Volunteers are of many kinds: "candy stripers" in hospitals, friendly visitors in nursing homes, people who deliver "meals-on-wheels" for the homebound, foster grandparents, big brothers and big sisters, and people who help run Special Olympics programs for the handicapped are some examples. In addition to their ability to relate closely and in a more informal way, volunteers make possible services that those in need could not afford if they had to be performed by paid professionals. Exhibit 2–1 in the "Reflections on Social Welfare" section at the end of the chapter looks at the volunteer experience in more depth.

The importance of volunteers for linking formal and informal services has been recognized by other societies for some time. This is especially true in less industrialized societies, which generally rely less on formal social welfare structures. Medical care in China is a case in point (Sidel, 1972).

Since the Cultural Revolution many paraprofessionals have been trained to help give medical care and be a bridge between the general population and the medical professions. In the rural areas "barefoot doctors" have been trained in immunization, health education, and the treatment of

Volunteers provide valuable services that would be difficult and expensive to provide in any other way. Just as important, the volunteers themselves benefit from their efforts on behalf of others.
(Colonial Penn Group, Inc.)

minor illnesses. Barefoot doctors are peasants who receive approximately
three to six months' formal training and then work half the time as agricultural workers and half the time as medical workers; they are paid as full-
time agricultural workers. "Red Guard doctors," usually housewives, are
the urban counterparts of the barefoot doctors, but are generally unpaid
and work in neighborhood health centers under the supervision of fully
trained physicians after only ten days' training. . . . The "worker-doctor"
with one to three months' training works half time as a medical worker in
his factory. Both in cities and rural areas "health workers" have been
trained by and are directly responsible to barefoot doctors or Red Guard

doctors. . . . All four categories of paraprofessional health personnel—barefoot doctors, Red Guard doctors, worker-doctors, and health workers—incorporate social-service functions into their medical work.

The Structure of Social Welfare Programs

So far we have been looking at issues relating to the overall social welfare institution: Are services accessible to everyone? How are services integrated into the basic fabric of society? Now we will turn to an analysis of how specific programs get structured.

Public and Private Programs

Services that are funded from public monies, are enacted by public mandate, or are administered in publicly funded agencies are called **public social welfare services. Private social welfare services,** in contrast, are generally funded from private monies (such as individual contributions, foundation grants, and corporate donations); they exist because an agency's policymaking body mandated them; and they are administered in an agency supported mostly by privately earned or donated funds. The distinction between public and private services is not always clear cut, however, because private agencies are increasingly providing services for public agencies on a contractual basis (Kamerman, 1983). Nevertheless, the basic distinction between public and private services continues to be significant: public agencies are sponsored by and accountable to society as a whole, and private agencies are not (Wilensky and Lebeaux, 1958:146).

Kramer notes several functions of particular significance for private agencies (Kramer, 1973). They are more likely to experiment with innovative programs because their governing structures are usually less cumbersome than those of public agencies. Private agencies can be more responsive to the needs of special-interest groups, an important factor in a multicultural society like our own. Private agencies can also serve as a stimulus to public agencies to improve their services (Anderson, 1982), besides helping people identify and obtain services from public agencies. Finally, because private agencies can be more flexible, they have traditionally tried to provide services that were not provided by public agencies. The medical community's efforts to provide care for the uninsured jobless is an interesting example (Smothers, 1983).

In spite of the potential of private agencies for innovative, flexible, specialized programs, they are a smaller part of the social welfare structure than public agencies. Public expenditures for social welfare are far greater than private expenditures (Greene, 1976). In addition, the public network of services most directly puts in operation the society's commitment to social welfare. The public network of services exists because society has mandated helping services, and is therefore more firmly rooted in the institutional structure of society than is the private professional helping network. The latter depends on the willingness of individuals to spend some of their own disposable income on charitable activities, a willingness that fluctuates according to economic conditions and changes in personal value systems.

Public services have traditionally protected the most needy and those groups most discriminated against. Members of these groups are often invisible to the average citizen, and those segregated or in need may represent value issues about which many people experience considerable ambivalence. These factors reduce the likelihood that people will ask private agencies to develop and provide services for such needy and oppressed groups. Because laws do mandate equal protection and nondiscrimination, the needs of these groups are more likely to be met by public agencies. This is especially true when general societal conditions create widespread need. Only the public sector is likely to have the resources to meet that level of need (Teltsch, 1983).

Public and private agencies are best understood as partners in service delivery (Kamerman, 1983). Together they meet the needs of specialized groups besides providing basic services for all citizens. They often cooperate in ways that make each more responsive and accessible to the many groups in society needing help. They guarantee society's commitment to the well-being of its citizens at the same time that individuals have opportunities to act according to their own personal charitable impulses. Each is important and each has a special role to play in the total social welfare institution, even though the public structure is dominant (see Table 2–1).

Income Maintenance Programs and Social Services

Services that improve a recipient's financial situation are called **income-maintenance services.** Income-maintenance services make it possible for people to pay their rent, buy food and clothing, pay for needed health services, and so on. In a market economy like our own, access to sufficient money is basic to staying alive and healthy, keeping family or family-like social units together, and maintaining a standard of living that provides for dignity and a sense of well-being.

TABLE 2-1   Examples of Public and Private Agencies

Public Agencies	Private Agencies
Social Security Office	Catholic/Protestant/Jewish Family
Department of Social Service	Service Agency
(Public Welfare)	Private Day Care Center
State Mental Hospital	Private Hospital
City-run Medical Center	Private Nursing Home
Unemployment Office	Big Brothers/Big Sisters Program
Community Mental Health Center	YM/YWCA
City-run Community Center	Doctor's Office
Public School	Marriage Counseling Center
Prison	Private School
Police Station	Blue Cross/Blue Shield Office
Fire Department Station	Women's Shelter
City-run Shelter for the Homeless	Alcoholics Anonymous
State-run Group Home for the	A Church-run Shelter for the
Retarded	Homeless
City-run Day Care Center	The Salvation Army
Public Housing Project	The Red Cross

Social services, sometimes called **personal social services,** help people with their nonfinancial needs. Examples include child-welfare services (adoption, foster care, protective services, residential facilities), family counseling, homemaker services, protective care of the aged, community centers, self-help and mutual-aid activities, information and referral services, recreational services, and so on (Kahn and Kamerman, 1976:4). Income-maintenance and social services are closely related. Stress created by financial need is often a significant source of personal and group problems. Families may be broken up when parents cannot earn enough to keep everyone together. Marital and marriage-like ties can be severely strained by the daily battle of making do with too little money (Rule, 1982). One's sense of personal integrity may be attacked by financial "failure," or feelings that one cannot provide adequately for loved ones. Similarly, a stronger sense of self, or the ability of members of a community to work together more effectively can improve access to and management of financial resources.

Social welfare services help to meet people's financial and social
needs. These elderly people are enjoying social services that help
them remain active and in contact with others. (Leonard Freed/
Magnum Photos, Inc.)

Grant-in-Aid Programs

A **grant-in-aid program** is one in which a money grant is given to those
who are financially needy. The money comes from funds to which the
recipients have usually not contributed. Let us look at a money-grant
program such as the Supplemental Security Income program (SSI).
This is a program that provides a very modest monthly income to

destitute elderly, blind, or handicapped people. These grants come from general tax revenues, to which the recipients are not contributing because they have no income other than the grant. In other words, the general tax-paying population is, through its taxes, making cash grants available to SSI recipients.

IN-KIND GRANT PROGRAMS. A grant program may also provide non-monetary support. It may involve some kind of commodity, such as food or clothing. This is called an **in-kind grant,** because what is given is a needed item rather than the money to purchase that item. Whether grants provide money or commodities, they are not usually repaid by those who receive them. Grant-in-aid programs are sometimes re-garded by average citizens as perpetuating financial dependency, something that is considered undesirable in American society because of the strongly held belief that people should be self-reliant. However, grants-in-aid do not promote irresponsibility unless they are structured so as to make it practically impossible for people to become indepen-dent if they receive help. For example, many people criticize the AFDC program for fostering dependency. Many states have a rule that a household receiving aid cannot contain more than one adult, yet it is known that single-parent families are more likely to remain mired in poverty (*Washington Social Legislation Bulletin,* 1983). Furthermore, the AFDC program discourages efforts to work because benefits de-cline in proportion to income earned, so one's income is the same, whether or not one works (indeed, the costs associated with going to work may actually lead to *less* income). Under such conditions, grant-in-aid programs may promote dependency, but not because of the laziness of the recipients, as is often assumed.

Social Insurance Programs

Our society much prefers a social insurance approach to service deliv-ery to any type of grants. A **social insurance,** like life insurance, is built on the principle of contributions. People pay premiums to the com-pany until they die, when their beneficiaries are paid a specified amount by the company. Some people pay for many years and never collect—the beneficiary may already be dead, or may die soon after. Other people die young, so their beneficiaries collect more than was paid in premiums. It is easy to see that an insurance program spreads the risk, and that money collected comes from a pool into which the recipient has contributed. Thus, as with life insurance, some will collect more than they paid in, while others will collect less.

A life insurance program, a pension program, and health insurances like Blue Cross are private social insurance programs, and they are very common. The best known public social insurance programs are the retirement and survivors programs of the Social Security Act, Unemployment Insurance, and Medicare. In general, social insurances are less stigmatized than grant programs because they are not considered "handouts." People contribute to them toward the time when they are in need; thus they "earn" what they get. This is simplistic thinking to some degree, because need is often caused by social conditions that victimize helpless people—economic recessions and racial or ethnic discrimination are cases in point (Gailey, 1982; Kerr, 1982; Kleiman, 1982). Nevertheless, in an achievement-oriented society such as ours, being seen as "earning one's keep" is considered important. Chart 2–2 summarizes major grant-in-aid and social insurance programs.

CHART 2–2   Major Grant-in-Aid and Social Insurance Programs

Grant-in-Aid Programs*

Aid to Families with Dependent Children (AFDC)—provides income maintenance for needy families with children.

Medicaid—provides medical services for needy individuals and families.

Supplemental Security Income (SSI)—provides income maintenance for needy elderly, disabled, and blind people.

Food Stamps—provides income maintenance for needy individuals and families; grants may only be used to purchase food.

General Assistance—provides income maintenance on an emergency basis for needy individuals and families.

Tuition Assistance Program (TAP)—provides grants for college tuition for needy students.

Social Insurance Programs**

Old Age and Survivors Disability Insurance Program (OASDI)—provides income maintenance for retired and disabled persons and their dependents

*All of these are public programs.
**The first four listed are public programs, and the last three are private programs.

(this program is commonly called "Social Security," although it is only one part of the Social Security Act).

Medicare—provides medical services for the elderly.

Unemployment Insurance—provides income maintenance for persons temporarily and involuntarily unemployed.

Workmen's Compensation—provides income maintenance for persons injured on the job.

Blue Cross/Blue Shield/Major Medical/Health Maintenance Programs (HMO)—provide medical service to subscribers.

Job Related Pension Plans—provide income maintenance for retired persons and their dependents.

Life Insurance—provides income maintenance for survivors.

Harriette C. Johnson and Gertrude S. Goldberg (1982), *Government Money for Everyday People* (Garden City, N. Y.: Adelphi University School of Social Work) can provide more information about any of the government-sponsored programs listed above.

Fee Programs

A few social welfare programs are operated more or less as commercial services are. Users are charged a fee that covers some or all of the actual cost of the service. Most therapists charge fees that cover the total cost of their time, as do hospitals. At other times a **sliding scale of fees** is used, by which fees are negotiated according to the ability of users to pay. In these cases, fees are not expected to cover full costs. They are instead met by a combination of fees and other sources of income (such as government funds and private contributions). A capitalistic society like ours tends to use the marketplace as much as possible, but it also recognizes that many people using social welfare services cannot afford to pay for them.

Evaluating Social Welfare Programs

Winifred Bell (1969) has developed eight criteria helpful in evaluating the effectiveness of social welfare programs, whether public or private. The greater visibility of the policy-making process in public programs makes it easier to apply Bell's criteria to such programs, but any program can be evaluated using these criteria.

Objectives

These are the purposes of the program as formally stated. A program may be successful in attaining these objectives, it may be partially successful, it may attain other objectives not planned for, or it may simply be unsuccessful. Although the stated objectives guide one's evaluation of a program, the attainment of unanticipated objectives should be included in the evaluation of a program. In some cases they may be as important as the original intended objectives.

Legislative Authorization

This will normally be applicable only to public programs. Considering legislative authorization helps to relate programs to others created at the same time, as well as establishing a historical perspective for such programs. When programs fail, it is often because legislation did not build in adequate implementation procedures.

Source of Funding

Funding is crucial to program implementation. In public funding, there is sometimes a distinction between legislation and the appropriation of funds to carry out the legislated program; both the authorizing legislation and the appropriations legislation are necessary for a functional program. Private agencies, also, may recognize the need for a program but may not have adequate resources to implement it.

Administrative Structure

We explored, earlier in this chapter, the several ways in which administrative structure can influence program effectiveness. Such structural considerations include the internal functioning of an organization (specified goals and means, structural problems such as technicism, and the like), and the relationships between several organizations that may be involved in a program (cooperation between the Department of Agriculture and local departments of social services that operate Food Stamp programs, for example). The systems nature of social welfare is also significant in administrative structure. A program can be greatly helped or seriously hindered, depending on whether its structure provides for meaningful system ties. For example, when the Office of Economic Opportunity was created, it had strong presidential backing and the authority to initiate action in many parts of the social welfare system. In its last days, it had virtually no support and little power to gain the cooperation of other parts of the system.

Eligibility Requirements

These determine who is eligible to participate in a program. If a program is universal in scope, need is the only criterion for eligibility. The more residual a program is, the more stringent the eligibility requirements are likely to be.

Coverage

Eligibility requirements establish the boundaries of the potential client population, whereas coverage refers to the number of those eligible who actually participate in the program. It is a good measure of the program's effectiveness in reaching the target population, and it is frequently the case that more people are eligible for a program than actually receive benefits.

Adequacy

Adequacy is a measure of the program's effectiveness in meeting the need of the target population. Sometimes programs are planned to meet only a percentage of the estimated total need, hoping to encourage self-help and to spread scarce resources as far as possible. However, the result is often a residue of unmet need, making the program inadequate for attaining its ultimate goal of need satisfaction. Many states, for example, pay AFDC recipients less than the budget calculated as necessary to meet minimum survival needs. Whereas some AFDC recipients are successful in finding some other source of help, many are not, with the unmet need being reflected in various social ills, such as the lead paint poisoning of desperately hungry children, and pregnant women suffering from malnutrition.

Equity

Whereas coverage is a measure of the actual population served by a program, equity measures the degree to which a program discriminates between categories of persons who qualify for coverage. One of the accusations against Social Security is that it is not equitable in its treatment of working married women, because they cannot receive separate Social Security payments upon retirement, in spite of the fact that they made separate payments during their working years. Instead, they receive a payment tied to their husband's benefits, and this is less than they would receive if they collected their benefits independently.

Exhibit 2–6 in the "Reflections on Social Welfare" section at the end of the chapter presents comparative data for Medicaid and Medicare. It is suggested that you take some time to use the above evaluative criteria to look at these two programs and try to evaluate their effectiveness. On the basis of your analysis, what changes do you think should be made? You might want to then compare your ideas with the material in Table 2–3, which presents data on cross-cultural social welfare programs. Looking at the ways in which other societies attempt to meet the needs of their citizens can be very instructive for our own society. Notice, however, that all societies face the same issue: what are the priorities in the allocation of social resources? When looking at Exhibit 2–6 you should also be alert to how it illustrates the differences between an insurance program and a grant-in-aid program. Notice in particular how funding, administration, coverage, adequacy, and equity are affected.

Comparative Social Welfare

With social welfare so completely embedded in the institutional structure of a society, it is to be expected that social welfare will vary from society to society. This variation reflects each society's distinctive values, priorities, and ways of organizing its resources. In general, industrialized societies tend to have more fully developed formal social welfare structures than do less industrial societies, owing to the greater availability of economic surpluses in highly industrialized societies and greater technology for reducing human need. For example, in a society in which safe water and a predictable supply of electricity are problematic, highly sophisticated hospitals are unlikely. Similarly, a society in which most people never progress beyond grammar school will simply not have the large numbers of specially trained professional practitioners required by an extensive, formal social welfare system.

This is not to say that less industrialized societies lack social welfare services. They do, however, tend to rely most heavily on informal structures rather than on the formal types of services we take for granted in this country. Kin networks and local community bonds are most often relied on to help people meet their needs. These countries also rely heavily on volunteers and **paraprofessionals**—people with specific technical training for dealing with particular types of problems. China's "barefoot doctors," discussed earlier, are examples of paraprofessionals. The limited numbers of professionals provide supervision, as well as direct service in the most difficult cases.

Among industrialized societies, those that are socialist democracies, such as Sweden, Great Britain, and West Germany, have the most fully developed formal social welfare structures. Our own society, being a capitalistic democracy, places less emphasis on social planning to meet human need. Here it is assumed that people will largely be responsible for themselves, with the government stepping in only as a last resort. Socialistic societies do much more social planning, which diverts societal resources into social welfare to ensure a certain standard of living for everyone (Bell, 1983:5–8). We are, of course, talking about degrees of planning, because all of the major western industrialized societies have relatively well-developed social welfare structures.

Let us compare the ways two different societies—the United States and West Germany—approach social welfare. Both societies cover basic needs: unemployment, retirement, medical care, compensation for job-related injuries, disability benefits, supports to help keep families intact, housing, nutrition, the needs of children and the elderly, and special benefits for veterans (Johnson and Goldberg, 1982). Nevertheless, there are noticeable differences in the way these needs are met and in the extent to which they are met. In general, West Germany is far more thorough and extensive in its coverage of people's needs (Windschild, 1978), placing a much greater emphasis on prevention, for example. Every employed person is required to have a pension plan, regardless of income. In the United States only about nine out of ten working people have Social Security protection, and even these benefits are not sufficient for survival above the poverty level for many recipients. In Germany, medical care is compulsory and comprehensive, including dental care, sick pay, and a death benefit. Our system is voluntary and far from comprehensive, even requiring copayments or deductibles in most cases. Unemployment benefits are similarly more complete in West Germany, including such things as bad-weather allowances and bankruptcy benefits for employees who lose their jobs because an employer goes bankrupt.

At the family level, West Germans enjoy children's allowances. Every family, regardless of income, receives a grant-in-aid for each child. The concept behind such payments is that children are costly for any individual family, and society as a whole has a stake in effective child rearing. Therefore, children's allowances help families to provide for their welfare and ensure that the children will become healthy, productive, adult members of society. Although children's allowances have been discussed in the United States, such a program has never been implemented. Services for children tend to be available only after the child (or its parents) has already experienced difficulty. Services are also fragmented, denying needy children access to an environment that supports all aspects of their development.

Can we then conclude that West Germany's welfare system is better than that of the United States? Using Bell's criteria discussed earlier in this chapter, we can certainly say that the German system has somewhat different objectives, that its funding and administrative structure are different, and that it is more comprehensive, adequate, and equitable than the American welfare system. However, this is not to say that one is "better" than the other, because each society has its own particular way of approaching issues. Many people in the United States would say, for example, that the West German system reduces people's independence and initiative, values that are very strongly held in our society.

Through this comparative approach to social welfare, we can learn alternative ways of approaching needs and structuring social welfare systems. Doing so, however, requires identifying approaches used in one society that would be compatible with the needs and approaches of another. If what we learn helps us to improve our own system, so much the better. We have to expect, however, that simply trying to impose what one society does on another society is not likely to work.

We also have to remember that social welfare is constantly changing in response to other changes in society. In the early 1980s, many industrialized nations experienced economic problems similar to ours. Even societies with highly developed formal social welfare structures—such as Sweden—began to reexamine them to see if they were too costly (see Figure 2–2). As the Reagan presidency made clear, societal commitments to social welfare can be changed. To summarize and conclude this discussion of comparative social welfare, Tables 2–2 and 2–3 and Figure 2–1 provide data on the welfare expenditures of several different societies.

SUMMARY

In this chapter, we have looked at the various ways in which social welfare as an institution can be structured, and some of the major issues in the development of specific programs. Questions of profes-

TABLE 2–2 Comparative Social Welfare

Social Expenditure in the Federal Republic of Germany 1980 in billion D-Marks

Old age insurance program	141.5	Public welfare assistance	13.9
Health insurance program	86.5	Accident insurance program	9.9
Civil service pensions	48.2	Tax benefits in housing	
Continued wage payments		construction	5.8
in case of illness	27.1	Youth programs	5.8
Unemployment benefits, re-		Education allowance	
training programs, etc.	22.6	(BAFöG)	3.3
Children's allowance	17.6	Restitution to Nazi victims	2.5
Social benefits in the public		Old-age assistance for	
service	17.6	farmers	2.7
Savings incentives	11.9	Equalization of war burdens	1.7
Assistance to war victims	13.4	Rent allowance	2.0
		Health service	1.4
		Other	14.0

total: 449.0
billion DM

= 30 per cent of the Gross National Product. This means that almost one third of all income is spent on social expenditure.

Source: Günther Windschild, Social policy—a comprehensive network, in *Meet Germany,* 18th ed. (Hamburg: Atlantik-Bruche, 1981), p. 88. Reprinted by permission of the publisher.

sional versus bureaucratic, residual versus universal, formal versus informal, public versus private, grants versus social insurances, are all significant aspects of the structure of social welfare. Programs can be evaluated in terms of objectives, legislative authorization, source of funding, administrative structure, eligibility requirements, coverage, adequacy, and equity, in order to identify who is or is not served, how they are served, and why certain needs are met and others are not. We also learn more about our own social welfare system by looking at those developed by other societies. Although each society will approach social welfare issues in ways that are appropriate to its own perspectives, societies can and do learn from each other. We now have a concrete sense of social welfare in United States society. In the next chapter, we will look at how this structure developed, and what might be ahead.

TABLE 2–3 Expenditures for Specified Social Welfare Programs

Country	Old age, survivors, and disability insurance				Public aid and other social welfare				Public health care programs			
	Expenditures (millions)		Percentage of GNP		Expenditures (millions)		Percentage of GNP		Expenditures (millions)		Percentage of GNP	
	1971	1974	1971	1974	1971	1974	1971	1974	1971	1974	1971	1974
Belgium[1] (francs)	70,583	123,983	5.0	5.9	14,547	23,981	1.0	1.1	56,147	96,270	4.0	4.6
Canada[1] (dollars)	2,205	4,121	2.5	3.1	2,147	2,754	2.5	2.2	4,153	6,150	4.8	4.8
France (francs)	38,139	56,803	4.2	4.3	(²)	43,240	(NA)[4]	3.3	41,062	65,704	4.6	5.1
Germany (Fed. Rep.) (marks)	58,550	74,482	7.7	7.9	7,621	9,243	1.0	.9	35,377	5,971	4.7	6.0
Japan[1] (yen)	297,829	723,449	.4	.6	431,228	936,534	.6	.8	2,719,300	3,524,000	3.7	3.1
Netherlands (florins)	12,636[3]	20,519[3]	9.8[3]	10.9[3]	1,325	2,846	1.0	1.5	5,969	9,919	4.6	5.3
Sweden (kronor)	11,045	17,854	6.1	7.2	5,968	8,814	3.3	3.5	11,789	18,386	6.4	7.4
United Kingdom (pounds)	2,002	3,320	3.8	4.5	1,079	1,802	2.1	2.4	2,087	3,049	4.0	4.1
United States[1] (dollars)	35,874	54,870	3.5	4.0	26,415	38,242	2.5	2.8	27,935	38,385	2.8	2.8

Source: Bureau of the Census, *Social Indicators* III (Washington, D. C.: U. S. Government Printing Office, 1980) p. 406.
[1]Some public expenditures for health care are included under public aid.
[2]Public aid expenditures are not separately identified.
[3]Includes expenditures for work-connected disability pensions.
[4]NA Not available.

FIGURE 2–1 Funding the Welfare State

The following graph shows the percentages of the gross national product that come from taxes in various industrialized societies. Societies with higher percentages have more comprehensive social welfare programs than the others. However, many societies are questioning whether they wish to continue to support the systems they have—even the United States, which has a less developed system than most other countries shown.

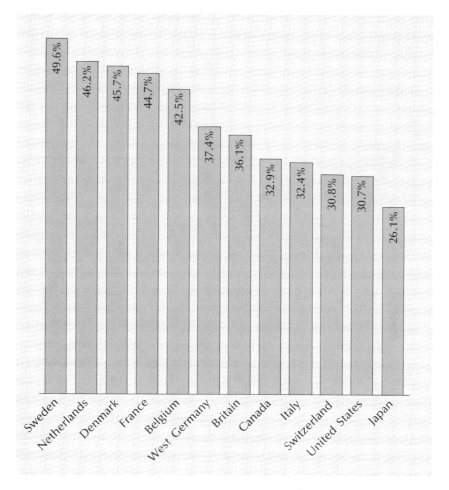

Source: The New York Times, April 25, 1983, p. D-11. © 1983 by The New York Times Company. Reprinted by permission.

REFLECTIONS ON SOCIAL WELFARE

The following six exhibits provide detailed analyses of some of the topics and issues addressed in this chapter. Reading them will help you to understand better how the social welfare institution is structured and how it functions.

EXHIBIT 2–1   The Volunteer Experience

The following excerpt examines the characteristics that competent volunteers should possess, discusses the kinds of tasks involved, suggests needed skills, and describes the relationship of the volunteer to the agency. It is interesting to note the use of the term friendly visitor *(rather than* volunteer*), a term that suggests how volunteers can reduce the anonymity of welfare bureaucracies, so that users perceive them as friends and neighbors rather than as impersonal specialists.*

We welcome you as a volunteer to aid in a Friendly Visiting Program among elderly or handicapped people. Without you this service would not be possible.

Your contribution is fourfold:

• It *enriches* the often cheerless and lonely life of an individual.
• It *supplements* the work of the professional staff.
• It is a *direct service* to your community.
• It enables *you* to grow in understanding and maturity.

Source: "A guide for friendly visitors" (mimeographed pamphlet) (Greensboro, North Carolina: Guilford County Department of Social Services). Used by permission.

What Is the Friendly Visiting Program?

The Friendly Visiting Program is an organized plan for visiting among people whose emotional and physical well-being is impaired by illness, injury, loneliness, or other misfortune.

Who Are the People Visited?

Elderly or handicapped people who live alone, in nursing or county homes, or in any situation where warmth or friendliness is needed. All have one need in common—the need for someone to take a personal interest in them.

Who Are the Friendly Visitors?

Volunteers—intelligent, friendly, dependable men and women who recognize the value of this program to the persons whom they visit and as a service to the community.

How Does the Program Operate?

Your local Social Services Department staff finds the need for this service among the people with whom they come in contact. If you want to volunteer you should contact the Social Services Department in your city or county.

Attendance at an orientation course is a prerequisite for each Friendly Visitor. This course, of no more than three sessions, is offered free of charge as the need arises.

The Friendly Visitor works with the agency caseworker or staff person requesting this service. The contact person provides the Friendly Visitor with further information and direction, has the story and pertinent facts about the person or persons to be visited and usually accompanies the volunteer on the first visit. Special emphasis is placed on matching interests on the basis of talents, hobbies, nationality. The Friendly Visitor reports directly to the agency contact person.

The above information pertains to Friendly Visitors volunteering as individuals or in connection with a group project.

What Do Friendly Visitors Do?

Create a warm and friendly relationship.

Chat of everyday affairs, except religion and politics.

Read aloud, write letters, play games, do puzzles.

Listen to and show respect for opinions and often-repeated stories.

Emphasize self-reliance but give assurance of help when needed.

Provide small, worthwhile jobs to do.

Assist with recreational activities.

Develop creative interests.

Admire and give importance to personal possessions.

Shop occasionally, with approval of the contact person.

Send seasonal greeting cards. Remember birthdays.

Take magazines, books, garden flowers, etc.

Cooperate with community affairs. Make posters, favors, place cards.

What Are the Duties of Friendly Visitors?

To observe the rules of the agency at all times.

To know and to keep within their privileges and limitations.

To visit regularly. If unavoidably detained, telephone. Should phoning not be possible, send an explanatory note.

To give full attention to the person visited.

To be a good listener. Consider the interests, likes and needs of each individual.

To refrain from discussion of controversial or depressing subjects.

To avoid criticism.

To guard against personal jokes and "talking down."

To respect names. It may be all there is left.

To help the older person assume responsibility for his own decisions.

To dress simply.

To keep confidential matters confidential.

To understand that all information about the residents, the staff, and the home are to be given out only by the person in charge. Publicity in any form is not the prerogative of Friendly Visitors.

What Qualifications Are Needed?

An *understanding* of and *liking* for elderly people.

A *sense of humor.*

Patience: Handicapped, confused, or senile persons are slow. Patience can go far to help a negative, irritable person to solve his own problems.

Tactfulness: To smooth over sensitive feelings.

Tolerance: To avoid unpleasant arguments.

Dependability: Disappointments are defeating.

Honesty: Admit mistakes. Don't be afraid to say you don't know.

Humility: Be willing to learn, and to accept constructive criticism with an open mind.

Generosity: Be willing for others to take the limelight.

Maturity: To communicate a sense of security and confidence. Understand that the elderly need to be useful and needed. They need to be loved and to have someone to love.

To recognize the spiritual values inherent in the warmth of friendliness.

Suggestions for Friendly Visitors

Establish a good rapport with the staff.

Check frequently with contact person to learn of developments.

Several visits may be required to gain the confidence of the persons visited.

Keep visits reasonably short. Do not stay through meal hours unless especially invited.

Be relaxed. When staying for only a few minutes do not appear hurried. Sit down in a chair where you can be easily seen. Do not sit or lean on the bed.

For the very ill, an affectionate pat may be better than a handshake.

Keep promises. Be careful what you promise.

Do not start anything that you are not prepared to carry through.

Refrain from talking in the corridors. Bits of conversation may be overheard, misinterpreted, and cause alarm.

Be a friend and companion. You are not expected to be a social worker, a pastor, a doctor, or a lawyer. Your visit means much to one who is shut away from normal family living. You may even be filling the place of the family.

Enjoy your visits. Cheeriness is contagious.

What Are the Responsibilities of the Friendly Visitors to the Agency?

To report regularly to the agency contact person. Any change in emotional, religious or physical problems should be reported immediately, and guidance and help requested.

To report to the contact person inability to accept or to continue an assignment once it has been accepted.

To recognize that Friendly Visitors supplement, not replace, the professional staff.

To avoid criticism of the policies of the agency.

To ask for a change if unhappy in the assignment.

Needs and Characteristics of the Elderly

The greatest contribution will be made by the volunteers who have a thorough understanding of the needs and characteristics of the elderly.

Some important factors are:

- Most older people are normal and have the same basic needs they have always had.
- They need to maintain their self-respect and as much independence as possible.
- Many have suffered loss of personal ties and are lonely. They feel rejected.
- They have to make adjustments continually to drastic and often tragic changes in their personal lives. These may include loss of husband, wife, or family; physical infirmities; changed economic circumstances; loss of employment and income; unfamiliar living arrangements; loss of community standing and influence. Many need reassurance. They are afraid of old age, of being alone, of illness, of not having enough money, or being pushed around. They fear death. They tend to be suspicious of anyone not connected with their own routine.

The Friendly Visitor can stimulate interest in the outside world and help renew a sense of personal dignity and worth.

Rehabilitation to self-care through personal attention, creative activity, physical exercise, and intellectual stimulation is worth all the time and effort that may be required.

Code of Volunteers

"As a Volunteer, I realize that I am subject to a code of ethics, similar to that which binds the professional. I, like them, in assuming certain responsibilities, expect to be accountable for those responsibilities. I will keep confidential matters confidential.

"As a Volunteer, I agree to serve without pay, but with the same high standard as the paid staff expect to do their work.

"I promise to take to my work an attitude of open-mindedness; to be willing to be trained for it; to bring to it interest and attention.

"I believe that my attitude toward volunteer work should be professional. I believe that I have an obligation to my work, to those for whom it is done, and to the community.

"Being eager to contribute all that I can to human betterment, I accept this code for the Volunteer as my code, to be followed carefully and cheerfully."

EXHIBIT 2–2   Social Work Professional Values

The following is the Code of Ethics implemented July 1, 1980, by the National Association of Social Workers (NASW), social work's largest professional association. Until 1969 only social workers holding the Master of Social Work

Source: Reprinted with permission of the National Association of Social Workers, Silver Spring, Md. Revised 1980.

degree were eligible for membership. In that year a membership category was also created for graduates of baccalaureate social work programs approved (now accredited) by the Council on Social Work Education. This NASW Code of Ethics is a good example of the codification of professional values that are expected to guide the behavior of members of particular social welfare professions.

This code should not be used as an instrument to deprive any social worker of the opportunity or freedom to practice with complete professional integrity; nor should any disciplinary action be taken on the basis of this code without maximum provision for safeguarding the rights of the social worker affected.

The ethical behavior of social workers results not from edict, but from a personal commitment of the individual. This code is offered to affirm the will and zeal of all social workers to be ethical and to act ethically in all that they do as social workers.

The following codified ethical principles should guide social workers in the various roles and relationships and at the various levels of responsibility in which they function professionally. These principles also serve as a basis for the adjudication by the National Association of Social Workers of issues in ethics.

In subscribing to this code, social workers are required to cooperate in its implementation and abide by any disciplinary rulings based on it. They should also take adequate measures to discourage, prevent, expose, and correct the unethical conduct of colleagues. Finally, social workers should be equally ready to defend and assist colleagues unjustly charged with unethical conduct.

Preamble

This code is intended to serve as a guide to the everyday conduct of members of the social work profession and as a basis for the adjudication of issues in ethics when the conduct of social workers is alleged to deviate from the standards expressed or implied in this code. It represents standards of ethical behavior for social workers in professional relationships with those served, with colleagues, with employers, with other individuals and professions, and with the community and society as a whole. It also embodies standards of ethical behavior governing individual conduct to the extent that such conduct is associated with an individual's status and identity as a social worker.

This code is based on the fundamental values of the social work profession that include the worth, dignity, and uniqueness of all persons as well as their rights and opportunities. It is also based on the nature of social work, which fosters conditions that promote these values.

In subscribing to and abiding by this code, the social worker is expected to view ethical responsibility in as inclusive a context as each situation demands and within which ethical judgement is required. The social worker is expected to take into consideration all the principles in this code that have a bearing upon any situation in which ethical judgement is to be exercised and professional intervention or conduct is planned. The course of action that the social worker chooses is expected to be consistent with the spirit as well as the letter of this code.

In itself, this code does not represent a set of rules that will prescribe all the behaviors of social workers in all the complexities of professional life. Rather, it offers general principles to guide conduct, and the judicious appraisal of conduct, in situations that have ethical implications. It provides the basis for making judgements about ethical actions before and after they occur. Frequently, the particular situation determines the ethical principles that apply and the manner of their application. In such cases, not only the particular ethical principles are taken into immediate consideration, but also the entire code and its spirit. Specific applications of ethical principles must be judged within the context in which they are being considered. Ethical behavior in a given situation must satisfy not only the judgement of the individual social worker, but also the judgement of an unbiased jury of professional peers.

Summary of Major Principles

I. *The Social Worker's Conduct and Comportment as a Social Worker*

A. *Propriety.* The social worker should maintain high standards of personal conduct in the capacity or identity as social worker.

B. *Competence and Professional Development.* The social worker should strive to become and remain proficient in professional practice and the performance of professional functions.

C. *Service.* The social worker should regard as primary the service obligation of the social work profession.

D. *Integrity.* The social worker should act in accordance with the highest standards of professional integrity.

E. *Scholarship and Research.* The social worker engaged in study and research should be guided by the conventions of scholarly inquiry.

II. *The Social Worker's Ethical Responsibility to Clients**

F. *Primacy of Clients' Interests.* The social worker's primary responsibility is to clients.

G. *Rights and Prerogatives of Clients.* The social worker should make every effort to foster maximum self-determination on the part of clients.

H. *Confidentiality and Privacy.* The social worker should respect the privacy of clients and hold in confidence all information obtained in the course of professional service.

I. *Fees.* When setting fees, the social worker should ensure that they are fair, reasonable, considerate, and commensurate with the service performed and with due regard for the clients' ability to pay.

---

*Note that this book uses the term *user of services,* rather than *client.*

III. *The Social Worker's Ethical Responsibility to Colleagues*

J. *Respect, Fairness, and Courtesy.* The social worker should treat colleagues with respect, courtesy, fairness, and good faith.

K. *Dealing with Colleagues' Clients.* The social worker has the responsibility to relate to the clients of colleagues with full professional consideration.

IV. *The Social Worker's Ethical Responsibility to Employers and Employing Organizations*

L. *Commitments to Employing Organizations.* The social worker should adhere to commitments made to the employing organizations.

V. *The Social Worker's Ethical Responsibility to the Social Work Profession*

M. *Maintaining the Integrity of the Profession.* The social worker should uphold and advance the values, ethics, knowledge, and mission of the profession.

N. *Community Service.* The social worker should assist the profession in making social services available to the general public.

O. *Development of Knowledge.* The social worker should take responsibility for identifying, developing, and fully utilizing knowledge for professional practice.

VI. *The Social Worker's Ethical Responsibility to Society*

P. *Promoting the General Welfare.* The social worker should promote the general welfare of society.

EXHIBIT 2–3 Three Examples of Social Welfare Bureaucratic Structures

---

Many types of bureaucratic structures exist in social welfare. These structures range from the federal Department of Health and Human Services to small private agencies. In this exhibit, three organizational charts are shown. They represent one federal-level and two state-level agencies. The first is the federal Department of Health and Human Services, the department most responsible for social welfare concerns. The second is the New Hanover County Department of Social Services in North Carolina. This is the structure of a multiservice agency that provides both income maintenance and social services. The third chart is for the Executive Department of the New York State Division of Probation, part of the State Department of Corrections. It illustrates how well-developed bureaucracies exist even in subparts of larger bureaucratic structures. (See pages 76–79.)

Organizational Chart of the Federal Department of Health and Human Services

(Reorganized May 1980)

ASSISTANT SECRETARY HDS/Deputy

- Executive Secretariat
- Public Affairs
- Equal Opportunity/Civil Rights
- Legislative Affairs

President's Commission on Mental Retardation

Work Incentive (WIN) program

Office of Management Services

- Office of Management Analysis & Reporting
- Division of Grants and Contracts
- Division of Budget
- Division of Administrative Services
- Division of Personnel

Office of Program Integration and Review

- Division of Regional Fiscal Operations
- Division of Technical Assistance
- Division of Training
- Division of Field Planning and Coordination

Office of Policy Development

- Division of Evaluation
- Division of Research and Development
- Division of Policy Coordination
- Division of Planning

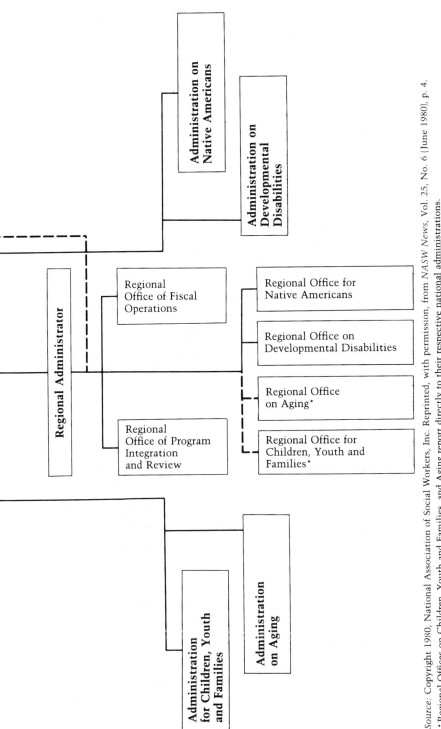

Source: Copyright 1980, National Association of Social Workers, Inc. Reprinted, with permission, from *NASW News,* Vol. 25, No. 6 (June 1980), p. 4.
* Regional Offices on Children, Youth and Families, and Aging report directly to their respective national administrations.

Organizational Chart of the New Hanover Department of Social Services

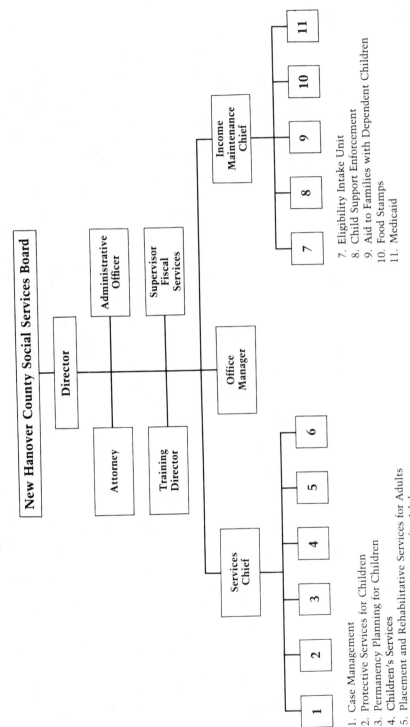

New Hanover County Social Services Board

Director

Administrative Officer

Attorney

Supervisor Fiscal Services

Training Director

Office Manager

Income Maintenance Chief

Services Chief

1 2 3 4 5 6

7 8 9 10 11

1. Case Management
2. Protective Services for Children
3. Permanency Planning for Children
4. Children's Services
5. Placement and Rehabilitative Services for Adults
6. Maintenance and Support Services for Adults

7. Eligibility Intake Unit
8. Child Support Enforcement
9. Aid to Families with Dependent Children
10. Food Stamps
11. Medicaid

Source: Courtesy New Hanover County Department of Social Services, Wilmington, N.C., F. Wayne Morris, Director.

Organizational Chart of the Executive Department of the New York State Division of Probation

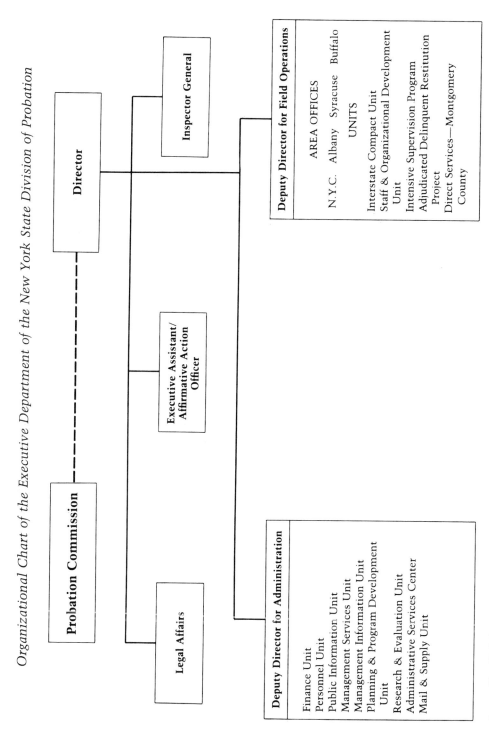

Source: New York State Division of Probation.

EXHIBIT 2–4 Battered Freddy

The following case excerpt is an excellent example of how bureaucracies can, though following all the proper procedures, fail to deliver needed services. In terms of fulfilling professional values, each bureaucracy was quite ineffective. This case also shows many parts of the social welfare system being brought to bear on a problem, with several social service professions becoming involved. Note the ultimate reliance on the family to mobilize the professional helping network in a meaningful way. Note also that the final ability of the system to act is based on the societal mandate given to certain professional systems (in this case the police) to forcibly intervene in the family. As the social service worker says, intervention in the family is a serious decision requiring a great deal of evidence because of its police-state implications. This case excerpt illustrates the delicate societal decisions often encountered in social welfare work.

At 17, one year after his parents were arrested for child abuse and he had had the benefit of warm professional care, Freddy was 4 ft. 6 in. and weighed 75 pounds. One of Freddy's doctors said, "I think he can grow to about five feet now, maybe a little more. . . . But it's pretty certain he'll always be stunted."

Before his aunt swore out a warrant for the arrest of Freddy's parents on child abuse charges, Freddy's name slipped in and out of the files of three city agencies, a private organization for retarded children, and the police, all to no avail:

1. A policewoman visited the home and, noting Freddy was small for his age, referred him to a special school at Rosewood State Hospital. "However, there were no vacancies at the time," and contact was ended.
2. Since Freddy was first brought to public school at age 12, he was not allowed to register as a regular student, and was referred to the Department of Education's Psychological Service Division for testing and evaluation. Contact was ended when "the Psychological Services Division was completely unsuccessful in getting the parents to bring Freddy in for an evaluation. . . ."
3. The Psychological Service Division referred Freddy to a public health nurse who noted "that although he was 12 years old, he seemed no more than 5." She made several attempts to get the parents to bring Freddy to the Health Department's diagnostic and evaluation center, which they never did. After more than a year of frustrated attempts to have the boy taken to a doctor, and after an appointment at Johns Hopkins Hospital was broken by the parents, the nurse gave up.

Source: Adam Kline, "Battered Freddy's new chance at childhood," *Baltimore Sun Magazine,* October 11, 1970, pp. 20ff. Used by permission.

4. The case was referred to the Baltimore Association for Retarded Children. After futile attempts at contact, "The Association notified the Health Department . . . that no progress could be made."

5. Referral was next made to the Department of Social Services. The worker there was allowed to take Freddy to the Department of Education for comprehensive psychological and intelligence testing. They recommended he be placed in a city school for trainable retarded children, but his parents refused to grant their permission. After another broken contact initiated by the parents, the Department of Education closed their file on Freddy. The Health Department did the same since it "had not been able to obtain evidence of physical maltreatment. . . ." This was followed by similar action by the Department of Social Services.

6. The warrant for the arrest of the parents was sworn out by Freddy's aunt.

Regarding this case, the agencies said:

HEALTH DEPARTMENT: "There was never any evidence of physical maltreatment that we could get a handle on. . . . If we sense a case of child neglect, we can only turn it over to Social Services; technically it would do no good to notify the school system of truancy, because he was never registered in a school to begin with. If there is any department that could have taken it to Juvenile Court then, it's Social Services, not us."

SOCIAL SERVICES: "A charge of contributing to the delinquency of a minor would be irrelevant. They kept him out of school, sure, but what school would have taken him anyway by the time it was brought to our attention? And not only that, he was almost 16, the age when school attendance becomes optional. If the parents weren't going to cooperate at that point, we felt there was nothing we could do. Look, it seems there was so much happening to the child, but we had no evidence of that; to tell the truth, we had no real evidence of anything other than that the boy was retarded and that they weren't doing anything to help him. The only way we could have found out more is by breaking down their front door, and this isn't a police state, we don't do things like that. The papers said the neighbors seemed to know what was going on, but, damn it, they never told us a thing."

EXHIBIT 2–5 Formal and Informal Helping

Formal and informal helping structures are very important to each other. The formal system would be far less effective if it did not have informal resources available. The following excerpt illustrates this point. Willard entered the

Source: Steve Bogira, "Casework," *Reader: Chicago's Free Weekly,* January 15, 1982, Vol. 11, No. 14, pp. 1ff. Copyright 1983 Chicago Reader, Inc.

formal helping system when he was brought to a psychiatric hospital by a family member. Since then, he has been in and out of formal and informal settings. Although the social worker agrees that the informal system would be best for the young man, he also believes that it cannot deal with Willard's problems. Only the formal structure has the needed resources. Ironically, it lacks other resources Willard needs that are best obtained in an informal structure, the family.

Willard is used to running—he is only 14, but he has been on the run regularly since late in 1979, when his grandmother decided she couldn't manage him anymore. Willard had been causing her all sorts of trouble; so she brought him to a psychiatric hospital and said she was through with him. Willard became a ward of the state of Illinois, which meant his guardian was the Department of Children and Family Services (DCFS). Since then, DCFS has found places for Willard to live, and Willard has run away from them. The police pick him up occasionally; that's why he jumps whenever he hears knocking.

This time it wasn't the cops at the door, but Jeff Jovien, Willard's DCFS caseworker. Jovien is bad news, too—he might be friendlier than the police, but he's more persistent, always tracking Willard down and telling him where to live. A few calls to people who knew Willard, and Jovien found out Willard was staying here, in this first-floor apartment of a dilapidated west-side two-flat that sits in the shadows of a housing project. A woman with a bunch of kids, call her Mrs. Booker, had taken Willard in after her kids said he was living in the streets this cold December.

Mrs. Booker gave Willard time to make his escape, and then she let Jovien in. It was late morning but the shades were drawn in the apartment; in the dimness Jovien could make out about a dozen people of assorted ages—a few toddlers, a few teens, a few adults. The teens eyed him suspiciously; satisfied he wasn't a cop, a couple of them ran out back and informed Willard, and he decided to come in. But he kept his wary eyes on Jovien, who was standing in the living room, and he would come no closer to the caseworker than the adjoining dining room. . . .

Jovien told Willard about a residential program outside of Cook County that might accept him. Jovien wanted to get him out of these surroundings, and he thought unfamiliar streets would be less of a lure for a chronic runaway. Of all his previous placements, Willard had stayed longest at a suburban institution.

"I ain't goin' way out there," Willard said.

"It isn't far."

"It *is* far."

Mrs. Booker walked into the living room, folding a tablecloth over her arm. "His shoes ain't got no bottoms," she told Jovien. "He wheezin' every night. To me, it seem he should be with a family. And he need school. See, I raised 12 kids. I know."

Jovien, too, thought it would be ideal if Willard could live with a family. But

Willard had been in a lot of hot water the past two years, getting picked up by the police for beating up a kid, for picking a pocket, and for pointing a gun at someone. He has behavior problems that foster parents wouldn't be equipped to handle; besides, with his record, finding foster parents who would take him would be nearly impossible. "He's been with a family," Jovien said. "It didn't work out."

EXHIBIT 2–6 Medicare and Medicaid Compared

The following comparison of Medicare and Medicaid provides a concise listing of the differences between these two federal social welfare programs.

	MEDICARE	**MEDICAID**
Objectives	Providing protection from financial need caused by medical-care costs.	Providing protection from financial need caused by medical-care costs.
Legislative Authorization	Social Security Act—Title 18.	Social Security Act—Title 19.
Funding	As insurance program: Medicare Hospital Insurance is financed by a separate payroll contribution (part of the regular Social Security withholding). Medicare Medical Insurance is financed by monthly premiums. The federal government pays half and the insured person pays half. Medicaid can pay the individual's premium for those who qualify for Medicaid coverage.	A grant program: Medicaid is financed by federal, state, and local governments. The federal government contributes from 50 percent (to the richest states) to 83 percent (to the state with the lowest per-capita income) of medical care costs for needy and low-income people who are aged, blind, disabled, under 21, or members of families with dependent children. Money is obtained from federal, state, and local taxes. States pay the remainder, usually with help from local governments.
Administration	Medicare is run by the federal government. Medicare is the same all over the United States. The Health Care Finance Administration of the United States Department of Health and Human Services is responsible for Medicare.	Medicaid is run by state governments within federal guidelines. Medicaid varies from state to state. The Health Care Finance Administration of the United States Department of Health and Human Services is responsible for the *federal aspects* of Medicaid.

	MEDICARE	MEDICAID
Eligibility	Medicare is for people 65 or older. Almost everybody 65 or older—rich or poor—can have Medicare. Some people 65 or older can have both Medicare and Medicaid.	Medicaid is for *certain kinds* of needy and low-income people: • the aged (65 or older) • the blind • the disabled • the members of families with dependent children • some other children Some states also include (at state expense) other needy and low-income people.
Coverage	Medicare paid medical bills for nearly 12 million people in 1977. Approximately 24 million people were covered by Medicare in 1975. Medicare is available everywhere in the United States.	Medicaid paid medical bills last year for more than 18 million people who were aged, blind, disabled, under 21, or members of families with dependent children. In addition, some states paid medical bills for low-income people *not* aged, blind, disabled, under 21, or members of families with dependent children.
Adequacy	Medicare pays part—but not all—of hospital and medical costs for people who are insured. Hospital Insurance pays inpatient hospital bills *except* for the first $256 (in 1982) plus additional co-payments after the first 60 days each year. Medical Insurance pays $4 out of each $5 of reasonable medical costs *except* for the first $75 each year (1981 figure). Medicare Hospital Insurance provides basic protection against costs of: • inpatient hospital care • post-hospital extended care • post-hospital home care • health care Medicare Medical Insurance provides supplemental protection against costs of physicians' services, medical services and supplies, home health-care services, outpatient hospital services and therapy, and other services.	Medicaid can pay what Medicare does not pay for people who are eligible for both programs. Medicaid can pay whatever Medicare does not pay in each benefit period for eligible people. Medicaid can pay any costs not paid by Medicare. Medicaid pays for at least these services: • inpatient hospital care • outpatient hospital services • other laboratory and x-ray services • skilled nursing home services • physicians' services • screening, diagnosis, and treatment of children • home health care services In many states Medicaid pays for such additional services as dental care, prescribed drugs, eye glasses, clinic services, intermediate care facility services, and other diagnostic, screening, preventive, and rehabilitative services.

Equity	Tied to Social Security which has not achieved universal coverage and tends to be least likely to cover the unskilled, transient worker. Is available only to those 65 or older. While hospital insurance is automatic for those covered by Social Security, medical insurance is optional and requires an additional payment.	Benefits are not the same in all states having programs. Tied to receipt of public assistance or Supplemental Security Income—public assistance is known to have incomplete coverage within the eligible population and to discourage participation through restrictive eligibility requirements and demeaning application procedures.

Source: "Medicaid, Medicare—which is which?", Department of Health, Education, and Welfare (Washington, D.C.: U.S. Government Printing Office, July 1972); Harriette C. Johnson and Gertrude S. Goldberg (1982), *Government Money for Everyday People* (Garden City, N.Y.: Adelphi University School of Social Work); "Your Social Security," Department of Health, Education, and Welfare (Washington, D.C.: U.S. Government Printing Office, May 1975); and *Social Indicators* III, Bureau of the Census (Washington, D.C.: U.S. Government Printing Office, December 1980), p. 399.

STUDY QUESTIONS

1. Make a chart that shows as many relationships as you can think of between the social welfare institution and the other major social institutions in our society. Do certain institutions have more of an impact on the social welfare institution than others? Be sure to include the impact the social welfare institution has on other institutions. After you have finished, compare your chart with someone else's chart and discuss the differences between the two with that person.

2. After reading the material on the characteristics of professions, are you convinced that professions are different from any other occupation? Compare a profession to a nonprofession (being a secretary, for example), and see what differences you find. On the basis of your analysis, should professions have the degree of autonomy that they claim? If professions were less autonomous, what regulatory mechanisms would you suggest?

3. What area of social welfare most interests you—social work, medicine, gerontology (working with the aged), child welfare, corrections, and so on? In your area of interest, explore the literature to discover where you can find what specific programs are available. Make a list of as many programs as you can find, and try to learn a little about each. Are you surprised that there are so many programs? or so few?

4. Select a specific program that interests you and apply Bell's evaluative criteria. Do the criteria help you to understand the program better? Do they help you to understand better whether the program actually helps people? Why or why not?

5. How do you feel about working in a social welfare bureaucracy? Many students think they wouldn't like it, because of the impersonality or the paper work. What do you think? Do you see any advantages to working in a social welfare bureaucracy?

SELECTED READINGS

Bell, Winifred (1983). *Contemporary Social Welfare*. New York: Macmillan.

Johnson, Harriette, and Gertrude Goldberg (1982). *Government Money for Everyday People*. Garden City, N. Y.: Adelphi University School of Social Work.

Kamerman, Sheila, and Alfred J. Kahn (1976). *Social Services in the United States.* Philadelphia: Temple University Press.

Pierce, Dean (1984). *Policy for the Social Work Practitioner.* New York: Longman Publishers.

Washington Social Legislation Bulletin. Published biweekly by the Social Legislation Information Service, a division of the Child Welfare League of America, 1346 Connecticut Avenue NW, Washington, D. C. 20036.

The Historical Development of Social Welfare

In early 1983, only one of the six emergency rooms in Mobile, Alabama
was open on weekends—one fully staffed emergency room for some
350,000 people.

The reason . . . is complex. The factors are competition among hospitals,
the flight of doctors and clinics to wealthy suburbs, skyrocketing medical
costs and high unemployment, and breakdown of the state's weak mechanism for coordinating health services.

But many agree that the heart of the problem is public resistance, reflected
in county and state politics, to provide adequate funds for health care of
the indigent. . . .

The city's medical plight became serious . . . when the University of South
Alabama Medical Center announced that it was closing its emergency
room on weekends and would no longer accept patients from out of the
county unless payment for their care could be guaranteed. . . .

"There is no Santa Claus," said . . . a state legislator who had been exploring additional financing for the hospital. "Everybody wants services, but
nobody wants to pay for them . . ." (Miller, 1983).*

At first glance, it may seem difficult to understand how the situation
in Mobile could have developed. The need for medical care is obvious,
so why was it so difficult for the various people involved to develop a
plan to provide it? The answer lies in a complex web of forces that
reach back to England, from which many of this society's ways of thinking and acting have come. To fully understand the present, then, it is
necessary to have some knowledge of the past.

This chapter will trace the major factors and events influencing the
development of social welfare. The special importance of values is
emphasized. Because the programs established by the Social Security
Act are of particular significance for the current structure of social
welfare services, we will examine them in some detail. Considerable
attention is also paid to recent developments, because they represent
a significant change of direction for the social welfare institution in the
United States.

The Bases of Social Welfare

There are two characteristics of the human condition that make social
welfare an integral part of our humanity. The first characteristic is that
human beings, compared to other animal species, have relatively little
behavior controlled by genetic programming. Most animals are born
with the developmental program that will lead them inevitably to perform the behaviors necessary for survival. Humans, on the other hand,
have to *learn* the behaviors that will enable them to survive physically
and socially. Unlike other animals that are primarily characterized by
genetic programming, humans have as a dominant inherited characteristic the ability to think, learn, and adapt (Berger and Federico, 1982).
We learn how to behave, making it possible to learn the ways of the
particular culture in which we live.

The adaptive capacity of humans leads to the second important aspect of the human condition: our humanity resides in our social interaction. We become human participants in an ongoing social unit by
interacting with others and learning appropriate behavior (Federico
and Schwartz, 1983). This interaction not only teaches us what to do,

---

*© 1983 by The New York Times Company. Reprinted by permission.

but also ultimately gives us a sense of ourselves. We acquire a group identity and a position within that group on the basis of our interaction with others. It is easy to see, then, how our minimal amount of genetic programming and our need for social interaction makes us dependent on others.

The goal of social welfare—to improve social functioning and minimize pain—can only be accomplished socially. Ultimately, our dependence on others can itself be a source of personal breakdown and suffering, but even in those cases, the solution lies within the social network. Human groups are formed because they are useful for their members. By banding together, human beings ensure their basic survival in terms of protection and reproduction. Beyond that, the group makes possible the highly complex social patterns we take for granted today.

The first human group to emerge was probably the family, a group built around the desire for sexual expression and the need for physical protection. The family can be regarded as the earliest social welfare unit, and it continues to be a basic social welfare resource today. Most societies have **extended family units**—families made up of three or more generations and a variety of kin members. This large family is well suited to agricultural societies in which work occurs close to home and in which all family members have work-related tasks they can perform. The family form dominant in industrial societies like the United States is the **nuclear family.** It is made up of two generations, adults and their children. This smaller family is better suited to wage economies, in which the home and workplace are separated. Because the nuclear family has fewer family members who can work together than does the extended family, its resources are limited. As a result, the nuclear family has been gradually supplemented with other social welfare services, resulting in a complex network of resources, of which the family is only one. Nevertheless, even today the family holds a special place in the social welfare institution. It has the right to make decisions that other social welfare units are legally prevented from counteracting (a point illustrated in Exhibit 2–4, "Battered Freddy").

Early Social Welfare Services Outside the Family

The church was perhaps the earliest formalized helping structure beyond the family for the poor, the sick, and the aged (Klein, 1968). The Judeo-Christian beliefs expressed in the Old and New Testaments, which commanded that the needy be served, led to early church-provided social welfare services through its network of parishes and monasteries. Only as the development of national governments during the Industrial Revolution gradually broke the power of feudal and church landholders were these services substantially reduced in importance. Today, the church continues to be instrumental in providing social welfare services. This occurs informally through such activities of individual churches as counseling the bereaved, opening churches as shelters for the homeless, and collecting food and clothes for the poor. Services are provided more formally through social agencies with religious affiliations, such as hospitals and residential homes for the retarded, the emotionally disturbed, or unwed mothers. Multiservice agencies under church auspices provide counseling and financial assistance. In addition to churches, early social welfare services were provided by fraternal membership organizations, such as guilds. These organizations were somewhat similar to present-day unions and groups such as the Shriners and Knights of Columbus, which continue to provide social welfare services for members in need.

The 1500s in England saw early attempts to formalize and unify social welfare services beyond churches, monasteries, guilds, and other benevolent groups (Steinberg, 1963). The **parish**, the local governmental unit most similar to what we call a county, began to organize the provision of charity by parceling out responsibility for the poor to both religious and secular organizations. Even though units of government were beginning to organize them, these services were still provided through private charity. The use of public funds to help those in need was an eventual result of the **Industrial Revolution.** Most broadly, the Industrial Revolution refers to replacing human and animal power with that from machines (Schenk and Schenk, 1981). Its social significance, however, lies in the profound social changes that resulted, starting in England in the 1600s.

There were three especially important social effects of the Industrial Revolution: the breakdown of the medieval feudal system, the centralization of political power in national governments, and the displacement of church power by secular governments. These changes shifted resources from the church and feudal landowners to emerging national governments (Notestein, 1954). At the same time, need increased. The mechanization of wool processing led to the wool trade becoming more productive in England than farming. Large amounts of land were removed from cultivation and given over to grazing. This process displaced many farm workers and reduced the value of land, in turn reducing the power of the feudal landholders. Monasteries, also large landholders, were broken up, thereby reducing the ability of the church to provide charity. By 1518 the swelling ranks of the unemployed and homeless generated efforts to block migrants and the unemployed from wandering in search of work or aid (you will recall similar actions taken in the 1980s by such communities as Phoenix, described at the beginning of Chapter 1). With the resources of churches and feudal lords reduced, the power and responsibility of local and ultimately national governments to care for the poor increased (Coll, 1969).

A commission appointed to study England's unemployment in the 1500s noted that it was caused by social changes rather than by the personal inadequacy of those affected (Mencher, 1967). Indeed, every study of widespread unemployment has reached the same conclusion throughout the history of social welfare. Nevertheless, as in our own day, much of the governmental response was to pass legislation to preserve the existing social order. The **Elizabethan Poor Law** was passed in 1601 for this purpose (Kurzman, 1970). This legislation was important for four major reasons:

First, it established three categories of the poor: the helpless, the involuntarily unemployed, and the vagrant (Leonard, 1965). These categories have influenced our thinking about the needy up to the present day. The helpless were those with a disabling condition over which they had no control, such as the aged, mentally ill, mentally or physically handicapped, diseased, and the orphaned. These people were generally considered unable to care for themselves, and so were accepted as a responsibility of the community. The involuntarily unemployed were those who had suffered some kind of misfortune, such as fire, robbery, or having more children than they could handle ("overcharged with children"). Those in this group were considered somewhat responsible for their condition, and were expected to work for what they got (or else be punished). The vagrant included drifters, beggars, and others who had no roots in the community. They were not considered to be the responsibility of the community and were forced to leave.

The parish welfare structure that resulted from concepts established by the Poor Law consisted of four main parts: almshouses, outdoor relief, workhouses, and indenture (Leonard, 1965:137). **Almshouses** provided housing and food for the group defined as helpless. They were a type of **indoor relief,** because assistance was provided in facilities established for that purpose. Although almshouses were far from appealing, they did meet people's basic needs and were an acknowledgment of the community's responsibility for those who were defined as not able to help themselves. Those in the needy category who could manage on their own, especially the aged and some of the handicapped, received **outdoor relief.** This was help provided in the recipient's own home, rather than moving that person into an almshouse. **Workhouses** were provided for the able-bodied needy, primarily those defined as involuntarily unemployed. These people were expected to work for the housing and food they received, and were stigmatized for being needy, because they were thought to bear at least some responsibility for their situation. Those who refused to work were sent to houses of correction.

Children of destitute families were **indentured.** They were removed from their own homes and placed with another family, which agreed to provide room and board in return for the child's work. Although indenture seems cruel by contemporary standards, and many children were in fact exploited by the families that agreed to care for them, it was intended to be helpful for the child. It was believed that removing children from destitute families would both provide for their physical needs and give them appropriate role models. The Poor Law makes it clear how social welfare is a way of thinking about the needy, and that this way of thinking is what determines the structure of social welfare services that result. This relationship between a conception of social welfare and a service-delivery structure is clearly seen in our contemporary network of services, as we will see later in the chapter.

A second important effect of the Elizabethan Poor Law of 1601 was its recognition of the desirability of national coverage and administration of public welfare, a feature of many contemporary public programs. It never accomplished total national coverage, however, and the parish continued to be the local unit through which the legislation was administered. Third, funds to support the programs created by the Elizabethan Poor Law came from voluntary contributions and, for the first time, public funds in the form of a public land tax. This was a significant recognition of the responsibility of the government for its citizens, a concept that is basic to our current efforts to strengthen the social welfare institution. Finally, the Law tried to strengthen the family, because it was felt to be the foundation of the community. It made parents and grandparents responsible for their children up to the age of twenty-four for boys and twenty-one for girls (unless they were married).

The Elizabethan Poor Law was a highly significant piece of legislation in a number of respects. It clearly stated the responsibility of the national and local governments for the well-being of citizens. It categorized recipients, according to how responsible for their own need they were thought to be. Services were provided differentially to those two groups, with those defined as having responsibility expected to work for what they got. The Poor Law also established the idea of communities only being responsible for their own members. Outsiders were simply turned away. Finally, the principle of removing children from homes considered unsuitable was established.

Although passed nearly 300 years ago, and in another country, it is remarkable how much of the Elizabethan Poor Law can be found in our own social welfare institution. Programs still differentiate between types of recipients, with those less stigmatized receiving more aid under less demeaning circumstances. Although the concept of a residence requirement was declared unconstitutional in 1969 (*Shapiro* v. *Thompson*), we have already seen how some communities in the Southwest tried to deter migrants seeking work during the depressed economic conditions of the 1980s. Children are still removed from their homes when that is considered to be in their best interests, but parents continue to have basic responsibility for their children. Houses of correction continue in the form of prisons, and some would say that many mental hospitals and nursing homes are not far removed from some of the demeaning conditions that were common in almshouses. It is easy to see, then, why a knowledge of history is important for fully understanding the present social welfare institution.

As the number of needy increased, attitudes became more punitive and, by the 1700s, harsher laws and the narrowing of poor relief occurred. Poverty and dependency were further stigmatized, and thrift, sobriety, and hard work were glorified. Amendments to the 1601 Poor Law went so far as to evict from a parish anyone who might become dependent. In 1776 Adam Smith published *The Wealth of Nations*, in which he recommended the amassing of wealth. He believed that people should be allowed to pursue economic activity with a minimum of societal restraints, a principle called **laissez-faire capitalism.** Though he did not call for the end of the poor laws, he felt that giving freely to people would only result in dependency and misery (Coll, 1969:9). Others followed in pointing out the evils of supporting those in need, with Thomas Malthus arguing in 1798 that population growth would soon outrun food production. The rise of Protestantism in Europe and England provided further impetus for making relief more punitive. It stressed the importance of individual effort, rather than the charity and the help-your-neighbor attitude of the Judeo-Christian tradition.

Gradually the punitive aspects of the poor laws came to be stressed over their rehabilitative components (Mencher, 1967).

Social conditions worsened between 1740 and 1850 as the Industrial Revolution gained momentum. The uncontrolled growth of factories and the towns that grew up around them created new social problems, especially those related to pollution, health, housing, and crime. In addition, the population was growing rapidly. In response to these conditions, the **Speenhamland Act** was passed in 1796. It established the **bread scale,** an income level guaranteed to all. The bread scale was based on family size and food costs, and those whose income fell below it were entitled to financial aid. The Speenhamland Act was probably ahead of its time in trying to establish a poverty level and a guaranteed income, but the direct cause of its failure turned out to be the greed of "law-abiding citizens." Because employers knew that workers would get at least the bread scale no matter what wages they were paid, the Speenhamland Act had the effect of driving wages down, thereby increasing welfare costs. This is an early example of how well-meaning, humane, social legislation is sometimes abused and exploited by the affluent so that it benefits them rather than those in need (an example of a conflict between the manifest and latent functions of social welfare). A more recent example of this exploitation is the rapidly rising cost of medical care that has escalated the costs of Medicare and Medicaid. As a result, numerous actions have occurred to control the services covered by these programs (Pear, 1983). Inevitably, either services are decreased or people have to use more of their own income to obtain them.

Early Social Welfare in America

Much in the new society was borrowed from the old one, and that included the basic approach to social welfare. Carried over with the Poor Law were the practices of residence requirements, parental responsibility, classification of the needy, and indoor and outdoor relief. Residence requirements in the colonies included the practices of **warning out** (the turning away of persons who might become dependent) and **passing on** (transporting people to their legal residence if they became dependent) (Coll, 1969:20).

A different approach to social welfare arose from the obvious needs created by the rigors of frontier life and the rise of Romanticism spawned by the American and French revolutions. Romantic ideals emphasized the goodness, uniqueness, and value of each individual,

thereby supporting attempts to increase individual autonomy and provide basic social welfare services to all. Values based in Romanticism
had some important practical results. Prison reforms were initiated,
starting with the opening of the Walnut Street Prison in Philadelphia in
1790. Conditions in almshouses gradually improved, and many were
converted into hospitals for the poor. This improvement was stimulated by the arrival of over six million immigrants between 1820 and
1860, many of whom arrived destitute, ill, and with language barriers.
These immigrants were highly motivated and usually needed only temporary care until they could regain their health and become acclimated
to their new society. In response to such needs, medical care in
almshouses was sometimes provided by some of the greatest physicians in the country, and many almshouses gradually became hospitals. Manhattan's Bellevue Hospital, Philadelphia's General Hospital,
and Baltimore City Hospital were all originally almshouses.

The period from 1830 to 1860 brought other reforms as well.
Thoreau, Emerson, and other intellectuals recognized the need for
social reform, and they stimulated attempts to establish experimental
social communities to find better ways of life. Brook Farm and the
Oneida Community were two examples of their day, and the com-
munes and planned communities of our day continue the search for
more satisfying community environments. In addition, movements to
correct the social ills of industry, eliminate religious intolerance, and
provide better treatment of the insane increased (Cohen, 1958). Education, women's suffrage, temperance, trade unionism, and slavery were
other important issues of the time that reflected society's struggles
with early industrialization and the values of freedom and democracy.

In spite of these reforms, conflicting views on welfare continued.
Some felt that hard-working individuals should not have to pay taxes to
support the idle, whereas others felt that those people who had once
contributed to society should be aided in troubled times. Some felt
volunteer charities should be the only source of aid, whereas others
believed that volunteer charities were too limited and unstable to bear
the sole responsibility for aiding those in need. These are, of course,
issues still being debated today.

New Patterns of Helping: The Legacy of the 1800s

From 1860 to 1900 the population of the United States rose from 31.5
million to 76 million, 13.7 million of them immigrants. The Industrial
Revolution was having a profound effect on the United States during

Immigrating to the United States has been an experience that has often entailed physical discomforts and painful changes in social relationships. This photo illustrates the crowded conditions that were common aboard immigrant ships in the early part of this century. (Museum of the City of New York)

this period, and the nation was rapidly becoming a large, urban society, increasingly aware of its problems. During the 1800s social welfare progress occurred in three major spheres: public social welfare services; private social welfare services; and services for special groups.

Progress in Public Social Welfare

From 1857 onward, outdoor relief became more generally accepted and gradually replaced almshouses. Studies had shown outdoor relief to be less costly than help provided in almshouses. The belief also grew that those temporarily in need should not be subjected to the degrading conditions of almshouse life. Outdoor relief payments were small, however, because many continued to believe that low payment levels would encourage recipients to seek work. These beliefs continued in spite of evidence indicating that the majority of the needy could not work (Coll, 1969:30–37).

The Civil War and its aftermath led to other changes in the public welfare system. In this period of intellectual and social upheaval, the equality of all people and the struggle between competing political and economic systems became issues of high priority. Congressional responses to these issues included the passage of the Morrill Act and the establishment of the Freedmen's Bureau in 1865. The former gave states land grants to build colleges and other public facilities. The latter was created to help the needy, especially former slaves, by providing financial assistance and free education in the South (Smith and Zeitz, 1970). The Freedmen's Bureau was supported by the first federal tax legislation to care for the poor, a clear governmental declaration of its responsibility for citizens who were the pawns of the political and economic dislocation of the Civil War.

Progress in Private Social Welfare: The Charity Organization Society

Although progress was being made in the public sphere, by the 1880s the limited help provided stimulated efforts to better structure private charity. The best known was the Charity Organization Society (COS). Begun in England in 1869, COS opened its first United States affiliate in Buffalo in 1877, and by 1892 America had ninety-two offices. The purposes behind the COS were ". . . to end the abuse of charity, especially by professional beggars; to make charity more effective for those who really deserved it; and to mobilize the forces of helpfulness" (Leiby, 1978). The COS followed the teaching of Josephine Shaw Lowell, as espoused in her book *Public Relief and Private Charity*. Lowell believed that all relief should be voluntary and made unpleasant enough so that few would stoop to ask for aid. She further believed that almshouses and workhouses should be rehabilitative, with those working there finding moral regeneration. On the other hand, careful records were kept and claims were carefully investigated.

Lowell based her system of helping on some insidious values. Her underlying belief was that most needy people were capable of work, a belief no truer then than it had been earlier or is today. She also continued to distinguish between deserving and undeserving poor, and required people to prove their need for aid. Such values and practices continue to undermine contemporary efforts to formulate an adequate social welfare system, and as such were unfortunate parts of Lowell's work. However, she did make beneficial changes, as well. The individual was considered for relief according to that person's own set of circumstances. However, if a person was found worthy of aid, the charity of relatives, the church, and others was sought before the COS offered help.

At first, COS workers were volunteers. However, keeping careful records and making regular visits to recipients were tasks that most volunteers didn't want to do, and soon both became the job of paid agents. These agents were the first "social workers," as we now define that term—that is, paid helpers using specified procedures to investigate need and provide resources. This professional development was greatly aided by the work of Mary Richmond, a major figure in the COS in the United States. In 1897 she called for the establishment of a training school for professional social workers, and she subsequently formulated the first statement of the principles of social casework (Lubove, 1969).

The COS played an important role in the development of social welfare in the United States. Besides spawning the profession of social work and improving the systematic, organized way in which private services were provided, it clarified the individual circumstances that might create need. It also influenced and enlisted the support of scholars from university campuses and set standards of case evaluation that all charity and relief organizations could use. Further, COS offered auxiliary services: an employment bureau; a savings and thrift class; a loan office; a workroom; legal aid; a day nursery for working mothers; and visiting nurses.

Public agencies were modeled after the private Charity Organization Societies. The first was the State Board of Charities in Massachusetts in 1863; by 1897 there were fifteen more states with similar agencies. They improved conditions in facilities for the needy, and created special services for children, the handicapped, and the mentally ill (Bruno, 1957). These agencies also tried to counteract the excessively moralistic and restrictive aspects of COS practices, supporting outdoor relief over almshouse care as the most effective and humane way to provide help. However, the battle over the effects of outdoor relief continued into the new century, as Lowell contended that it would lead to shiftlessness and dependence. As a result, many states vacillated between outdoor relief and almshouse care.

Other Private Social Welfare Developments

In response to continued criticisms of outdoor relief, other solutions were sought. The settlement house movement caught on as a possible alternative: in 1887, Neighborhood House in New York opened; Hull House and the Northwestern University Settlement in Chicago opened in 1889 and 1891, respectively; and the South End Settlement in Boston opened in 1892. The settlement houses were community centers that met special community needs for practical education, recreation, and social cohesion. They were especially supportive in helping immigrants get a foothold in America. The settlement houses formed ties with universities and the community in which they existed, and proved more understanding of the causes of poverty than the COS.

Contemporary self-help movements to reduce inequality and improve the quality of life in society are logical successors to the principles established in the settlement house movement. Today we speak of consumer advocacy, participation of the poor, community organization, and the like. Although the terminology may be modern, the ideas were sown in the earlier settlement house movement, which exemplified a community approach to problem solving.

Progress in the provision of services for special groups occurred during the late 1800s. Of particular importance was the labor union movement that grew out of workers' attempts to protect themselves against abuse and exploitation in America's expanding but often dangerous and unpleasant factories (Cohen, 1958). Two events aided those who were physically and mentally ill. The founding of the American Medical Association in 1847 improved standards of medical care and practice (illustrating an important function of any social welfare professional association, discussed in the last chapter). At about the same time, Dorothea Dix was working to improve the treatment of the mentally ill by removing them from houses of correction. Children and prisoners were also helped. Legislation passed in the late 1800s prohibited the removal of children from their homes solely because of poverty, improved foster-care procedures, and better protected juvenile offenders. In addition, conditions of prison life and sentencing procedures were made more humane and more equitable (Cohen, 1958).

Social Welfare Before the Great Depression

Between 1900 and 1925 the population of the United States reached 100 million, with 50 percent of the people living in cities. The United States, by then an important industrial nation and world power, had attained a unique level of prosperity and wealth. The gross national product reached $104.4 billion just before the stock market crash of 1929. In the period from 1900 to World War I, a group of concerned citizens called Progressives sought to expose the evils of low wages, long hours, bossism, health hazards, and other problems facing the poor in the cities. Social workers also tried to help, and at the 1912 Conference on Charities and Correction, the Committee on Standards of Living and Labor recommended a liberal list of much-needed reforms. Among them were the eight-hour workday for women, children, and some men, and a six-day work week (Coll, 1969:63). In 1912, Woodrow Wilson took office on the platform of New Freedom, and before the outbreak of World War I, he pushed strongly for reform.

Child-labor laws were developed to protect young people from the pain and fear this boy so eloquently expresses after being injured in a mill near the turn of the century. (Library of Congress)

The protection of children was a prime concern in the early 1900s. Theodore Roosevelt held the first White House Conference on Children in 1909. The conference dealt with the care of dependent children and resulted in the formation of the Children's Bureau in the Department of Labor in 1912. The bureau, in the capable hands of Julia Lathrop and Grace Abbott, carefully regulated the laws and reforms concerning children's rights in this country (Coll, 1969:72). Special health services for children were also sought, and by 1934 thirty-seven states had developed programs for diagnostic services, medical treatment, and convalescent care for crippled children (Miles, 1949:200).

By the 1920s, reformers had generated a greater awareness of the need that often resulted from such factors as poor sanitation facilities, low wages, poor safety precautions in industry, and various other occupational hazards. Unemployment, illness or incapacity, death of the breadwinner, and old age were also accepted as legitimate causes of need. Work-related problems were especially obvious in early factory systems, and by 1920 forty-three states had passed workmen's compensation laws (Coll, 1969:74). This legislation was especially important because it was an early form of social insurance, a type of social welfare program that was to figure prominently in the Social Security Act of 1935.

Workmen's Compensation is a program to cover work-connected injury. Each state must develop its own program, as the federal government does for federal employees. The program is considered a cost to an employer of doing business, and employers are required to have a plan with a private insurance company, a state-run plan, or be self-insured. Although the scope of coverage, benefit provisions, and administrative procedures vary by state, in all states covered workers injured on the job receive benefits from the employer's insurance plan. Workmen's compensation is a plan that does not entail a direct cash grant out of public monies. Instead, employers have paid into a fund from which workers are paid in the event of injury on the job. As with any insurance, some employers pay in more than their workers ever collect, while others have workers collecting more than the employer paid. This sharing of risk is characteristic of any insurance plan. It is easy to see how a particularly salient problem of the time, industrial safety, combined with a social welfare program that did not disrupt societal values of self-reliance, resulted in a workable solution to the problem. When the need for the Social Security Act was recognized in the 1930s, it is little wonder that the Congress turned first to the social insurance concept.

Workmen's compensation is a good program to use in examining some characteristics of the relationship between the states and the federal government with respect to social welfare policy. In recognition of states' rights, a basic principle of the society's political structure, each state has developed its own workmen's compensation plan within broad federal guidelines. This has led to variations in coverage among states that result in unequal benefits: residents of different states get different benefits. This trade-off of nonuniform and therefore inequitable programs in return for maintaining state autonomy is one that characterizes several other important programs, Aid to Families with Dependent Children being another major example.

State autonomy in welfare policy also makes it possible for some states to have programs that others do not, creating another type of inequality among states. In the Aid to Families with Dependent Children program, for example, some states allow families with an unemployed father to live with the family, whereas others will not provide benefits if there is an employable adult male present, unemployed or not. The effect of this difference in programs is that in some states families can remain together while receiving AFDC benefits, while in others men must abandon their families in order for the family to receive help.

On the other hand, state autonomy often has a beneficial impact on national programs by allowing for state experimentation that may ultimately result in national legislation. Workmen's compensation is a case in point, because it was the recognition by individual states of the need for compensation for work-related accidents that finally led to federal legislation requiring all states to have such programs. This history illustrates once again the close interaction between the social welfare institution and other major social institutions (the economic institution, in this instance).

Social welfare programs were gradually developed to aid various special groups besides those already mentioned. By 1920 forty states had passed acts to aid needy mothers, and soon after, similar aid was made available to the aged. Lobbies were formed to improve facilities for the destitute aged, and by the Depression, the lobby for the aged was one of the most powerful groups pushing for social security legislation. The early 1900s also saw the continued growth of voluntary organizations financed by dues, donations, and subscriptions. Some of the best-known groups were the Boy Scouts, Girl Scouts, National Tuberculosis Association, American Cancer Society, the National Association for the Advancement of Colored People (NAACP), and the

National Child Labor Committee (Bremner, 1960:117). Another voluntary organization, the Red Cross, performed important functions under the directorship of Harry Hopkins during World War I.

The Impact of the Great Depression

The stock market crash of 1929 ushered in the Great Depression. People lost thousands and even millions of dollars as stock became worthless and banks failed. People who had always worked and who desperately wanted to continue working could no longer find jobs as the entire economic system came close to collapse. Social events prevented people from working and generated massive need. Individuals were no longer in control, and the American value system would never be the same. Hard work and thrift were suddenly not enough to ensure economic security, and it was this realization that made possible the

Problems in the nation's economic system have created periods of economic depression and high unemployment. This unemployment line in Memphis in 1938 illustrates the fact that minorities have always been most hurt by high unemployment. (Library of Congress)

sweeping changes enacted during the presidency of Franklin D. Roosevelt. These changes became known as the **New Deal,** a program to restore the country's economic health. Naturally, this would in turn aid the individuals who were suffering because of the economic problems created by the Great Depression.

The Depression answered the question of whether financial assistance should be primarily public or private. The crisis was so widespread that private agencies could not begin to alleviate the unemployment and resulting need (Coll, 1969:81). It was this impetus that finally made the federal government assume the major responsibility for economic stability and personal economic security. The economic crisis had caused poverty and unemployment, and only the federal government had the power to stem the rising tide of business and banking failures. As a result of the Great Depression, people came to view poverty as a societal rather than an individual problem (Mencher, 1967:363).

Early Social Welfare Responses to the Great Depression

Early responses to the economic crisis were partial and fragmented. Efforts were directed at dealing with specific parts of the problem, especially unemployment. Some states established emergency relief administrations to help the unemployed. The federal government passed legislation in 1932 to authorize the Reconstruction Finance Corporation to make loans to states for public works projects and to help fund unemployment relief programs (Miles, 1949:219). President Roosevelt also established the Federal Emergency Relief Act (FERA), to make grants-in-aid to states for work-relief and unemployment-relief programs. The Public Works Administration was also designed to stimulate employment by increasing the demand for heavy or durable goods and stimulating purchasing power.

Although much of the early legislation passed in immediate response to the Great Depression was at least partially successful in alleviating need, it soon became apparent that a more fundamental change in the nation's economic and social welfare structures was necessary. Early legislation carefully tried to protect the traditional relationship between the states and the federal government. Many programs were developed by states, sometimes with federal assistance. This created a patchwork of programs that created inequalities across the country in terms of services available to people. In addition, no state had the power that the federal government possessed to address what was truly a national problem. At best, individual states could try to relieve the suffering of their citizens by stimulating local industry and providing local services. As long as the whole nation was in an economic depression, however, state efforts were bound to be only partially successful. The nation was obviously reluctant to bring sweeping changes at the federal level, because doing so would permanently alter the whole pattern of federal-state relations. Yet there seemed no alternative, after early efforts to solve the crisis proved to be insufficient.

The Social Security Act of 1935: The Enduring Legacy of the Great Depression

The Social Security Act was proposed by President Roosevelt and passed by Congress in 1935. It laid the foundation of the present public social welfare structure in the United States, and proved to be the badly needed national response to the crisis of the Great Depression. The original Social Security Act established two insurance programs and three grant programs. Before looking at each in turn, you will recall that the last chapter discussed the differences between social insurances and grant programs. Social insurances involve the creation of a fund to hold contributions made by insured persons. When benefits are received, they come from this fund. In contrast, grant programs are funded by general tax revenues; those who receive benefits have not necessarily paid anything for them. As a result, grant programs are seen as giving people "something for nothing," and tend to be stigmatized. Social insurances, on the other hand, are seen as a type of forced savings. People get back their own money, although this is an oversimplification of the way in which any insurance program operates to spread risk (that is, some people die before they ever collect, and others live long enough to collect more than they contributed).

Social Security Act Social Insurance Programs

Two social insurance programs were created in 1935: Old Age and Survivors Insurance (OASI) and unemployment insurance. **Old age and Survivors Insurance** was intended to provide income for workers when they retired, and to protect the widows and minor children of such workers. This program is tied to employment, with both employed people and their employers each paying a tax on the employees' in-

TABLE 3–1   Funding Retirement Benefits Through Social Security

The following table shows how the tax to support retirement benefits through Social Security have increased over the years. Note that only a certain amount of income is taxed—in 1983 it was $35,700. Earnings over that amount are not taxed, making this tax **regressive.** *This means that the less income a person has, the larger the percentage of it that will be taxed. For example, someone earning $20,000 paid 6.7 percent retirement tax on all of this amount. Someone earning $100,000 in that year paid 6.7 percent retirement tax on only the first $35,700 of income.*

Earnings and Social Security Taxes

	Annual earnings base	Tax rate	Maximum tax		Annual earnings base	Tax rate	Maximum tax
1937	$3,000	1.0 %	$ 30.00	1972	$ 9,000	5.2 %	$ 468.00
1950	3,000	1.5	45.00	1973	10,800	5.85	631.80
1951	3,600	1.5	54.00	1974	13,200	5.85	772.20
1954	3,600	2.0	72.00	1975	14,100	5.85	824.85
1955	4,200	2.0	84.00	1976	15,300	5.85	895.05
1957	4,200	2.25	94.50	1977	16,500	5.85	965.25
1959	4,800	2.5	120.00	1978	17,700	6.05	1,070.85
1960	4,800	3.0	144.00	1979	22,900	6.13	1,403.77
1962	4,800	3.125	150.00	1980	25,900	6.13	1,587.67
1963	4,800	3.625	174.00	1981	29,700	6.65	1,722.35
1966	6,600	4.2	277.20	1982	32,400	6.7	2,170.80
1967	6,600	4.4	290.40	1983	35,700	6.7	2,391.90
1968	7,800	4.4	343.20	1985	*	7.05	
1969	7,800	4.8	374.40	1986	*	7.15	
1970	7,800	4.8	374.40	1990	*	7.65	
1971	7,800	5.2	405.60				

Source: The New York Times, February 4, 1983, p. A-12. © 1983 by The New York Times Company. Reprinted by permission.
*Wage base will automatically increase with growth in average wages.
Tax rates from 1983 and beyond are scheduled in existing law. Employers and employees pay these taxes.

come. Tax rates have gradually risen over the years, as shown by Table 3–1.

Taxes that are collected are kept in a Social Security Trust Fund, and benefits are paid from this fund. Originally, workers could only retire at 65, later changed to allow for the option of early retirement with reduced benefits at age 62. However, retirement benefits from Social Security were never intended to be the sole source of support for retirees. Therefore, benefit levels have never been high enough to live comfortably, even though Figure 3–1 below shows that many people rely on these benefits for a substantial part of their income.

Table 3–2 examines the adequacy of OASDI benefits from another perspective. It compares the average OASDI benefit with the federal poverty level for various categories of recipients. In two categories, OASDI benefits are less than $500 above the poverty level, and in one category, OASDI benefits are actually *below* the poverty line. In only two categories are OASDI benefits nearly $1000 or more above the poverty level. Obviously, then, retirement benefits by themselves permit a comfortable standard of living, even though Figure 3–1 showed that OASDI benefits comprise as much as 75 percent of total income for some retirees.

Since it was enacted in 1935, the Social Security Act has been amended many times. These changes have generally included more people under existing and newly created benefit programs. Among the most significant new programs was the covering of disabled persons regardless of age in 1957, and the introduction of two health programs in 1965, Medicare and Medicaid (examined in depth in Exhibit 2–7). As a result, the original OASI program is now expanded to Old Age, Survivors, Disability and Health Insurance Program (OASDHI). In 1983, approximately 115 million workers participated in Social Security, and about 36 million retired people, disabled workers, and their families received benefits (*The New York Times*, 1983). Of these, 66.4 percent received old-age retirement benefits, 12.4 were disabled workers, and 21.2 percent were survivors.

The second social insurance established by the Social Security Act of 1935 was **unemployment insurance.** It was intended to provide income during periods of temporary, involuntary unemployment. Each state has its own unemployment insurance program, established within federal guidelines. Each also establishes its own methods of computing benefits. The program is supported by a payroll tax paid only by employers on a specified amount of earnings per employee. It is administered by the federal government, and the taxes collected pay for benefits, administrative expenses, and to support the U. S. Employment Service. Recipients must register at the state employment office, seek work, and be available for work in order to qualify for benefits. Because each state has its own program, the program varies among states. Also, not all workers are covered, especially many low-income,

FIGURE 3–1   Social Security Benefit Levels

This graph shows the importance of Social Security benefits for persons over 65.

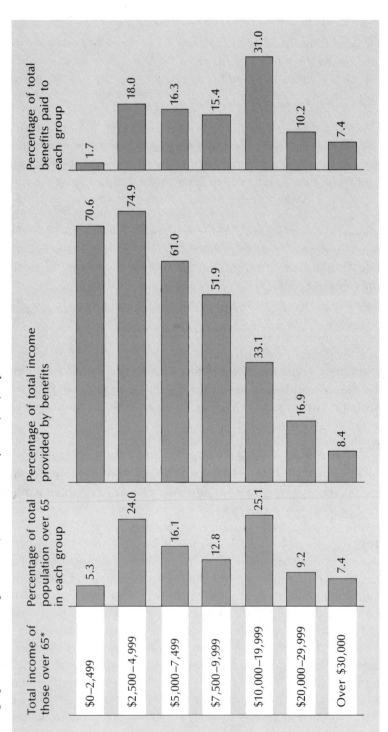

Source: The New York Times, February 4, 1983, p. A-12. © 1983 by The New York Times Company. Reprinted by permission. Data from 1979. Numbers do not add up to 100 because of rounding. *Individuals and households.

TABLE 3–2   Social Security Benefits and Poverty Standards

This table shows the average benefits, for various categories of recipients, from OASDI, and compares them with the poverty level. The figures are for 1981.

Category of Recipient	Social Security Average Benefit	Poverty Standard
Retired worker	$4,476	$4,360
Aged widow	$4,176	$4,360
Retired worker and spouse	$7,656	$5,501
Surviving mother for father and children (based on four people)	$10,260	$9,289
Disabled worker, spouse, and children (based on four people)	$9,708	$9,289

Source: Gertrude S. Goldberg, Center for Social Policy, Adelphi University School of Social Work. Cited in Harriette C. Johnson and Gertrude S. Goldberg, Government Money for Everyday People (Garden City, N. Y.: Adelphi University School of Social Work, 1981), p. 4. Reprinted by permission.

unskilled, marginal participants in the work force whose work history is often too unstable to qualify them for coverage. Nevertheless, the program, with only minimal criticism, has adapted to fluctuating economic conditions, with states especially hard hit by depressed economies able to extend the duration of benefits and the level of benefit payments.

Grant Programs

Besides two social insurances, the Social Security Act of 1935 established grant programs for the blind, dependent children, and aged persons not covered by OASI. A grant program for the partially and totally disabled was added later. Because these grant programs were so controversial, they were restricted to helpless groups with obvious need. Unlike the social insurances, the grant programs involved complex federal-state cooperative funding and administrative arrangements. The goal was to leave as much power as possible at the local level, where it was assumed that the needs of the people could be more easily expressed and assessed. Federal guidelines assured some level of uniformity and equity within and among programs, but specific characteristics of the programs, including major eligibility requirements and benefit levels, were left to the discretion of each state. Inequitable benefits among states have resulted. For example, in 1980 average monthly payments to families receiving money under the Aid to Families with Dependent Children program ranged from a low of $88 in Mississippi to a high of $399 in California (*Statistical Abstract of the United States*, 1981:345).

It might seem odd that the Social Security Act provided both a social insurance program and a grant program to meet the economic needs of the elderly. The reason was that it would take some years for the OASI trust fund to be developed from the contributions of workers. The grant program could meet the needs of the elderly during this period, because it was funded from current tax revenues. It was assumed that all of the grant programs would decrease in importance as more and more people were covered by the social insurance programs. However, poverty has created a continuing need for the grant programs.

In 1974 the grant programs for the blind, disabled, and aged were transferred to a newly created program called **Supplemental Security Income Program.** It is funded and administered completely by the federal government, leaving the program for dependent children the only one of the original grant programs still funded by the federal government and the states, and operated by the states. This program, now called **Aid to Families with Dependent Children (AFDC),** illustrates society's continued bias in favor of the work ethic and personal responsibility. Although AFDC deals with a helpless group, dependent children, it also recognizes that they must be cared for by adults. This creates a host of potentially explosive value issues, such as unmarried women having children, mothers staying home to care for the children rather than working, mothers having companionship with males they do not marry, and so forth. Society's response to these issues has been to keep benefit levels low, and to impose a number of restrictions on beneficiaries. Leaving the program under state jurisdiction has perpetuated the differences in benefit levels noted earlier. The aged, blind, and disabled can be clearly defined as helpless and are therefore helped with a minimum degree of stigma. Dependent children and their guardians, however, mix helplessness with an assortment of other less acceptable values and behaviors, and society's assistance to them comes grudgingly and minimally. Exhibit 3–1 in the "Reflections on Social Welfare" section at the end of the chapter illustrates the differences between SSI and AFDC.

In summary, the Social Security Act of 1935 marked the recognition of governmental responsibility for needs in a new and creative manner. The act continues to support the basic framework of the social welfare system in the United States. However, it has been modified on a regular basis, and we will see later in the chapter that changes made in the 1980s have begun to redirect its focus.

Movements Toward Social Justice, 1940–1970

The period directly following the passage of the Social Security Act focused mostly on World War II and its effects. The volunteer and public agencies tried to provide for the needs of men and women in the military and their dependents at home. Postwar plans for the economy were somewhat undirected. The Servicemen Readjustment Act of 1944 (better known as the G. I. Bill), which provided for medical benefits and a maintenance allowance for education, was the major social welfare legislation of the 1940s. Government support of social welfare was continued with few major changes.

The 1950s saw a continued concern with foreign policy rather than social issues. This was in part a reaction to the anticommunist hysteria generated by Joseph McCarthy and the investigations over which he presided. Congress reorganized the welfare structure in 1953 to achieve more administrative efficiency and coordinated planning, but no major substantive changes were implemented. The Social Security Act was modified in 1954 and 1956 to include many members of the labor force not covered by the original act. In addition, unemployment insurance coverage was broadened, and the amount of assistance and the duration of coverage were increased. Further amendments in 1962 made significant new funds available for the training of public assistance workers, and social services were added to financial aid in public assistance programs. The concept of public welfare as a rehabilitative program was stressed during this period. Public assistance continued to be seen as temporary until people could once again independently participate in a competitive society.

A new dimension of social welfare came into focus in the 1950s: social justice. In 1954, the Supreme Court found school segregation unconstitutional on the grounds that the "separate but equal" is inherently unequal. It ordered desegregation of the nation's public school systems "with all deliberate speed." President Eisenhower ordered federal troops to Arkansas to enforce integration of Little Rock Central High School in defiance of Governor Orval Faubus in 1957. In the same year, Eisenhower signed the Civil Rights Act, which authorized the

Justice Department to bring to federal courts cases involving discrimination in voting. The Civil Rights Act of 1960 went further by making possible legal action against state and local officials. The Supreme Court's action established its role as a powerful force for social change and social justice. It has the power to mandate the enforcement of civil rights legislation and to strike down legislation and interpretations that violate human rights. This mandate by the Supreme Court has made it possible for progressive legislators and law-enforcement officials to act to preserve social justice when it has been threatened by people motivated by bigotry, ignorance, or greed (see Exhibit 3–2 in the "Reflections on Social Welfare" section at the end of the chapter).

As the Supreme Court's actions changed the climate for social justice, courageous members of groups traditionally discriminated against were encouraged to accelerate their ongoing quest for justice and equality. Blacks were the first to make major assaults against institutionalized inequality. Under the leadership of people like Martin Luther King and his associates, the 1960s and 1970s witnessed a series

Dr. Martin Luther King was a powerful advocate of peaceful protest, a strategy he used very successfully to push for civil rights legislation. He and his wife are shown here leading a civil rights march in Montgomery, Alabama, in 1965. (United Press International, Inc.)

of nonviolent confrontations to demonstrate the existence of inequality and the need for social change. Blacks, often joined by white college students, carried out planned sit-ins at places of business that practiced discrimination. They organized peaceful protest marches to Washington, D. C., state capitols, and local power centers. They also carried out voter registration drives to help people denied their legal voting rights through fraud and intimidation to exercise this right. These nonviolent attempts to enforce existing laws and to seek new nondiscriminatory legislation were frequently met with harassment, intimidation, and physical violence (even murder) from law-enforcement officials and others. In spite of this, these courageous groups succeeded in gaining new legislation and widespread public support for their goals. By their successes, blacks stimulated similar attempts by other repressed groups, especially Chicanos, Native Americans, women, and homosexuals.

The election of John F. Kennedy as President in 1960 ushered in a period of extraordinary concern with social issues. Drawing on the expertise of the nation's foremost intellectuals, Kennedy spoke of a **New Frontier** that offered numerous opportunities for social development. Liberal Social Security revisions were enacted, and the Redevelopment Act was passed in 1961. This was followed by the Manpower Development and Training Act in 1962, and the creation of food stamps as a new method to help meet the nutritional needs of the poor. The enthusiasm generated by Kennedy turned abruptly into a profound sense of loss when he was assassinated in 1963 in Dallas. Vice-President Lyndon Johnson succeeded to the presidency and was able to channel the nation's desire to honor Kennedy into a series of significant pieces of social legislation that continued the directions set by his predecessor. This legislation fell under Johnson's concept of a **Great Society:** "The Great Society was envisioned as a perfectible society in which social justice (could) be created by the development of institutions to meet the needs of the citizens" (Smith and Zeitz, 1970:200). Under Johnson, several significant pieces of social welfare legislation were enacted—the Mental Retardation and Community Mental Health Centers Construction Act of 1963, followed in 1964 by civil rights legislation and the Economic Opportunity Act. More civil rights legislation passed in 1965, as well as the Appalachia Regional Development Act, Department of Housing and Urban Development legislation, and the amendments to the Social Security Act, which created Medicare and Medicaid. 1966 saw another housing act passed, and 1967 brought legislation further revising the Social Security Act.

The Economic Opportunity Act was the heart of what became known as the **War on Poverty.** It created several important programs housed in the Office of Economic Opportunity (OEO): VISTA, which was modeled after the Peace Corps and which organized volunteers to spend a year or more working at community-development projects among the poor in America; the Job Corps, which provided work training and work projects for unemployed young people coming from backgrounds of poverty and deprivation; and Head Start, an educational program for disadvantaged children to prepare them to succeed in the public school system.

A strong component of the Economic Opportunity Act was the con-cept of the **participation of the poor** in planning the programs that would affect them. This was rarely done prior to the Economic Oppor-tunity Act, and it threatened local political structures and entrenched welfare organizations. Unfortunately, it mandated participation with-out the opportunity for deprived communities to learn the necessary skills first. As a result, many programs floundered under the squab-bling of several deprived groups in communities, all competing for resources and not knowing how to work together for mutual advan-tage. These problems were accentuated by inadequate funding for many programs and exploitation of OEO contracts by powerful busi-nesses and social welfare agencies.

Always a political target because of its potential for shifting power to powerless groups, the Office of Economic Opportunity was abolished in 1974 and replaced by the Community Services Program. This pro-gram dispensed with most of the concept of participation by the poor, and many specific programs like Headstart were moved to other agen-cies, especially the Department of Health, Education, and Welfare (now known as the Department of Health and Human Services). In effect, the Great Society, as visualized in the Economic Opportunity Act, was dead, and America entered a period of retreat on many social concerns. Nevertheless, The Economic Opportunity Act succeeded in creating a new focus on community organization and planning, and on the value of having users of services participate in planning. It also underlined the need for more adequately conceptualized and imple-mented legislative solutions to the nation's welfare needs. Finally, it demonstrated the entrenched complexity of most social problems and the obstacles created by the social welfare bureaucracy itself.

The first massive violence in the civil rights movement broke out in 1965 in Watts, a section of Los Angeles. Similar rioting later broke out in other cities. These riots reflected the accumulating frustrations with the steady but slow pace of civil rights progress. As greater social justice was attained, incidences of inequality—and the poverty and humiliation associated with them—were both more visible and less tolerable. A period of conflict within the black civil rights movement developed. One side continued to argue for nonviolent protest, pointing to the real progress attained using this approach. Another view argued for a more activist and, if necessary, violent approach. Proponents of this direction pointed to the slow pace of progress and the high price blacks continued to pay in terms of poverty, illness, and discrimination.

Martin Luther King's murder in 1968 weakened the forces pushing for nonviolence. Dissipation of the peaceful-protest phase of the civil rights movement was signaled by the ineffectiveness of the Poor People's Campaign in Washington, D. C., that same year. Thereafter, more militant and more politically sophisticated approaches were adopted, as exemplified by the National Welfare Rights Organization (NWRO). Formed primarily of public assistance recipients, it sought changes in social welfare legislation to make benefits more adequate and equitable. It also sought greater involvement of welfare recipients in social policy by organizing them into an effective political force. After several years of protests and other activities, by the early 1970s NWRO had lapsed into inactivity.

Further protests on behalf of social justice occurred during the late 1960s and early 1970s. The escalation of the Vietnam War in 1966, the assassination of Robert Kennedy in 1968, and the United States invasion of Cambodia in 1970 were all factors that promoted massive unrest on college campuses during this period. The Students for a Democratic Society (SDS) was the leading campus group organizing protests. They focused on the costly and inefficient bureaucracy of government, the depersonalization of universities, the inhumanity of war, the social and economic deprivation of minority groups and the poor, and the discrepancy in some areas between what America stands for and what it practices. These protests were carried out mostly by college students, middle-class youth, and discontented blacks. America's eventual withdrawal from Vietnam and Cambodia helped to reduce protests on campuses.

Nixon and the 1970s

The early 1970s saw renewed efforts to grapple with some long-standing social welfare problems. The passage of the Supplemental Security Income program, which took effect in 1974, was a step forward in providing a uniform, federally administered and financed, guaranteed income program for the needy aged, blind, and disabled. The exclusion of AFDC was unfortunate, however, as noted earlier in this chapter. Medicare and Medicaid had begun to address people's needs for medical security, and national health insurance was heavily debated during the 1970s. Whereas most highly industrialized societies provide comprehensive medical care for their members, Americans must purchase health care individually or through their place of work. Health insurance programs generally do not provide for routine check-ups and other preventive medicine. Also, the high unemployment of the early 1980s demonstrated how quickly medical insurance is lost when people lose their jobs. Nevertheless, the American Medical Association continued to strenuously resist national health insurance, and no legislation was enacted. The closest to it was legislation supporting the development of health maintenance organizations (HMO) as an optional type of medical care. The HMO charges a flat fee for which it provides all needed care. This approach encourages preventive medicine, because reducing the costs associated with illness is obviously in the HMO's best interest. However, most people choose traditional health insurance, in part because it is generally cheaper but also because they can use whatever doctor and medical facility they wish, rather than having to go to the facility and staff used by the HMO.

The election of Richard Nixon as President in 1968 ushered in the beginning of an era of attacks on social welfare programs and, more importantly, values and principles. His resistance to school busing as an effective civil rights tool stimulated antibusing legislation in 1972 that has seriously weakened school busing in concept and practice, a discouraging reversal of hard-won gains. He also supported the idea of public assistance applicants making themselves available for work as a condition of receiving aid, in spite of high unemployment rates, low wages, and the unsuitability of most assistance recipients for gainful employment (Romanyshyn, 1971:173–232).

Perhaps the most significant and potentially destructive legislation enacted under Nixon was Public Law 92-512, revenue sharing, passed in 1972 as part of his **New Federalism.** This refers to an effort to transfer as much decision making as possible from the federal government back to the states. The legislation provided for the following:

> . . . financial assistance to states and localities, one-third to the states, two-thirds to the localities. The localities are restricted in their use of funds to (1) "ordinary and necessary capital expenditures" and (2) "ordinary and

necessary maintenance and operating expenses" in eight priority areas. These are public safety, environmental protection, public transportation, health, recreation, libraries, social services for the poor or aged, and financial administration (Hardcastle, 1973).

Revenue-sharing funds replace in whole or in part grants from the federal government earmarked for the support of specific programs. Those programs that continue to be funded with government money have usually had their funds reduced, whereas the others have to compete within the pool of money provided for the general areas outlined above. Within these areas, the revenue-sharing funds can be used at the discretion of the local and state decision makers.

In theory, revenue sharing allows states and localities to allocate funds more wisely than is possible by the federal government, because these units of government are closer to the people and presumably more responsive to their wishes. However, Hardcastle notes the following (Hardcastle, 1973:7):

> The trend represented by revenue sharing shows that nationally, a commitment to domestic programming, especially in social services, is simply not there. The political implications are clear. Federal protection for social services will be removed and they will have to compete with the entire array of fiscal demands for public funds. Mental health programs, for example, will have to compete for funds at the state and local level not only with child welfare services but also with street improvements.

Revenue sharing marks a step backward in a process that had been developing for some time—namely, increased federal planning and supervision of the social welfare system. An expanded role for the federal government in social welfare planning and supervision reflects the impact of large-scale social forces on individual and community functioning. The return to more local control opens up possibilities for less efficient and more inequitable use of funds, as well as an inability to see long-range human needs and plan appropriately for them. Social welfare has always been enmeshed in the societal need to set priorities in the use of relatively scarce resources. Revenue sharing reemphasizes the need for establishing priorities, but it vests much of the decision-making power with those having perhaps the weakest grasp of the significance of their decisions.

> The assumption is that citizens participate in decisions as to how local revenues are spent and that this participation would be extended to revenue-sharing expenditures as well. The assumption is erroneous. Citizens generally are not involved in complex local and state budgeting

processes. Revenue sharing has not changed this fact of life (*Washington Bulletin*, 1974).

Revenue sharing has continued to create problems for the funding of social welfare programs, because it was a program eagerly endorsed by President Reagan after his election in 1980. The problem is best summarized in the following (*Washington Social Legislation Bulletin*, 1982:120):

> The consequences of enactment of the President's proposal would be a lower level of service for people in need, because inherent in New Federalism is a vast withdrawal of Federal funding as well as Federal concern, and States would not be able to pick up much of the slack created by the loss of Federal funds. This has already been demonstrated by the inability (and in some cases the disinclination) of States to make up for more than a small proportion of the reduction in Federal social program funding dictated by 1981 budget action.
>
> Human service needs now addressed by Federal programs are those which have been identified as being essentially national in scope and beyond the capacity of State and local governments to adequately serve. The social problems that created the need for a responsive program derive from forces beyond the control of States and localities.
>
> In addition, the enactment of the New Federalism would mean the increase in the disparity among the States. The rule in many States is that, if the Federal government is not interested in a problem area, then the State will not move into that area. Some States will be better off than others, and some States with more of a tradition of helping people, will end up with programs that are more comprehensive than those in neighboring States. Thus New Federalism will mean a weakened national response to national problems and greater disparity among States. The happenstance of residence will affect the services available to needy persons.

President Nixon resigned in 1974 as a result of the Watergate scandal. The Watergate affair caused a profound distrust of the government to develop. As confidence eroded, so did people's willingness to trust the government to manage money and programs honestly and effectively. This distrust had a serious effect on social welfare. At first, it enabled Jimmy Carter to gain the Presidency in 1976 on a platform of simple, honest government. A well-meaning man, he supported several improvements in the social welfare system. The Housing and Community Development Act of 1977 included subsidies to low-income families as well as homeowners and the housing industry. It also extended the Community Development Block Grant program, and established a new Urban Development Action Grant program, which sought to improve the quality of housing, especially for the poor. The Juvenile Justice Amendments of 1977 extended the Juvenile Justice Act of 1974, emphasizing citizen participation and prevention. These amendments also extended the Runaway Youth Act. The Child Abuse Prevention and Treatment Act Amendments and Adoption Reform Act were passed in 1978. The former strengthened the role of the National Center on Child Abuse and Neglect in contracting for research and for publishing results in the area of child abuse. It also established a new program on the sexual abuse of children. The latter act established a National Adoption Information Exchange that uses computers to locate children who would benefit from adoption and to assist in placing them.

In spite of these advances, the mood of the country was mixed. The economic picture was darkened by inflation that proved difficult to control and that stimulated an economically conservative approach to social welfare expenditures. The passage of Proposition 13 in California, which limited the property tax and hence the funds available for public services, was one indication of this conservative mood. It was followed by similar legislation in other states. Affirmative Action efforts to protect education, employment, and housing opportunities for minorities became less visible. The Equal Rights Amendment for women did not pass; racially motivated riots flared up sporadically; two liberal elected officials were murdered in San Francisco by a conservative man who was unhappy over civil rights gains in that city; and Anita Bryant led a crusade against homosexuals. The climate for progress in social welfare became noticeably worse.

Social Welfare in the 1980s

Jimmy Carter's inability to control inflation and his lack of political skill led to his defeat in the 1980 presidential election. Ronald Reagan became President, supported by a well-organized and well-funded rightwing faction that sought to dismantle the social welfare system and some basic civil rights structures. Reagan believed that the federal government was too large, expensive, and inefficient, and set out to reduce its expenditures (one reason why he favored the New Federalism so strongly). He also sought to control inflation by practicing **supply-side economics.** By increasing incentives for people and businesses to invest in business expansion, production would be stimulated, employment increased, and people's income increased. He believed that this would result in lower prices, increased economic activity, and lower inflation (O'Neill, 1982).

Unfortunately, Reagan saw social welfare expenditures as interfering in the operation of the economic marketplace. Government expenditures on social welfare programs were thought to sap funds from other, more important activities, the major one being a substantial increase in the military budget to protect against what he perceived as a Russian threat. Besides, he felt that stimulating the economy and reducing inflation would eventually "trickle down" to the poor. More jobs would enable them to work and earn enough money to survive. He was not altogether clear how they were to survive in the meantime, however. Although he spoke of a "safety net" for the "truly needy," his policies eroded programs in all areas of social welfare year by year.

The Reagan administration set about reducing or eliminating a wide range of social welfare programs. A strong conservative faction in Congress supported these efforts, and by 1983 many social welfare programs had been seriously affected. Exhibit 3–3 in the "Reflections on Social Welfare" section at the end of the chapter summarizes some of these cutbacks. Predictably, the results of these cutbacks were disastrous for users of the programs, especially low-income Americans (*Washington Social Legislation Bulletin*, 1983; Pear, 1982).

Another area in which the Reagan administration's actions have been hurtful to social welfare is that of civil rights. The Reagan administration has taken a stand against busing for the purposes of achieving desegregation, but has not proposed viable alternatives (*Civil Rights Update*, 1982). Leaders of various minority groups have lamented the retreat by the Reagan administration from active enforcement of existing civil rights laws (*Perspectives*, 1982). The administration has also been criticized for engaging in other practices to undermine civil rights. These include changing the composition of the Civil Rights Commission (*Civil Rights Update*, 1982:2) and reinterpreting laws without amending any statute or regulation, thereby preventing oversight by either Congress or the general public (Pear, 1983). In addition, the President indicated his willingness to support racist schools, prayer in the schools, and antiabortion measures, all issues that raise serious concerns about social justice and equality. Furthermore, he has openly sought support from right-wing conservatives, such as North Carolina Senator Jesse Helms, who espouse programs that deny people their civil rights.

Two problems inherited by the Reagan administration were funding for both Social Security and Medicare, both of which have been in danger of running out of funds (see Figure 3–2). In early 1983, Con-

---

FIGURE 3–2   Funding Problems of Social Security and Medicare

The following two charts document why Social Security and Medicare have run into funding problems. In part, they reflect demographic changes in the society, which has a population that is gradually aging. As a result, the balance is shifting between those who are working and those who must be supported by the Social Security taxes paid by those who are working.

Although Social Security taxes have risen steadily over the years, benefits have grown even faster, and the gap between expenditures and receipts is widening. Last month, a special commission appointed by President Reagan and Congressional leaders suggested a number of modest changes in the law, including

What Was Paid Out and What Was Paid In

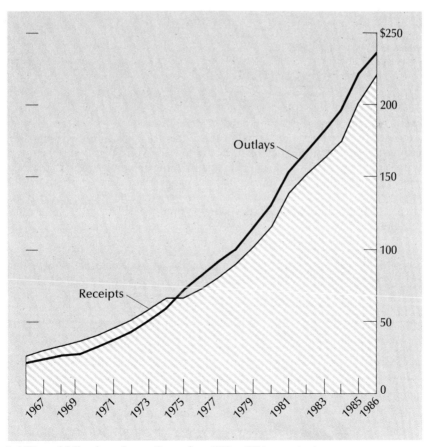

In billions of dollars for each year. Figures from 1982 to 1986 are projections.

Projections for Medicare Trust Fund

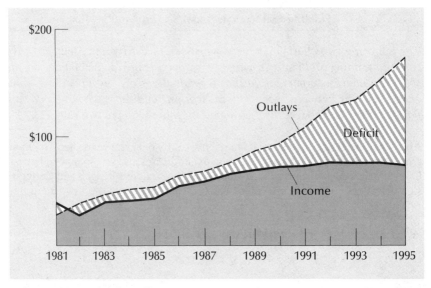

Source: Congressional Budget Office.

Data for each calendar year in billions of dollars. Figures for 1981 and 1982 are actual, all others are preliminary estimates.

postponement of cost-of-living benefit increases and higher tax levels, that would bring revenues and spending into balance for the time being. But, primarily because of the high birth rate following World War II and the lower birth rate recently, the country is changing demographically. Early in the next century, when those born during the baby boom begin to retire, there will be relatively fewer workers to pay taxes to support the increased number of retirees. Many experts believe that this long-term problem will prove more difficult for Congress to resolve than the short-term imbalance in the system.

Source: These graphs are taken from *The New York Times,* February 4, 1983, p. A12 (Social Security) and February 21, 1983, p. 137 (Medicare). © 1983 by The New York Times Company. Reprinted by permission.

gress passed legislation to salvage the Social Security system. It entailed several changes: increasing payroll taxes; postponing cost-of-living increases in benefits; raising the retirement age to 66 in the year 2009 and 67 by 2027; and levying an income tax against part of the Social Security benefits received by some retirees (Shribman, 1983;

Washington Social Legislation Bulletin, 1983a). Congress chose these alternatives rather than to support the Social Security trust fund partly out of general tax revenues or to have payroll taxes paid on a person's total income. Thus far, no action has been taken to deal with the funding problems of Medicare.

In spite of the devastating impact of program cuts initiated by the Reagan administration, perhaps the most serious effect of the Reagan presidency on social welfare relates to values. Explicit in many of the President's statements, and implicit in much of what he has tried to do, is the assertion that this society has little responsibility for those who are in need. Reagan has been unique as a President in his willingness to initiate policies that he knows will increase need without also trying to generate programs to help those in need. This is a stunning reversal of prior beliefs about the society's commitment to social welfare. The subtle assertions that many who receive help don't really need it are not new, but they serve to reinforce prejudices and stereotypes about the needy that are no truer now than they were in years past. In some ways, the rapidity with which the Reagan administration could undo programs and values that have taken decades to develop and nurture can only be viewed as shocking and frightening. It will take additional decades for the social welfare institution to recover. Meanwhile, the cost in human suffering will be enormous.

SUMMARY

The social welfare institution has grown slowly from one based in the family to one embedded in the social organization of our society. It has always reflected societal values, and it continues to do so. Our ability to study and learn about social processes has enabled us to develop new programs to better meet the needs of an increasingly diverse range of people. This has helped in the quest for greater social justice and equality for all groups. However, the Reagan administration demonstrated how very fragile the social welfare institution is. It continues to rely on society's mandate to care for its citizens. When that mandate is destroyed or weakened, social welfare programs will be seriously affected. Ultimately, it is the task of the citizenry to determine what this mandate shall be, and to make sure that it is carried out effectively. The chapter concludes with Exhibit 3–4 in the following section, "Reflections on Social Welfare." It summarizes some of the major trends of the history of social welfare that will continue to affect the shape of the social welfare institution.

REFLECTIONS ON SOCIAL WELFARE

The following four Exhibits explore various aspects of past and current societal events of importance to social welfare. Exhibit 3–1 compares AFDC and SSI, two grant-in-aid programs with rather different structures and effects. Exhibit 3–2 summarizes some of the major decisions relating to social justice that have occurred over time, some of which are threatened by political events summarized in Exhibit 3–3. Exhibit 3–4 provides a broad overview of some of the most significant themes in the historical development of the social welfare institution.

EXHIBIT 3–1   AFDC and Supplemental Security Income Compared

Some of the differences between AFDC and the Supplemental Security Income program are illustrated in the following data, which look at eligibility requirements and benefit levels, as well as administrative procedures. The stigma against AFDC recipients turns out to be a costly one for them, and illustrates the importance of values in the determination of social welfare programs, a fact as true today as it has been throughout the development of social welfare concepts and programs. The AFDC data in this Exhibit are from North Carolina.

	AFDC	SSI
Eligibility Requirements		
Age	Under 21 years. If 16 or 17, must be regularly enrolled in and attending school; if 18 or over and under 21, must be regularly and successfully attending school, college or university, or a course of vocational or technical training.	None, except for the aged category (age 65 +)
Residence	Child is making his home in the state.	U.S.A.

	AFDC	**SSI**
Need	Deprived of parental support or care by reason of death, continued absence from home, or physical or mental incapacity of one or both parents, and living with relatives listed in federal act as interpreted, or in foster care as permitted under the federal act.	65 or older Blind Disabled
Financial/ Property Eligibility	Ownership of real property used as a home does not of itself disqualify. However, in determining need and amount of payment, resources (shelter, rent, etc.) from such property are taken into account. Real property not used as a home and all personal property (savings, cash value of insurance, bonds, and any other cash reserves) are limited to $1,100 for adult and one child, plus $50 for needy spouse and for each eligible child up to $2,000 maximum. When application or budget does not include needy adult, limitation on reserve for one child is $1,000; for two children, $1,100; with $50 for each additional child in family unit up to $2,000 maximum. (Administrative) May have equity in essential motor vehicle not to exceed $1,000; excess equity plus equity in the loan value of non-essential motor vehicles and non-essential personal property such as cameras, television sets, etc. are treated as reserve. Transfers of property must be made at fair market value; the proceeds are treated as a reserve.	Assets of $1,500 for single person. $2,250 for couple excluding house lived in as well as household goods, personal effects, insurances, car. Nonwage income over $20 a month reduces benefits. Wage income over $65 a month reduces benefit $1 for each $2 earned. Living in someone else's home usually reduces benefits.

Administration

| State | State Board of Social Services[a] (policy-making), for aged and disabled. Seven members appointed by Governor for 6 years, overlapping terms, one to | None. Administered by the Social Security Administration (federal), and checks sent directly to recipient. Apply at Social Security offices. |

	AFDC	SSI
	be a woman. Commissioner appointed by Board, with Governor's approval and serves at pleasure of Board. State-supervised program.	
Local	County Department of Social Services (100). County Board of Social Services—usually 3 members, 1 appointed by Board of Commissioners, 1 by State Board, and 1 by the other two for 3-year overlapping terms; in 51 counties, 5-member boards. County Director appointed by County Board of Social Services.	None (see above).
Financing	Assistance costs: State and local funds. Source of state funds: general fund. Of nonfederal share, state not less than 50 percent, local not more than 50 percent. Administrative costs: Nonfederal share, state and local funds. State's participation varies according to county's financial ability (on an equalizing basis) from a small percent to 50 percent of the balance after having deducted federal participation.	General funds of the U.S. Treasury (Social Security funds are not used to pay SSI).

Average Benefit Payments (per month)			One Person	Married Couple
	(Data for 1980)	*Family*		
	North Carolina	$164 ⎫	Uniform throughout U.S.A.:[b] (Data for 1978)	
	Mississippi	88 ⎪		
	New York	371 ⎪		
	California	399 ⎬	$177.80	$266.70
	Montana	228 ⎪		
	Indiana	203 ⎪		
	Arizona	174 ⎭		

Sources: The data on Supplemental Security Income is taken from U. S. Department of Health, Education, and Welfare pamphlet No. SSA 74-11000 (January 1974), and the data on AFDC in North Carolina is taken from pages 76 and 77 of *Characteristics of State Public Assistance Plans*—January 31, 1973 (Washington: U.S. Government Printing Office, 1973). North Carolina data are illustrative, since each state's plan is somewhat different. Data on comparative payments by state are taken from *Statistical Abstract of the United States 1981*, Bureau of the Census (Washington, D.C.: U.S. Government Printing Office), p. 345.

[a] Operated within Department of Human Resources.
[b] May be higher if state supplements federal SSI payments, or lower if recipient has other income as noted above. These figures are for 1978.

EXHIBIT 3–2　A Proud Tradition of Civil Rights Progress

The major civil rights legislation and Supreme Court decisions supporting civil rights summarized below are in the best tradition of American concepts of justice. These actions have been highly significant in moving the society toward greater equality for all of its members. As we saw in this chapter, actions by the Reagan administration in the 1980s sought to undermine some of the principles established in these actions.

Major Federal Civil Rights Laws 1957–1978

Civil Rights Act of 1957	Established the U. S. Commission on Civil Rights.
Equal Pay Act of 1963	Prohibits employers from compensating members of one sex at a lower rate than members of the other sex for equal work.
Civil Rights Act of 1964, As Amended	Prohibits discrimination based on race, color, religion, or national origin in places of public accommodation or in the use of public facilities owned, operated or managed by state or local governments; prohibits discrimination based on race, color or national origin in any federally-assisted program or activity; prohibits discrimination based on race, color, national origin or sex in employment practices; empowers Equal Employment Opportunity Commission to eliminate unlawful employment practices.
Voting Rights Act of 1965, As Amended	Requires that no state or political subdivision shall impose a voting qualification, standard, practice or procedure or prerequisite for voting to deny the right of any citizen of the U.S. to vote based on race, color, age or membership in a language minority group.
Age Discrimination Act of 1967, As Amended	Prohibits employers, employment agencies and labor organizations from discriminating on the basis of age (40–70) in employment practices.
Indian Civil Rights Act (1968)	Guarantees rights to individual Indians. These rights, patterned after the Bill of Rights and the 14th Amendment to the U. S. Constitution, must be respected by Indian tribal governments.

Source: John W. Blassingame, The revolution that never was: The Civil Rights Movement, 1950–1980, in *Perspectives: The Civil Rights Quarterly,* Vol. 14, No. 2 (Summer 1982), pp. 3–15 (published by the U.S. Commission on Civil Rights).

Civil Rights Act of 1968, As Amended	Prohibits discrimination based on race, color, national origin, religion or sex in the sale or rental of most residential property, in advertising such sales or rentals, and in the financing and provision of brokerage services.
Education Amendments of 1972	Prohibits discrimination based on sex in federally-assisted education programs; prohibits discrimination based on blindness or impaired vision in admission to any federally-assisted education program.
Rehabilitation Act of 1973	Requires Federal government and certain Federal contractors and subcontractors to develop affirmative action programs for handicapped individuals; prohibits discrimination based on handicap in federally-assisted programs.
Equal Education Opportunities Act of 1974	Prohibits state and local governments from denying equal educational opportunity to an individual based on race, color, sex or national origin.
Equal Credit Opportunity Act of 1974	Prohibits discrimination based on race, color, religion, national origin, sex, marital status or age by a creditor in any aspect of a credit transaction.
Age Discrimination Act of 1975	Prohibits discrimination based on age in federally-assisted programs.
American Indian Religious Freedom Act (1978)	Protects Indian religious beliefs and practices.

Significant Supreme Court Civil Rights Cases

1954 *Brown* v. *Board of Education*	Ruled racially segregated educational facilities in violation of the equal protection clause of the 14th Amendment because they are inherently unequal.
1966 *South Carolina* v. *Katzenbach*	Upheld the major provisions of the Voting Rights Act of 1965 including the special procedures protecting minority voters in states having a history of voting discrimination.
1968 *Green* v. *County School Board of New Kent County, Va.*	Found a freedom-of-choice desegregation plan ineffective and ordered an end to the delay in desegregation, calling for realistic desegregation plans "now."
1968 *Jones* v. *Alfred H. Mayer Co.*	Held that the Civil Rights Act of 1866 bars all racial discrimination in the sale or rental of public or private property.

1971 Graham v. Richardson	Found that classifications based on alienage, like those based on nationality or race, are inherently suspect and subject to close judicial scrutiny; state statutes that deny welfare benefits to resident aliens or to aliens who have not resided in the United States for a specified number of years violate the equal protection clause of the 14th Amendment.
1971 Griggs v. Duke Power Co.	Held that any employment practice that results in disproportionately higher percentage of minority persons or women being excluded from employment opportunities violates Title VII unless the practice can be justified as job-related or a business necessity; found that lack of discriminatory intent is not a defense to a claim of discrimination under Title VII.
1971 Swann v. Charlotte-Mecklenburg Board of Education	Approved busing and using race in student assignments as appropriate remedies to eliminate unconstitutionally segregated schools.
1973 Frontiero v. Richardson	Found that Federal statutes denying female members of the military the right to claim their spouses as dependents on an equal footing with male members in violation of constitutional guarantees of equal protection of the law.
1973 Keyes v. School District No. 1, Denver, Colorado	Held that in defining a "segregated" core city school, Hispanics should be placed in the same category as blacks, since both groups suffer the same economic and cultural deprivation and discrimination; found that de jure segregation can result from official actions or policies as well as statutes.
1974 Lau v. Nichols	Held that under Title VI, a public school system must make an effort to ensure that non-English-speaking students are equipped with language skills necessary to profit from their required school attendance.
1974 Morton v. Mancari	Upheld a statute giving Indians preference in Bureau of Indian Affairs hiring since Indians were singled out not as a racial group, but as members of quasi-sovereign tribal entities.
1976 Craig v. Boren	Held that a law prohibiting the sale of beer to males under the age of 21 but to females under the age of 18 constituted gender-based discrimination that denied 18–20-year-old males the equal protection of the laws since the classification was not substantially related to the attainment of an important governmental objective.

1980 *Fullilove* v. *Klutznick*	Upheld a provision in the Public Works Employment Act of 1977 requiring a 10 percent setaside of Federal funds in local projects to procure services or supplies from minority-owned or controlled businesses.
1980 *Plyer* v. *Doe*	Prohibited states from withholding state education funds for the education of illegal alien children, and from authorizing local school districts to deny enrollment to such children.
1982 *Youngberg* v. *Romeo*	Held that under the due process clause of the 14th Amendment, states must provide an involuntarily committed mentally retarded person with safe conditions of confinement, freedom from unreasonable bodily restraints, and such minimally adequate training as reasonably may be required by these interests.

Civil Rights Executive Orders

1962 E.O. 11063	Prohibits discrimination based on race, color, creed, or national origin with respect to residential property and related facilities that receive Federal financial assistance.
1964 E.O. 11141	Prohibits Federal contractors and subcontractors from discriminating on the basis of age in employment practices.
1965 E.O. 11246	Requires Federal contractors and subcontractors to eliminate employment discrimination based on race, color, religion or national origin and requires affirmative action to provide equal employment opportunity.
1967 E.O. 11375	Adds sex to the prohibited bases for employment discrimination by Federal contractors and subcontractors covered in E.O. 11246.
1969 E.O. 11478	Requires Federal agencies to provide equal opportunity, prohibit discrimination, and develop affirmative action programs in employment practices.
1978 E.O. 12067	Transfers authority to coordinate equal employment opportunity laws, regulations, and policies in Federal departments and agencies to the Equal Employment Opportunity Commission.

EXHIBIT 3–3　**The Reagan Administration's Attacks on Social Welfare**

The Reagan administration began attacking social welfare programs as soon as it gained office. The result has been serious decreases in most social welfare programs. (Figures on all graphs represent billions of dollars.)

Medicaid

In 1981, Mr. Reagan failed in his attempt to impose a limit on the increase in Federal spending for Medicaid, the Federal-state program that provides medical care for the poor. His proposal called for a 5 percent cap in the fiscal year 1982 and similar limits, equal to the inflation rate, in later years. Governors of both parties opposed the idea, saying it would tie their hands.

Congress did order Federal Medicaid payments reduced below the amounts that states would otherwise have received. The reductions were 3 percent in the last fiscal year, 4 percent this year and 4.5 percent next year. However, Congress did not place any limit on the overall growth of Medicaid spending, which rose about 10 percent last year.

Mr. Reagan said the changes he sought in 1981 would save $1 billion in the fiscal year 1982 and $2 billion in 1983. The Congressional Budget Office estimates that the changes approved by Congress saved $800 million last year and will save $1.1 billion this year. Actual Medicaid spending last year totaled $17.4 billion. That is remarkably close to the $17.2 billion level Mr. Reagan originally proposed.

Many of the people forced off the welfare rolls in 1981 also lost Medicaid benefits because eligibility for the two programs is linked. Many states have trimmed medical benefits because they cannot afford to pay their share of Medicaid costs.

Congress saw the 1981 cuts as severe and resisted major changes in 1982. Congress agreed to let states charge nominal fees such as $1 or $2 for Medicaid services, but did not require states to impose such fees, as Mr. Reagan wanted them to. Congress accepted Mr. Reagan's proposal to let states impose liens on the property of nursing home residents so the states might ultimately recover part of the cost of Medicaid benefits.

Source: Robert Pear, The Reagan revolution, in *The New York Times,* January 31, 1983, pp. A18–A19. © 1983 by The New York Times Company. Reprinted by permission.

But the savings from such optional changes are always difficult for the Federal Government to predict.

Disability Insurance

Congress went along with Mr. Reagan's proposal to trim Social Security disability benefits. The Federal payments are reduced to take account of disability benefits provided by other Federal, state or local programs. The total from all sources may not exceed 80 percent of the worker's prior earnings. However, the savings were modest because veterans' disability benefits were not included in the calculation.

The Administration has been extensively criticized for its intensive review of the disability rolls, the results of which ended benefits for thousands of people who said they were eligible. But the review, which reversed the growth in disability rolls, was an administrative action taken by Reagan appointees on the basis of a law passed in 1980.

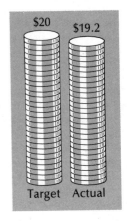

Welfare

President Reagan persuaded Congress to adopt nearly all the changes he proposed in 1981 to restrict eligibility and reduce benefits in the main Federal-state welfare program, Aid to Families with Dependent Children. Mr. Reagan had much less success with a second round of proposals in 1982: Many members of Congress complained that the combined effect of his budget and tax cuts was to penalize the poor and reward the wealthy.

The changes enacted in 1981 were remarkable because they were so numerous and technical. Congress limited eligibility to families with gross incomes at or below 150 percent of the "standard of need," a subsistence level determined by each state. The effective tax rate on income earned by welfare recipients was increased; Congress eliminated a provision that had permitted the recipients to keep the first $30 of their monthly earnings plus one-third of the remainder.

Congress also required welfare officials to count the income of stepfathers and stepmothers in determining child's eligibility and benefits. The old law did not assume that such a parent's income was available to the

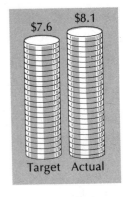

child. Under the 1981 law, a family with assets of more than $1,000 was ineligible for welfare. In the past, regulations set the limit at $2,000.

The cutbacks have halted the growth in welfare costs even at a time of high unemployment, when many people might have been expected to seek welfare after exhausting their unemployment benefits. The welfare program cost $8 billion last year.

Social Services Grant

Mr. Reagan originally proposed consolidating 40 Federal programs in one lump-sum grant to the states. He wanted to cut Federal spending for the programs 25 percent below the level of the fiscal year 1981. Congress ultimately put only two programs into the block grant and reduced spending by 20 percent, to $2.4 billion. Many program regulations were eliminated, so state officials have much more authority over use of the money.

The money can be used for a wide variety of social services to children and adults. But Congress, having just created a special Federal program for foster care and adoption assistance in 1980, refused to include it in the block grant, as Mr. Reagan wanted.

Food Stamps

President Reagan achieved the full amount of savings he sought in 1981. Indeed, Congress cut slightly more than he requested. The changes, according to the Congressional Budget Office, trimmed an average of $2 billion a year out of a program that would otherwise have cost more than $12 billion annually in the fiscal years 1982 through 1984.

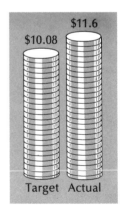

$11.6

$10.08

Target   Actual

Congress basically accepted the President's proposal to limit eligibility to households with income at or below 130 percent of the poverty level. For a family of four, the income limit is about $12,000 a year.

Congress reduced benefits for households with earned income, permitting only 18 percent of earnings as a deduction for taxes and work-related expenses. In the past, 20 percent was allowed. Congress also froze the standard deduction, designed as an allowance for medical and shelter costs, further reducing food stamp benefits for most households. Congress deferred the cost-of-living adjustment scheduled for January 1982 by nine months, to October.

But Congress overwhelmingly rejected the President's proposal to reduce a family's food stamp allotment to reflect the value of free meals served to children at school. This proposal would have significantly reduced benefits for some of the nation's poorest families.

Congress also accepted Mr. Reagan's suggestion to replace the food stamp program in Puerto Rico with a lump-sum grant. The amount of the grant was $825 million a year, representing a 25 percent reduction from what would otherwise have been spent on food stamps in Puerto Rico. Because of Puerto Rico's high poverty rate, more than half of its people had been receiving food stamps.

Social Security

President Reagan initially persuaded Congress to eliminate the minimum benefit of $122 a month. He said a welfare program known as Supplemental Security Income would meet the needs of the elderly poor adequately without diverting $1 billion a year from the Social Security system. The action aroused such a furor that Congress soon restored the minimum benefit for all people who were on the rolls or became eligible for benefits before January 1982. There is no minimum benefit for people who become eligible after that date.

Congress adopted Mr. Reagan's proposal to end payments to full-time students ages 18 to 21. No additional adult students are being enrolled in the program. Benefits for current students are being reduced 25 percent a year; there will be no more checks after April 1985. The President argued that other student aid programs would make up for the loss of this benefit.

Congress also accepted Mr. Reagan's proposal to eliminate death benefits where there was neither a spouse nor a minor child to receive the payment. In the past, such benefits had been paid to funeral homes and adult children.

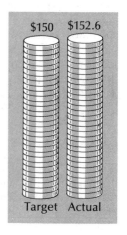

Target   Actual

Education

President Reagan proposed consolidating 45 separate Federal elementary and secondary education programs in two lump-sum grants. The block grants, he said, would shift control to state and local governments, where the authority "constitutionally and historically belongs."

Congress agreed, up to a point. Thirty to 35 programs were consolidated in a single block grant for states, which in turn can distribute the money to local agencies. Some of the original programs, such as metric education, were so small that they may, in effect, have been eliminated. Civil rights advocates and school officials in large cities have expressed particular concern about a sharp reduction in Federal money for desegregation.

The programs consolidated in the block grant cost $575 million in 1981. Mr. Reagan had wanted to consolidate programs totaling $5.1 billion. But Congress refused to relinquish control over compensatory education for poor children, the Title I program, and special education for the handicapped, which together cost $4.1 billion a year.

Congress has consistently appropriated more money for education than President Reagan requested. In the current fiscal year, for example, the actual budget for the Department of Education is $15.1 billion, compared with the President's request of $10 billion.

Housing

Mr. Reagan proposed new appropriations of $18.7 billion for subsidized housing programs in the fiscal year 1982, a one-third reduction from the Carter request. Congress ultimately approved $17.4 billion.

Congress cut the programs more deeply the next year, but not as much as Mr. Reagan wanted. In his 1983 budget, he proposed to cancel $15 billion of spending authority granted in earlier years. Congress agreed to cancel only $4 billion, but then appropriated $8 billion more for subsidized housing in 1983.

Congress approved the President's request to increase rents for tenants of subsidized housing, to 30 percent of their adjusted incomes from 25 percent, over five years. But Congress rejected his proposal to count food stamps as income when computing the rent.

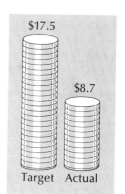

Unemployment Insurance

Congress, at Mr. Reagan's request, sharply cut back the extended benefits program for workers who are unemployed more than 26 weeks. Under this program, the Federal Government pays half the cost for 13 weeks of assistance beyond the first 26 weeks of state benefits.

But with rising unemployment, the cutbacks proved a political liability for some lawmakers. Congress has twice authorized temporary supplemental benefits for workers who would otherwise have run out of benefits.

Extended benefits would now be available in all states if Congress had not changed the law in 1981. In fact, the extended benefits are now paid in only 20 states. Such benefits are available only when a special statistic known as the insured unemployment rate rises above a specified level. Congress accepted Mr. Reagan's proposal to change the method of computing this rate, so unemployed people already receiving extended benefits are not included in the calculation. As a result some states with high unemployment rates, even for a time Michigan, which has the highest unemployment rate of the 50 states, lost eligibility for extended benefits.

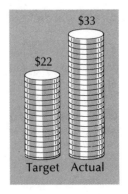

The surge in unemployment has washed away the savings that Mr. Reagan expected. The Congressional Budget Office says outlays from the unemployment trust fund rose from $18.7 billion in the fiscal year 1981 to $24.3 billion in 1982, and it forecasts outlays of $33 billion this year. President Reagan was predicting two years ago that unemployment would decline and that the changes he requested would hold the annual cost of the program to $22 billion.

Congress rejected another Reagan proposal that would have established a more stringent work requirement for people receiving regular unemployment benefits. Under the proposal, workers who had received 13 weeks of benefits might have been required to take jobs paying wages equal to the amount of their unemployment benefit or the minimum wage, whichever was higher. Congress showed no interest in the proposal.

CETA Jobs

Congress acquiesced in Mr. Reagan's request to cancel $1.2 billion of subsidies to state and local governments for the hiring of poor people. The Federal Government had provided such money under the Comprehensive Employment and Training Act since the 1974–75 recession.

The public service job program was costing $4 billion a year and there were 306,000 people in subsidized jobs when Mr. Reagan took office.

The program ended in September 1981, but many in Congress are trying to revive a public service employment program, now that 12 million Americans are jobless.

Child Nutrition

President Reagan proposed eliminating school lunch subsidies for children from middle- and upper-income families. Congress reduced but did not eliminate the subsidies. The lunch program cost $2.5 billion in the last school year, or $1 billion less than it would have cost under the old law. The President's original proposals would have saved an additional $500 million.

White House officials now acknowledge that they did not fully understand the economics of the program. When the Government reduces the subsidy for children from middle- and upper-income families, they tend to drop out of the program because meal prices generally rise. School lunch operators have found it is not economical for them to run a small program just for poor children. The total number of youngsters in the school lunch program dropped by 3.2 million last year, to 23.6 million.

Student Loans

The volume of guaranteed student loans, one of the main sources of Federal aid for college students, declined 22 percent last year, partly as a result of tighter eligibility criteria enacted at Mr. Reagan's request in 1981. New loan commitments for students attending college in 1982–83 totaled $6.1 billion, as against $7.8 billion in the prior school year. The loan volume had been rising steadily since 1977.

Congress made two major changes in the program in 1981. Students from families with adjusted gross income of $30,000 or more a year were subjected to a test of financial need. In addition, all students were required to pay a 5 percent "origination fee" to the lender, which could be a commercial bank or a state loan agency.

T. H. Bell, the Secretary of Education, said the changes had squeezed "fat" out of the loan program. But educators said some low-income families were no longer able to send their children to higher-priced colleges.

President Reagan proposed further cuts last year, but Congress balked after thousands of college students converged on the Capitol in a show of opposition.

EXHIBIT 3–4   The Threads of History in Social Welfare

To summarize this chapter's review of the historical development of the concept of social welfare, the major stages of welfare growth are presented on the following pages, along with a brief discussion of their enduring effects on social welfare concepts and programs.

Informal Welfare Structures

The highly formalized and specialized welfare structures we take for granted have their roots in informal attempts to meet people's basic needs. The family was the earliest structure in which this occurred, and, in spite of the highly formalized and professional programs that exist today, informal attempts to help others continue to exist and be important—the family, friendship groups, mutual aid groups. As long as the magnitude of need was small, and the definition of who was responsible for helping whom was narrow, informal welfare structures were adequate. When need and responsibility grew beyond immediate kin or friendship groups, more formal structures became necessary.

The Causes of Need

The incidence of need has generally been related to social conditions. The Industrial Revolution, including its earliest phases that broke up the manorial system, generated need of many kinds—housing, food, illness, and others. During periods of economic depressions, or during periods of war, it is common for people to experience need. Institutionalized inequality in whatever form—slavery, child labor, indenture, lack of women's rights, and religious persecution, to name a few—serves to make people helpless and dependent. Although there is always some need caused by willful neglect and deviance, the lessons of history demonstrate that need is most often a social phenomenon.

Categorizing the Needy

With the formalization of welfare services came the desire to categorize the needy in order to determine who qualified for what services (formalized in eligibility requirements). The Elizabethan Poor Law established three categories of the needy, which have proven remarkably long-lived. These categories, the services provided in each, and the present-day forms of both, are summarized below:

The helpless were persons who could not be blamed for being needy because of age, illness, or disablement. These persons received outdoor relief or were placed in almshouses. The helpless are still with us (the aged, dependent children, and the physically and emotionally disabled), and they continue to be considered worthy of assistance. Such aid today is normally provided in their own homes rather than in almshouses (although there are still some vestiges of almshouse-like residential facilities).

The involuntarily unemployed were persons who were the victims of misfortune, but who were generally ablebodied. They were usually sent to workhouses or houses of correction, where they were expected to work in return for help. The involuntarily unemployed are today generally helped through outdoor relief, although there is still a tendency to try to make receipt of aid dependent on going to work if at all possible.

The vagrant were persons without a stable place of residence. They were usually ostracized, or, if they had to be accepted by a community, placed in workhouses or houses of correction. They were considered willfully indigent, and despised as a result. Vagrancy today has a somewhat different connotation. Persons who exist outside the normative structure are our contemporary vagrants, whether or not they are physically mobile—skid-row alcoholics, drug users, persons who have committed a crime, sexual deviants, etc. They are likely to inhabit the modern-day houses of correction—prisons and mental hospitals—and they continue to carry the scorn of their society.

Public and Private Responsibility for the Needy

The enduring dislocations of industrialism created need on a scale beyond the resources of the informal welfare system. The result was the development of two types of structured social welfare: public and private. Publicly supported social welfare has always been the more important of the two because it is societal recognition of its responsibility to its members. Private social welfare depends on the personal sense of responsibility of individuals, and requires that they voluntarily forego some of their own resources to help others. In some this sense of responsibility does not exist, while in others available resources are too limited to allow any to be contributed to help others. Private contributions are also heavily dependent on societal economic health. On the other hand, until the 1930s private social welfare often met people's needs more adequately and comprehensively than did the then-minimal public system. Private services also served to stimulate the development of more adequate public services. However, public services have always been the barometer of societal attitudes toward the needy. Especially since 1935, public social services have come to dominate the society's social welfare system, reflecting changed attitudes toward helping.

Financial Aid, Social Services, and Special Groups

Two of the enduring issues in the provision of social welfare services have been deciding for whom society is responsible, and what needs should be met. Beginning with a focus on basic survival needs (food, money, shelter, health care) there has been a gradual expansion to include more socially oriented services—marital counseling, job skills, mental health, recreation, group participation, and the like. One way in which this has occurred is by focusing on special groups—children, the aged, the handicapped, the mentally ill, and prisoners—and developing a comprehensive network of services to meet their needs. This has generally led to a fragmented service delivery network (the aged are helped by programs different from those for children, or veterans, or the retarded), but still a gradually expanding network of increasingly comprehensive services has developed. Part of the reason for the initial focus on just one type of service (such as financial aid) or a special group whose needs seem so obvious (dependent children, for example) lies in society's struggle to define those who are deserving of need. Another part of the reason lies in changing and developing awareness of the causes of and solutions to need. And a third factor lies in historical accident—the existence of a Dorothea Dix, Jane Addams, or Michael Harrington to document need in a particular group, and often to fight for the development of services to meet identified need.

Professionalizing Social Welfare

There has been a progression in social welfare from informal services, to structured services, to structured professional services. Several factors have contributed to this progression: the increasing numbers of services provided and users served; the growth of the social sciences, making the measurement of social behavior possible and demonstrating the complexity of social behavior; and the expansion of the concept of social welfare beyond mere survival to include complex social behaviors. Although some other societies have well-developed social welfare systems that are informal in structure, in contemporary Western industrialized societies the professionalization of social welfare is an indication of the society's commitment to social welfare goals.

The Quest for Social Justice

The very concept of social welfare suggests a concern with social justice in its attempt to share social resources with those in need. Early attempts to meet need were focused on physical needs for food, shelter, and nurturance. Gradually individual autonomy became another right recognized by society, and was reflected in a concern with adequate psychological functioning and personal care in such places as prisons and mental hospitals. The professionalizing of social welfare emphasized individualizing people and problems, so that services were adapted to individual needs. A much later development has been recognition of a need for social participation, the right of people to have input into social policy-making and service delivery. Paternalistic views of minority groups by majority groups are increasingly repudiated as unjust. Racial, ethnic, age, and sex groups are all being seen as having the right to determine their own destinies. Social justice means the right to equal participation in societal decision-making, and equal access to social resources. As the survival needs of people as physical beings have been more adequately met, society has been able to turn to the survival of people as social beings. Much of the future of social welfare will be in the development of a society characterized by higher levels of social justice.

STUDY QUESTIONS

1. The family has traditionally been an important part of the social welfare institution. However, the contemporary American family is undergoing a number of changes. Identify three such changes, and discuss how each affects the family as a part of social welfare. Consider the family's ability to meet the needs of its members, the way the family relates to other social institutions, and the need the family has for other kinds of social welfare services.

2. Civil rights is an issue with which this society has struggled for most of its existence. For which groups do you think civil rights are especially problematic at the present time? Why does that particular group have difficulty obtaining its civil rights? What efforts are currently under way to try to strengthen the civil rights of members of that group?

3. In what year were you 15 years old? Starting from that year, review this chapter and list the social welfare issues and legislation that have occurred since then. Try to remember what social conditions and events were taking place when these issues or legislation were being debated, and identify as many as you can. How do you think they influenced the legislation or the treatment of the issues?

4. Visit your local Social Security office and get booklets describing the present programs that are available under OASDHI. Then visit your local Employment Office to get information about the present unemployment insurance program, and your local Department of Social Services (Public Welfare) to get information about the AFDC program. Take the information you get and compare it with the provisions of the original Social Security Act as described in this chapter (and through additional research that you may do).

5. Write down as precisely as you can what your political beliefs are. Then discuss how they are likely to influence your attitude toward social welfare in general, as well as specific social welfare programs. Who have you (or would you have) voted for in the last two presidential elections? Assuming your candidate won (whether or not he actually did), what impact would your choice have had on the social welfare institution?

SELECTED READINGS

Axinn, June, and Herman Levin (1982). *Social Welfare: A History of the American Response to Need.* New York: Harper and Row.

Coll, Blanche (1969). *Perspectives in Social Welfare.* Washington, D. C.: U. S. Government Printing Office.

Leiby, James (1978). *History of Social Welfare and Social Work in the United States.* New York: Columbia University Press.

Lubove, Roy (1969). *The Professional Altruist.* New York: Atheneum.

Trattner, Walter (1974). *From Poor Law to Welfare State.* New York: Free Press.

The Helping Process in Social Welfare

Helping is fundamental to the idea of social welfare. We have seen that helping can be done informally as well as formally. Formal helping is provided by people who most often work in bureaucratically organized social welfare agencies, and who have had some kind of special training to prepare them for the helping tasks they perform. The formal helping process used in social welfare can be divided into four major parts. We will look at three in this chapter:

1. *The basic content or elements involved in any helping effort.* These include people, place, problem or need, purpose, specific helping activities, and the outcomes.
2. *The characteristics of helping people.* These include self–awareness, professional commitment, knowledge and practice

skills, objectivity, empathy, energy, and persistence and re-silience.

3. *Specific helping skills.* Social welfare professions use a variety of specific helping skills. In this chapter we will look at a few of the most important skills needed in any helping effort: relating to others, communicating with others, assessing situations, planning with others, carrying out plans, and evaluating results.

The fourth part of the helping process used in social welfare is knowledge. It will be discussed fully in the next chapter. Helping requires a good deal more than simply wanting to help, as important as such motivation is. Trained helping people must have a significant body of knowledge that underlies their helping activities. The type of knowledge needed will depend on the functions to be performed in the formal social welfare structure. Paraprofessionals, who work under close supervision in carrying out treatment plans developed by others, have a less extensive knowledge base than the professionals under whom they work. Highly skilled specialists will have a different knowledge base than people responsible for planning holistic care, although certain basic knowledge is shared by specialists and generalists. In other words, skill is built on knowledge, a connection we will explore in more depth in the next chapter.

The Content of Helping Efforts

Six elements are of particular importance for understanding the helping process (Eriksen, 1977):

People

Helping is a cooperative venture that involves at least two people, and often many more. Normally we think in terms of a person providing help (the **helper**) and people seeking help **(users of services).** Helpers and users of services may be single individuals or they may be groups of people. For example, Konle (1982) shows how a multiprofessional team (the helpers) is needed to accurately assess the needs of young people needing special-education services. Although the immediate user of services is a young person, Konle emphasizes how important the whole family unit is to the success of whatever service delivery plan is proposed by the team. Seen in this way, the users are the people who make up the family unit. Another example of a group of people who are users of services are the tenants of the apartment building at 165 Howell Street (see Appendix) who are helped to organize to improve the quality of their housing. Most of us are familiar with individual helpers and users of services. A doctor treats a patient, for example, or a tutor reviews study skills with a student. Helping is most commonly thought of as a one-to-one activity, but in reality many helpers work in groups and many users of services are groups of people.

Helpers and users agree to work together to meet needs or solve problems, and the work of both is essential in this process. Helpers do not solve the problems of users; people solve their own problems with the assistance of the helper. Helping, therefore, is an activity that is best entered into voluntarily. In some situations the user does not voluntarily seek help, such as when a delinquent youngster is ordered by a judge to see a probation officer. However, a probation officer cannot be helpful if the youngster refuses to accept the help offered (Veronica in Exhibit 1–2 is a case in point). In a sense, every helping situation is a *self-help* situation, in which users accept the resources provided by the helper in order to help themselves.

Place

Formal helping usually occurs through organizations specifically designed for that purpose. As a generic group, these organizations are usually called social welfare agencies, although they have specific names as well: mental hospital, probation office, well-baby clinic, welfare agency, Red Cross office, community center, rape-crisis hotline, employment office, to name a few. The organization designed for helping activities usually has basic resources needed in the helping process. These may include such items as clerical help, office space, recreational facilities, medicines, and books. Agencies frequently provide services to people within the structure itself—a hospital room, an office for counseling, or a gymnasium, for example. The conditions under which help is provided can usually be more controlled in these settings, as when doctors have access to sophisticated medical equipment in a hospital. However, professional helpers may also go outside their agencies to provide help. Meals may be taken to elderly people's homes, homemaker services may be provided for a struggling mother, a tenants' organization may meet in their own apartment building, and a city planner may go to a city council meeting to testify.

In informal helping situations, the place may be quite impromptu or unexpected. An automobile accident that occurs on a hilly dirt road requires that some helping activities occur there or nearby. A distraught woman who has just been raped in a city park needs help either there or at the first point of contact with others from whom help is sought. An isolated elderly woman may need to be counseled by a helper who remains out in the hall until the user feels safe enough to admit the helping person into the apartment. Often help is required where resources have to be quickly improvised and where conditions are far from ideal. Ultimately, however, the nature of the place is less important than the fact that help is found when sought.

Problem (Need)

The interactional nature of helping requires that there be basic agreement about what the problem or need is for which help is sought. Helping may be seen as a type of *contract* between the helper and the user, in which both agree to cooperate in order to reach a clearly specified goal using identified resources. Unless such a contract is reached, the helper and user may only too late discover that they see the problem or need differently, and that their objectives are different. Even in the above-cited instance of rape, perspectives may be surprisingly different. The helper may assume that a woman is primarily concerned with getting medical care and physical protection and with contacting the police to try to apprehend the rapist. However, she may actually be most preoccupied by the wrenching emotional impact of her experience and the fear that loved ones may reject her.

The need for agreement between the helper and user raises the possibility that agreement may in some cases not be achieved. What happens then? For one thing, helping cannot occur, because unless both parties agree and work together, helping is unlikely. In formal helping situations, lack of agreement may result from the helper feeling inadequate to the task because of a lack of expertise, perceived inability to avoid emotional involvement, lack of needed resources, or some other factor. A failure to reach agreement may also stem from the user, who may distrust the helper's motivations, may question the helper's competence, or may simply feel uncomfortable with that particular helping person. If at all possible, the helper refers the user to a more appropriate person under these circumstances. In informal helping situations, lack of agreement usually results in a rather spontaneous and mutual disengagement between the potential helper and user.

Purpose

As we have already discussed, helping takes place for agreed-upon purposes. These may be of many kinds. People ask others for directions, opinions, recommendations. They also ask to use objects—the car, a book, or the clothes washer and dryer. These are everyday kinds of purposes around which informal helping may occur. Professional helpers generally deal with more complex and difficult situations. Usually we think about a particular **task goal** that we are seeking to accomplish when we speak about a helping purpose. The task goal could be getting needed money or a job, locating safe housing, obtaining medical care or educational opportunities, eliminating a dependency on alcohol or another drug, and others. However, professional helping in social welfare also includes **process goals.** These focus on enabling the service user to develop the skills necessary to accomplish future tasks. Rather than finding better housing, for example, the purpose may be to help residents learn to act as advocates for their own needs, so that their existing housing can be improved. Another example of a process goal would be job training that prepares people to obtain better jobs. Helping people to accomplish a specific task and helping them to learn how to carry out tasks for themselves are both important purposes in the helping process.

Helping Activities

Many specific decisions and activities are part of helping efforts, ranging from the decision that help is needed through the actual interactions in which helping occurs. Although it is often overlooked, David Landy (1965) has emphasized the importance of the helping process. Landy points out that the process of seeking help is often difficult and complex. It begins with a recognition that something is wrong, but such recognition is hampered by the common tendency to deny failure in some aspect of our lives. This is encouraged by a societal value system that preaches self-reliance and the belief that individuals can and should solve their own problems. Under these circumstances, it is not surprising that people often seek help only when they are desperate and when the problems are so complex that they are very difficult to solve. People seeking help are admitting to themselves and others that their own attempts to cope with their personal problems have failed. The stigma attached to seeking help is one reason why people

Enabling people to work together to attain their goals is an important goal of professional helping. These women have formed a tenants' group to improve the public housing in which they live. (Eric A. Roth/The Picture Cube)

tend to turn first to the informal helping network: family, friends, or clergy. Here problems can be discussed with minimal risk. Entry into the professional social welfare network implies that the problem is serious (Schoen, 1983).

Landy also noted that the act of seeking help places users of services in a dependent position. They relinquish some autonomy over their own lives, and must answer endless questions, travel to an inconvenient agency location, keep appointments, and the like. Being helped is often uncomfortable, involving confrontation with painful memories, unpleasant insights into oneself and others, and emotional stress. A person with problems may not be eager to temporarily endure more stress to achieve ultimate solutions. Landy's point, therefore, is to remind the social welfare practitioner that asking for help is a major step that is likely to be stressful. Some of these stresses are vividly described in Exhibit 4–1 in the "Reflections on Social Welfare" section at the end of the chapter.

Once the decision to seek help has been made and a working relationship between the helper and the user established, a variety of specific helping activities may be used. Concrete needs may be best met through activities to identify resources and link people with them: financial assistance programs, medical care, housing, physical security, and so forth. Task needs often involve activities to bring people together so that they can work collaboratively toward goal attainment. Process needs may require activities in the areas of teaching and learning, as well as emotional support and personal growth. The range of specific helping activities used by social welfare professionals will be discussed later in this chapter.

Outcome

In evaluating the outcome of a helping effort, there are at least three general criteria that can be used:

1. *Evaluation of involvement.* Were all of the relevant people involved, or did the helper try to do everything alone? Effective helping involves working with others, not dominating or ignoring them. The user, and others who influence the user's situation, must be involved to the fullest extent possible.
2. *Socioemotional evaluation.* How did the people involved in the helping effort feel about it? Did the users feel that the decision to seek help was a wise one? How did others who were involved in the helping effort feel?
3. *Task evaluation.* Were needs met and problems solved? This, the most concrete way to evaluate a service, must always be a major part of the evaluation of the helping process.

Helping, therefore, is a complex interaction of helpers and users through which resources are identified and used to solve problems and meet needs. All of us are regularly involved in helping and being helped at many levels. The formal helping network requires a higher level of awareness, purpose, and skill than the informal helping network, in order to achieve more consistently effective results to often difficult and complex problems. Formal helping, however, should never entail controlling the lives of others. People need to be helped to control their own lives, and that is a significant goal in competent, professional, social welfare helping efforts.

The Helping Person

It is impossible, as much as it would be useful, to know exactly what the perfect helping person looks like. This is so because the perfect helper does not exist. The mix of person, problem, and purpose in the helping process is constantly shifting. The strengths that a particular helping person may have with one type of user (such as the elderly) or a particular type of problem (like child abuse) may be weaknesses with other users and problems. There are some general characteristics that experience has shown ought to be part of the professional social welfare helping person's overall profile, but the blend differs for each person. Precisely because each person is different, all persons seeking help, no matter what the problem or purpose, can find a helping person who can assist them. Each helping person has a "style," and as long as that style includes some strength along each of the dimensions that follow, one can predict that the style will be effective most of the time.

Self-awareness

Helping people must know themselves reasonably well, and on the whole, they should like themselves. The motivations for helping others should revolve around a belief in one's own ability to be useful to others. The balance of personal strengths and weaknesses should allow the helping person to focus on working effectively with others, and their values should support activities to help people gain control over their own lives and gain access to needed societal resources. Skills in social interaction should be used consciously and skillfully. Because all of us have limits, helping people must know when theirs have been reached. To know that a given situation is beyond one's abilities is sensible; to persist regardless is dangerous and often harmful. Although we never completely understand ourselves, successful professional helping people know their own basic parameters.

Professional Commitment

The social welfare professional should have a strong commitment to the goals of social welfare and to the ethical standards of social welfare professions. The professional helper has a fundamental drive to improve social and individual life conditions and reacts to situations of injustice and disadvantage. Commitment and self-awareness are closely related. The desire to participate in achieving the goals of social welfare means a constant evaluation of one's own professional behavior within professional standards of ethical behavior and practice competence. Professional commitment is not a blind, uncompromising assault on the institutions and structures of society that seem to be creating obstacles for people. It is instead a commitment and determination to work collaboratively with others to use professional knowledge, values, and skills to bring about the changes necessary for people to achieve their life goals more easily. Professional helping people work together; the world is too large and too complex for individuals to think that they can single-handedly solve its problems, although each person can certainly make a contribution to that overall effort.

Knowledge as a Base for Practice Skills

The activities of the professional helper are grounded in relevant social, behavioral, and biological science knowledge. Though the initial helping impetus flows from caring and commitment, the helping activities of the professional flow from knowledge of human behavior. The helper has to understand why people act as they do and the ways that behavior can be changed when that is desired. To be sure, the current state of much of our knowledge leaves many gaps in our understanding of human behavior. Nevertheless, the professional helper works with the best available knowledge to make conscious choices about what skills are needed in particular practice situations.

Objectivity

Problems are often multifaceted and complex, and sometimes it is difficult to separate the person from the problem. People sometimes do hurtful and morally troubling things, such as abusing helpless others, abusing themselves through the use of injurious chemical substances, and maintaining destructive personal relationships. Professionals have to understand that what someone has done is different from who that person is. People retain their rights as human beings in spite of their behaviors.

This is not to suggest that professional helpers have no moral standards or sense of outrage. They do. However, when working with users, the purpose is to help them solve problems and meet needs. This cannot happen if the helper begins to deny users the right to control their own lives, and to accept the consequences of their choices. A helper may hate the act of rape, but when working with a rapist, personal feelings have to be kept out of the way so the user can come to understand the resources and choices available.

Sometimes helpers confuse objectivity with distance. Objectivity involves being able to systematically evaluate people and their situations in an unbiased, factual way. This can be done while still being warm and caring toward those with whom one is working. Distance is creating barriers that reduce the user's perception that the helper is warm and caring. This usually reduces the willingness of users to share information and become fully engaged in the helping process. Distance can be created by expressions of personal disapproval of the behavior of users of services, by communication problems such as language difficulties or the excessive use of professional jargon, by the helper's inattention and seeming lack of caring, and by aspects of the physical environment like noise and difficulty in reaching the place in which helping is to occur. Being able to objectively assess and work on a situation is critical for professional helpers. All users have a right to this approach. Rejecting people because of their situations, or creating barriers for those seeking help, will destroy the helping process.

Empathy

Empathy is the ability to comprehend another's subjective reality and feelings. Empathy is more objective than sympathy because it does not include sharing feelings with the other person. It is instead sharing an understanding of those feelings and their importance. This enables the helping person to understand without being overwhelmed by what may be very upsetting and immobilizing feelings. Empathy and support are necessary to enable the person who needs help to use resources, both personal and outside resources, and to develop and implement a solution to the problematic reality.

Energy

Helping is an exhausting activity. Not only does it require the careful use of knowledge and skill, but it is also a constant drain on feelings and emotions. If there is a commitment to help, however, there has to be the energy to carry out the necessary helping activities. Sometimes professionals burn out, meaning that they become too physically or psychologically exhausted to care anymore. There are a number of ways to avoid burnout. A critical one is emphasizing the helping person's enabling role. Helpers facilitate the work of others, enabling them to understand resources and issues, to use resources more effectively, and to develop new skills. The professional's own resources go much further for far longer if they are invested in cooperative and facilitating interactions with colleagues and users of services.

Persistence and Resilience

Helping can be a very discouraging endeavor. Sometimes problems are so complex that they seem overwhelming, or needs so widespread that it seems they can never be adequately met. Sometimes people become so frightened by change that they become hostile and resistant. Occasionally, painfully won gains are wiped out through an unusual or unanticipated event. And sometimes the progress is so slow that it is easy to forget it is even happening. Yet these are the realities of change. People are not always grateful for efforts to help them achieve their goals, and some people wish to block the goal attainment of others. The bureaucracies in which we live and work seem to proceed with excruciating slowness. In spite of it all, the helping professional has to keep working in a methodical way toward the established goals and to keep finding better ways when the old ones are inadequate. Discouraged often, disappointed occasionally, and tired daily, the professional commitment that supports the helping professional nevertheless provides the core motivation for trying again and again, seeking to be better and better.

What makes an effective professional helping person? There is, of course, no simple answer to such a question. There are many people who make effective helpers. Keith-Lucas (1972) suggests the following:

> Courage, humility, and concern may then give us some characterization of the helping person. Other qualities such as dependability, patience, integrity, or a sense of humor are of course also desirable, or perhaps simply facets of these. Intelligence and imagination can be of help. But the helping person is an essentially human being, with many of the faults that all of us share.

Whatever the individual characteristics of the professional helper, this person must possess self–awareness and be aware of any particular strengths and weaknesses, skills and deficiencies, preferences and pet peeves. As Keith-Lucas notes, all of us have limitations and weaknesses, and helping professionals are no exception. They must recognize their limitations so that these characteristics will not interfere with the helping process as they work.

To conclude this section on characteristics of professional helping people, let's return to Jeff Jovien, whom we met in Exhibit 2–5 in Chapter 2. In Exhibit 4–2 in the "Reflections on Social Welfare" section at the end of the chapter, we will look at how he represents characteristics of professional helpers in his work with the Department of Children and Family Services (DCFS) in Chicago.

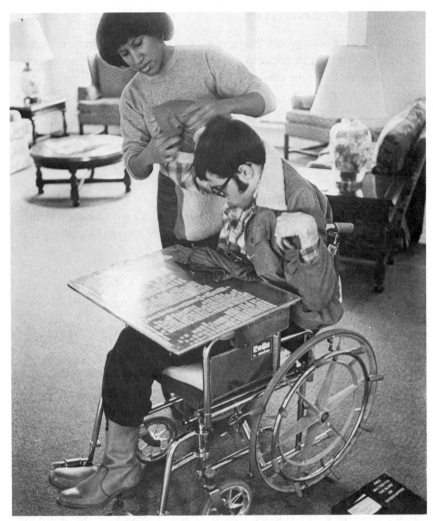

Helping occurs in many settings. This is a group home for the handicapped, in which residents live in comfortable, informal surroundings, rather than in large, restrictive, impersonal settings. (Bohdan Hrynewych/Southern Light)

Helping Skills and the Problem-Solving Process

In addition to understanding the elements of helping and the characteristics of helping people, professional helpers know how to combine them into consciously chosen helping activities. Each helping profession has its own specific approach to providing services to people. These reflect that profession's particular social welfare purpose, and the knowledge and skills needed to attain it. The surgeon's skill with a scalpel differs from the occupational therapist's skill in developing job-related abilities in people with physical or emotional limitations. Nevertheless, there is a set of practice activities used by all helping professionals, regardless of their particular profession. It is based in the **problem-solving process,** a systematic approach to combining knowledge, values, and skills in order to help others solve their problems (Brill, 1978; Devore and Schlesinger, 1981; Loewenberg, 1977). The problem-solving process has six parts:

communicating effectively with others

relating effectively to others

assessing situations

planning with others

carrying out plans

evaluating the results of the helping effort

We will look briefly at each in turn.

Communicating Effectively with Others

Communication is basic to any effort to understand people and situations, and to act in helpful ways. Communicating is a shared activity involving senders and receivers of information (Day, 1977). The message exchanged is encoded by the sender and decoded by the receiver—that is, the sender puts the message in a form that seems sensible, hoping that the receiver will be able to understand it in such format. Often this is not the case. Interferences in the encoding/transmission/decoding processes, which are generally referred to as static, may block communication. Static includes the physical conditions in which the communication is attempted (a noisy room, for example), the transmission skill of the sender (such as knowing what the receiver wants to know and in what form the receiver can process the information), and the motivation and emotional state of the receiver (McQuail, 1975). Finally, communication involves feedback, the response of the receiver to the sender, which in turn evokes further responses by the sender, and through which ongoing communication occurs.

Communication occurs through three major forms: verbally, in writing, and through the use of body language. Verbal communication involves the use of language, essentially the use of a commonly understood set of symbols that represent ideas, objects, and events. For verbal communication to be effective, all the people involved must understand the language. Obviously, people who only speak different languages—English and Spanish, for example—will not be able to communicate very effectively verbally (although they can communicate in other ways, as we will see shortly). Verbal communication using language may not work well for other reasons: The way a language is used affects its clarity. Dialects, for instance, affect grammatical structure and vocabulary, and may present difficulties for people who are speaking different dialects of the same language. In addition, some groups develop jargon, their own specialized vocabulary. This is true of the helping professions, with nurses referring to the ICU (intensive care unit), social workers talking about Title XX (of the Social Security Act), and police officers discussing a DOA (a crime or accident victim who was dead when the officers arrived or when they reached the hospital). Social welfare professionals should avoid jargon when communicating with users who don't understand it. It is also important that they understand the jargon or dialects of those with whom they are trying to communicate. These features of people's verbal communication frequently reflect important cultural characteristics and life experiences.

Written communication may also be based on language, as are letters, case records, books, and memos. The characteristics of language discussed above are also significant in these instances. However, written communication need not depend on language, as when someone draws a picture. Drawing and painting can be very significant when done by people unable to verbalize or use language—people too ill to speak, children, the mentally ill, and persons lacking the fine motor control needed to make letters. Written communication is especially important when helping professionals communicate with each other. Agencies expect that records will be kept. A professional may send a letter to refer a client, exchange memos to arrange case conferences, or prepare written testimony for a legislative hearing.

The third major kind of communication is body language, the messages that people are constantly sending by the way they walk, dress, sit, and act. Often we are unaware of our body language, yet we are constantly communicating with others through its use. It is common for helpers to note that a user looks tense and worried by his or her facial expression, clasping and unclasping of hands, or shifting in the seat. Helpers try to put anxious people at ease with body movements, such as smiling, maintaining eye contact, shaking hands, and nodding the head to acknowledge what someone has said. How people act is an important supplement to what they say. It is not uncommon for them to say one thing but act quite differently, to say "I'm OK" but to stare at the floor unsmiling, wince, or tremble. In addition, people who have difficulty speaking or writing may instead communicate with body language. A grateful person who hugs, a person who reaches out by offering a gift, and people who bury their face in their hands are all examples. Because body language is so important, helping professionals have to be astute observers of behavior to make sure that they "read" everything that is being communicated.

Much communication is informal—we chat with family and friends in a relatively unplanned way, for instance. Other times, we communicate in a very structured, planned way. The most commonly used, structured, purposeful, communication mechanism is the **interview.** Helping professionals frequently have to obtain information from people in order to understand problematic situations, people's life goals, and available resources. Interviews are used for these purposes and may occur with people seeking help, with friends or family members, with colleagues who can be helpful in a particular practice situation, with political officials whose actions are relevant to people's needs, and in many other situations. Interviews also enable helpers to provide information to others, and to provide an environment for the examination of feelings. Chart 4–1 provides a useful summary of the major components of interviewing.

Communication does not occur only between two people. Often groups of people are involved, and in such situations additional skills are needed. The ways to facilitate communication among groups depend on the type of group involved. Groups whose purpose is recreational provide a natural, nonthreatening context for interaction and communication. Therapeutic groups can provide opportunities for the ventilation and analysis of feelings in a supportive, nonjudgmental context. Task groups help people to establish communication and support each other by working together to attain common goals. These groups can help their members, in the process of working on tasks, to identify their own resources and find effective ways of using them by collaborating with others. Groups are not restricted to user and user-related groups, either. Most professional helpers practice in organizations in which they need to communicate with colleagues. They may also have to communicate with decision makers, such as judges, boards of directors, community-planning groups, and legislators. In these instances helpers provide data obtained in their work to decision

CHART 4–1   An Outline of the Interviewing Process

Following is an outline of the interviewing process used in the Social Worker Technician program of the U.S. Army Medical Field Service School at Ft. Sam Houston, San Antonio, Texas. It is an excellent summary of the major components of interviewing, and it provides a useful overview of the activities that are part of skillful interviewing.

1. *Beginning of interview*
   a. Begin where the patient is
   b. Attempt to set patient at ease
   c. Attention to patient's comforts
   d. Efforts to establish rapport
2. *Interest in patient*
   a. Courtesy
   b. Treating the patient with dignity
   c. Individualize patient
   d. Warmth
   e. Tone of voice
   f. Demonstrated sincerity of involvement
   g. Attentiveness and eye contact
   h. Remaining patient-centered, not note-centered
3. *Drawing out affect*
      Encourage patient to express feelings, i.e., anger, sadness, warmth, joy, despair, hostility, and others
4. *Skill in responding to patient's behavior*
   a. Recognition and appropriate use of verbal communication
   b. Recognition and appropriate use of nonverbal behavior
5. *Clarification and consistency of role*
   a. Self-control of stress, prejudice, and judgmental feelings
   b. Appropriate appearance
   c. Conveying one's purpose in the interview
6. *Questioning technique*
   a. Proper balance between general and specific questions
   b. Questions which guide the patient in telling story in his own words
   c. Transitions
7. *Listening techniques*
      Proper use of silence which encourages the patient
8. *Ending*
   a. Brief summarization of interview content
   b. Opportunity for patient feedback on interview
   c. Proper explanation of future plan/view in regard to the patient

makers. This information is critical for decision making that is helpful to users, either directly or by improving the environments in which they live.

Relating Effectively to Others

Through communication a relationship is established (or, if things are not working well, not established). It is useful at this point to reemphasize that helping is not a linear series of steps. Many things go on at the same time, and they are differentiated here only for conceptual clarity rather than to suggest that they always occur in a particular order. The **relationship** is the bond that is developed between professional people and those with whom they interact. This bond is built on mutual trust and confidence, and makes it possible to work on problems that are often difficult, painful, and exhausting.

A number of factors facilitate the development of relationships. Trust and confidence are fundamental, with all parties believing in the goodwill of the others. The professional person must be perceived as having the interest, commitment, and skills to be helpful. The helper, in turn, trusts that users will try in good faith to achieve the identified intervention goals. **Nonjudgmentalism** is an important part of trust, especially for the helper. Users must feel that regardless of how difficult, unpleasant, illegal, and even destructive the problem, they as people retain their basic self-worth and self-respect. As representatives of society, social welfare professionals are obligated to inform people of behaviors that are likely to lead to undesirable physical, emotional, or social consequences. However, this must be in the context of the separation of behavior and self-worth. Behaviors may be destructive, but the basic worth and human rights of each person remains, regardless of their behavior.

Relationships also require **empathy,** the ability to understand the feelings of another. Experiencing need is fraught with many feelings, such as despair, embarrassment, fear, and unacceptability as a person. These feelings are part of the situation, and they must be dealt with during the helping effort. Feelings can be handled only if they are recognized in a way that acknowledges both their existence and their significance. Mutuality and sharing are also part of relationships. All parties bring strengths, points of view, and goals to the helping effort. Through mutual exchange, strengths can be maximized and help becomes more possible. This also allows for self-determination, the ability of people to decide what they want their life goals to be. No one has the right or the resources to control the lives of others, not even highly trained professionals. Through mutuality and sharing, people can work together without feelings of inferiority or incurring obligations that can never be repaid. Such feelings build resentment and hostility and block helping. Attempts to impose help on others will almost surely fail, whereas allowing people to work together to achieve goals maximizes the effectiveness of helping efforts.

Interest and confidentiality provide encouragement for people to communicate in an open and frank way without fearing that information will be used inappropriately. The helping person's interest is strictly professional rather than voyeuristic, and so whatever is shared is kept within the professional helping relationship. Finally, a relationship is based on listening, support, and realism. One way interest is conveyed to another is through listening carefully to what is said and seeking clarification as necessary but avoiding repetition caused by inattention. Listening includes being sensitive to the many levels of communication and the mechanisms through which it occurs. By using interest, listening, mutuality, sharing, trust, and nonjudgmentalism, the helping person supports the efforts of others to communicate, to relate, and to engage in the helping process. However, supporting someone is different from false assurances. The successful outcome of an effort to organize a tenant's council cannot be guaranteed, but its members can be supported in their efforts. Persons with a terminal illness cannot be restored to perfect health, but they can be supported as they try to cope with their approaching death as constructively as possible. False assurances destroy trust and ultimately undermine a relationship, even though the helping person may want desperately to assist others in achieving their life goals.

Finally, there are special problems in relating to involuntary users of services. Sometimes groups of people are forced to accept social welfare services—criminals who are sent to prison, for example, or welfare mothers who must accept job training (Sheehan, 1978; Piven and Cloward, 1971). Frequently, the provision of such services occurs in ways that violate one or more characteristics of a relationship—lack of confidentiality with prisoners, or lack of mutuality and self-determination among welfare mothers. These situations create serious value and ethics dilemmas for professional helpers and may seriously impede efforts to develop a professional relationship. The helper is obligated to act as ethically as possible under the circumstances, explaining to users what the limits of the helping situation are. Within these limits, helping may occur, but the mutuality and sharing that is only possible when people are free to make their own decisions will inevitably be missing.

Assessing Situations

Assessment is the process of collecting and organizing information needed to understand a situation and ways of intervening in that situation. Assessment is holistic—that is, it seeks to analyze systematically the full range of biological, psychological, social, and cultural systems involved in a particular situation. However, assessment also involves partializing the situation so that the whole situation is divided into its parts. Usually problematic situations have to be worked with piece by piece, although always with an understanding of how each piece relates to the whole. For example, a social worker confronted with a battered wife's plea for help first has to obtain the information necessary to understand the woman's present situation: How is she handling the emotional stress? Is she in further danger? Does she have financial or other resources, such as a job, that can provide needed financial support, or family and friends who could house her temporarily if needed? Are there children involved? If so, where are they and what are their needs? Every situation is tied into a system of ongoing relationships, each of which has to be explored in a systematic way. Throughout, a balance between the whole and its parts must be maintained.

Assessment is done with the people involved in the situation. Events have to be understood in terms of their meaning to the people who experience them. Otherwise social workers risk imposing their own meaning, which may be quite foreign to the biological, cultural, or social characteristics of the people involved. For instance, whether a sick and elderly person is seen as a burden or a readily accepted responsibility varies between groups. As information is obtained, it has to be processed for meaning with those who are seeking assistance. Objectives, like meanings, vary among individuals and groups. A better job that requires geographical mobility is not necessarily preferable to staying close to family and friends, and scientifically validated medical treatment is not always seen as more desirable than folk remedies or spiritual healing.

Planning with Others

Planning involves using knowledge to create a procedure through which change will occur. Planning must involve the participation of those who will be affected so that people's rights to self-determination are respected and so that their cultural, biological, and social needs will be met in appropriate and acceptable ways. Based on the information obtained through holistic assessment, the helping person tries to foresee what the effects of various helping strategies will be. Although helping a single parent get a job may solve financial needs, it may disrupt important cultural patterns with the parent's children, peers, and parents. Solving a community's need for safe, comfortable, low-cost housing with a high-rise housing project may lead to increased crime and disrupt existing neighborhood support networks.

After the alternatives have been carefully considered in terms of available resources and possible obstacles, and the foreseeable effects of various strategies considered, contracting occurs. A contract specifies the following:

> what activities the various people, groups, and organizations involved in the change effort will perform
>
> what the time frame for the performance of these activities will be
>
> how and when the evaluation of the helping effort will occur

The contract involves ordering objectives and arranging them in a feasible time sequence. A large-scale goal, such as building a shelter for homeless people, usually results from the progressive attainment of smaller goals. It might be agreed, for example, that the local legal-aid office will clarify laws and policies about the establishment of a shelter. Social workers, medical professionals, and law-enforcement officers might contact legislators and business people to interpret the need for a shelter and seek funding for it. Meanwhile, homeless people might be organizing self-help support groups and seeking employment or job training. Each goal is appropriate to each group and is reasonably small in scale. In the aggregate, they add up to the larger objective.

Carrying Out Plans

Carrying out the plans made with and for others entails a number of specific activities. Teaching and providing information are frequent activities, because people often lack the information they need to find and use resources that could be helpful to them. For example, many young couples do not know that genetic counseling is available to them, and residents of a housing project may be unaware of their legal rights in situations in which they encounter landlord difficulties. Following up to ensure that people who have been referred to services actually receive them is another activity frequently performed by helpers.

Making people aware of resources often entails teaching them skills related to gathering and using information. By making people aware of sources of information (such as a community service directory or a community hotline), they can use these in the future as needed. Similarly, people can be taught how to make the best use of resources and services—how to dress for a job interview, how to check on eligibility, or how to use informal support systems in times of stress, for example. Teaching people how to better use themselves and their environment leads to personal growth and increased independence and control over their own lives. These are important goals for professional helping people.

Sometimes people need to be supported during their efforts to learn about and use resources. Emotional support is helpful as people reach out to make contact with others, to develop personal support systems for themselves, and to participate in social and personal change efforts. Other people for whom support is necessary are those who face a short-term crisis (such as rape, a natural disaster, divorce, the loss of a loved one), or who must learn to cope with a long-term debilitating illness, a handicap, or the prospect of death. These situations require that people be helped to clarify their respective situations, express their feelings about them, and explore their impact on their future lives. They will also have to be helped to accept that anxiety, resentment, inaction, and the need to depend on others may be appropriate short-term responses to their situations. In the long run, of course, these feelings and behaviors will be modified, so that more positive and productive self-concepts and behaviors are built. Even when a difficult situation cannot be changed, people can develop their own best ways to cope with it. These coping mechanisms should enable them to continue to work toward their own life goals with positive and humane feelings about themselves and others.

The great majority of social welfare professionals work in large-scale formal organizations like departments of social welfare, courts, mental health centers, hospitals, and others. Therefore, professional helping requires organization skills if plans are to be carried out effectively. These organizations become the immediate system within which professionals work. Each has its own particular procedures, including:

regulations specifying service delivery procedures (such as hours the agency is open, services available, and eligibility criteria)

record-keeping procedures (what kind of records must be kept, who has access to them, what form of written, filmed, or dictated records are required, for example)

procedures to use in carrying out activities (forms to be filled out, use of the telephone, appropriate use of support-staff people, such as secretaries, and scheduling facilities, to name a few)

These procedures are basic to organizational functioning, and professionals have to use them effectively in order to make the agency's resources available to users.

Evaluating Results of the Helping Effort

As we noted earlier, built into the contracting process is a time frame for evaluating progress toward attaining the objectives of the helping effort. Have the various people, groups, and organizations involved done what was anticipated? If so, were the results those expected? If not, what obstacles impeded their activities? What planning is now indicated, building on experience from previous efforts? Evaluation is an on-going activity that is responsive to the interplay of the dynamics involved in the problem-solving process. As situations change, perhaps in part because some goals have been attained, strategies to attain remaining goals must also be modified. Evaluation is important for reasons other than goal attainment, however. It is also a significant source of continuing growth for professional helpers. It provides the information they need to assess their own effectiveness, and to identify areas in which further professional growth is needed.

SUMMARY

This chapter has attempted to give you a reasonably concrete sense of how the work of social welfare is done—what elements are involved, who is involved, and what they do. Helping is a mutual activity that involves many people, some of them neither the helper nor the user of services. Formal and informal helping structures are used, although the special knowledge and skills of professional helpers enable them to use the problem-solving process in a very planned and effective manner. I hope that by now you are beginning to see the work of social welfare as complex but not mysterious. It results from the interplay of many people, groups, and organizations, and from the very deliberate use of a wide range of helping activities. These have been derived over time from knowledge and experience. In the next chapter, we will focus on the knowledge from the social, biological, and behavioral sciences that underlies professional helping activities.

REFLECTIONS ON SOCIAL WELFARE

The following two exhibits provide in-depth examples of what it can be like to seek help and to be a helper. Reading them will help you to understand better what the helping process is like for helpers and those who use their services.

EXHIBIT 4–1   When Seeking Help Becomes a Problem

In 1976, the Community Services Society of New York City sponsored a study of how the New York City Department of Social Services (DSS) was implementing existing procedures and regulations for applications for public assistance. The following case is one of the examples used in the report of this study. It is an excellent illustration of the difficulties people sometimes have in entering the formal helping network. Had the woman involved not been desperate, one could easily conceive her becoming so angry and upset that she would have ceased her efforts to find help. One could as easily imagine her dropping out of the helping effort if transportation to the agency had been especially difficult, as it is in many communities. As it turned out, this woman had the courage and stamina (plus help from ACCESS*) to persist in her efforts until she was successful. However, her account focuses attention on the procedures that are used in leading people to the social welfare services that have been created for their use. These procedures can become important determinants of the success or failure of helping efforts.

Mrs. B., an eighteen-year-old mother of one child, was nine months pregnant. She was separated from the father of both children and was staying with another man. The man told Mrs. B. that she had to leave because his wife was coming back to live with him.

Her father allowed her to stay in his home one night and a friend let her stay a second night. The next morning, June 8, she was "homeless" and went to the DSS Center to apply for public assistance. She was denied an application for public assistance because the worker said she had to have a place to stay before they could give her help. She should have been allowed to apply at the Center

Source: Daniel Reich, *Applying for Public Assistance in New York City* (New York: Community Service Society of New York, 1977), pp. 22–23.

*ACCESS is a service to help people apply for public assistance which is sponsored by the Community Services Society of New York.

since her family was undomiciled. According to City Procedure 75-13, p. 10, the application for a homeless person "should be taken by the first IM Center at which the applicant appears." She was referred to Project ACCESS by an ACCESS worker, and ACCESS provided assistance so that she could have shelter.

On June 9, she returned to the Center but was told that she had to go to Family Court to report the missing father. On June 10, she returned to the Center but was told that because the room where she was temporarily staying was out of the district, she could not receive help from that Center. This again violated City Procedure 75-13, p. 10. DSS Central Office was called by AC-CESS on June 10 to request intervention of this case by the administrative staff.

On June 15, Mrs. B. had her second child. She still had not received an application for public assistance. An appointment at the Center was made for June 18. On that date the applicant arrived at the Center at 9:00 a.m. but was told by the General Receptionist that she was too late to be helped. Mrs. B. finally received an application on her fifth visit to the Center on June 21. On June 22, Mrs. B. returned to the Center and was granted assistance.

EXHIBIT 4–2   The Professional Helper

This exhibit explores some of the personal and professional issues involved in being a professional helping person.

Does he see such successes often enough to feel he makes a difference? Jovien says yes, but he sounds as certain as a new waiter recommending wine. "I'd like to think I make the maximum gains under the circumstances," he says. "By setting realistic goals and formulating good plans, you can make an adequate amount of progress. . . ."

DCFS caseworkers can't be thin skinned. Even the best ones take abuse from parents, kids, and juvenile court judges, and they are regularly under fire in the media. Caseworkers worry that when the department takes heat in the press, they'll be the fall guys. . . . "We don't get a lot of positive strokes. I mean, it can be a self-rewarding job, but we don't get the pat on the back that we do deserve at times". . . .

Jovien's supervisor . . . calls Jovien "one of the best. He's systematic, organized, sensitive to the needs of kids". . . .

"I didn't want to be tied to a desk five days a week. I wanted to be in the field, with people. I like helping people solve their problems. . . . It's not a boring job at all," he says. "Every family's different. The variety appeals to me. And it's making a contribution to society. That's part of it, too". . . .

Source: Steve Bogira, "Casework," in *Reader: Chicago's Free Weekly,* Vol. 11, No. 14, January 15, 1982, pp. 1ff. Copyright 1983 Chicago Reader, Inc.

Jovien manages to keep his hours mostly 8:30 to 5. "I usually do not bring paperwork home, and I try not to make phone calls at home. But some people you can only get hold of at night. And the job tends to follow you home. If something's happening, it's going to be on your mind. It might be a runaway, and you're afraid the kid's going to get hurt. You'll be kicking it around. . . ."

He always thought it would be hard for dwellers in the world of poverty to escape, and "the job reinforced that for me. I've come to realize how difficult life is in a ghetto neighborhood and how hard it is to climb out. In some situations, I see that if they really wanted to work at it, some families could better themselves . . . but yet they don't. But for other families, the circumstances are overwhelming. . . ."

Because of that, Jovien says he has to be satisfied with bits of progress. "I don't try to shoot for the stars on all my cases. If I did, chances are I'd burn out."

STUDY QUESTIONS

1. How would you define the ideal helping person? Include personal characteristics, knowledge possessed, and skills at the helper's disposal. If you aspire to be a social welfare professional, how would you rate yourself at present in terms of this ideal?

2. Go to a public place, such as a bus station, airport, or bank and observe the people you see. What kinds of different behaviors do you observe between those providing help and those receiving it? Select someone and try to observe as many things about that person as you can. After doing so, try to construct a portrait of the person's life: Where does s/he live? Is s/he married? What kind of work does s/he do? Is s/he happy or sad? How could you go about getting additional information about this person if you had to?

3. Analyze your own verbal and written communication. Are you very verbal? Do you speak more than one language, or a particular dialect? Do you use jargon? How are your written skills? Do you write with facility, or is it generally a dreaded chore for you? Given your present level of verbal and written communication skills, how effective do you think you would be in communicating with people in social welfare settings? Would you feel more comfortable with particular users? Which ones, and why?

4. Now think about your body language. Are you aware of what you do—any mannerisms you have, for example? Do you ever consciously use body language to help accomplish a goal—dressing a certain way for a particular event, smiling a lot, or perhaps even purposefully crying in certain situations? How sensitive are you to the body language of others? What actions by someone else appeal to you, or repel you? Why? What do they communicate to you?

5. Do you believe that people have the right to control their own lives? Are there limits to this right, if it exists? For example, should people be allowed to choose to die if they are ill? Should a 15-year-old be allowed to leave home if unhappy? Should poor people be allowed to have children, knowing they will most likely have to rear them in poverty? What, to you, are the most important issues involved in the whole question of freedom of choice?

SELECTED READINGS

Brill, Naomi (1976). *Teamwork: Working Together in the Human Services*. Philadelphia: J. B. Lippincott.

———— (1978). *Working with People*. Philadelphia: J. B. Lippincott.

Davies, Martin (1981). *The Essential Social Worker*. London: Heinemann Educational Books.

Day, Peter R. (1977). *Methods of Learning Communication Skills*. New York: Pergamon Press.

Ivey, Allen (1983). *Intentional Interviewing and Counseling*. Monterey, Ca. Brooks-Cole.

Kahn, Si (1982). *Organizing*. New York: McGraw-Hill.

CHAPTER 5

The Knowledge Foundations of Professional Helping

The knowledge foundations of social welfare are found primarily in the liberal arts and the biological, behavioral, and social sciences. Of particular relevance are disciplines such as sociology, psychology, biology, political science, economics, and anthropology, which address various facets of the human condition with which social welfare is concerned. However, if behavior is to be viewed and assessed holistically, and the many dimensions of particular life situations understood, concepts from these many disciplines must be integrated. This chapter will look at specific knowledge areas that enable us to understand particular life situations, and explore ways to integrate and apply in practice this vast amount of knowledge. The link between professional practice and knowledge is a critical one. Without knowledge there can be no professional helping (although obviously other kinds of helping may occur). Before discussing specific knowledge, however, the chapter will begin with some criteria useful for selecting knowledge for use in practice.

Selecting Knowledge for Practice

Particular kinds of knowledge for use in practice are not selected at random. Three significant factors influence the choices: values, the existence of evidence about the accuracy of knowledge, and the practical applicability of knowledge. In this section we will look at each in turn.

Values

Everyone has a value stance from which he or she approaches the search for knowledge. For some, religious beliefs form an important part of their world view and their perceptions of cause and effect. For others, scientific methodology and empirically verified concepts and relationships are basic to their understanding of themselves and others. Still others may have an existential approach to the human condition. All of these attempts to understand the world are appropriate, but each suggests different bodies of knowledge that are most compatible.

It is important to know one's own values regarding acceptable sources of knowledge. This awareness not only aids us in our search for knowledge but also helps us understand what knowledge we reject, and why. The following brief excerpt from an article discussing social work with American Indians illustrates what happens when a user group uses knowledge that has its foundations in tradition, whereas the professional uses knowledge based on scientific research or practice experience (Good Tracks, 1973).

> The worker must not intervene unless the people request an intervention, and (s/he) is likely to wait a long time for such a request. The credentials of (his or her) profession, (his or her) position, status, knowledge, skills, achievements, and authority, although respected by the agency, are in most cases completely without merit among the Indians. Such things belong to Anglo culture and are not readily translatable into Indian culture.

(His or her) standing in the Anglo community does not give (him or her) a license to practice intervention among Indian people . . . In every case, the people utilize the established, functional, culturally acceptable remedy within their own native system.

Evidence

A second criterion that can be used in choosing theory for practice is the evidence that supports it. What is acceptable evidence relates to values as discussed above. Nevertheless, the theory that has the most evidence to support it, however "evidence" is being defined, would appear to be the most promising as a basis for intervention. For example, within a scientific perspective, more empirical evidence demonstrates the greater effectiveness of behavior modification than psychotherapy for resolving certain types of problems. This might be one criterion to use in deciding among two or more bodies of knowledge on which to base one's approach to helping.

Practical Implications

Another way to choose between available bodies of knowledge is the practical implications of each. For example, which theories suggest interventive approaches that will achieve results more rapidly? at lower cost? with all user groups rather than with just selected ones? When faced with racial discrimination in a school, for example, one can select from at least two competing sociological theories. One says that values must first be changed, which obviously is a long, slow process. The other says that changing behavior will automatically change values, something that can be done much more rapidly (as President Eisenhower proved in Little Rock). The first approach will take a generation or more to yield results, whereas the second approach could potentially be effective within a matter of a few years. Therefore, the latter approach might be preferred, all other things being equal (such as the amount of evidence available for each).

The Concept of Holistic Knowledge

In Chapter 4 a holistic view of human behavior was introduced. Let us now look at this concept in more detail. Human behavior is need meeting, in the sense that people act in ways that will enable them to attain their goals. Defining goals is, of course, a very individual activity. As professional helpers, we sometimes disagree with the goals people set for themselves. A person who decides to smoke regardless of the health risk, the person who elects to commit a crime to obtain money, and the person who chooses to deal with his or her personal despair by committing suicide are all making choices that helping professionals would consider destructive.

Most people, of course, engage in less dramatic and more life-affirming kinds of activities. They go to school to prepare themselves for a career. They get married to have a meaningful long-term relationship. They exercise and watch their diet to stay healthy. And they exchange favors so that everyone can get along. As they go about trying to meet their needs, people encounter **resources** and **obstacles.** Resources can be understood as whatever helps people function, meet their needs, or solve problems (Siporin, 1975). Obstacles, on the other hand, make it more difficult for people to function, meet their needs, or solve problems.

Resources and obstacles are encountered in many places and in many ways. Betty Baer (1981) has developed a view of resources built around what she calls "resource systems." These are the following:

The Society at Large

The way a society uses and distributes its resources through its social institutions affects what is available to people in that society (Pierce, 1984). Societal decision making can provide resources (free public education, for example) or create obstacles (economic insecurity, which decreases the likelihood that people will be able to go to school). Naturally, resources and obstacles are different for different groups, a point to which we will return later in the chapter. For now, we can note that the same societal decision can be a resource for some groups and an obstacle for others.

The Social Welfare Institution

We have already looked at how the social welfare institution provides resources and creates obstacles. For example, Medicare provides important and much-needed resources to help the elderly obtain medical care. However, the deductibles in Medicare and the limitations on how long services can be received create obstacles for those with long-term health-care needs and limited finances.

The Local Community

Communities may be geographical (where we live) or social (cultural, ethnic, and social groups to which we belong). Geographic communities provide housing, employment, and personal and social services. Social communities provide networks of relationships that support us as people. The family, and contemporary family-like units, are especially important social groups. Communities may also provide obstacles, of course. High crime rates can make people afraid to go out or talk with others. Families can withhold resources or even physically harm their own members (Reinhart, 1981).

The Helping Professions

Helping professions have professional associations that function to improve the delivery of social welfare services by influencing legislation, agencies, and professional helpers. They develop and enforce the profession's code of ethics and standards for professional education. They are important support systems for professional helpers, and they provide an organized voice for the profession and for users of its services in societal policy making. Professional associations, however, can also create greater distance between professional helpers and those they serve—for example, if they support legislation reducing opportunities for users to get needed services. The American Medical Association's opposition to national health insurance has had this effect.

The Helping Person

The helping person is a critical link between decisions made in the society at large, the way these decisions are carried out in the social welfare institution, and the actual delivery of services to specific people. The characteristics of helping people discussed in the last chapter are resources available to users of services. When these characteristics are lacking, the ability of the person seeking to provide help will be greatly reduced. The result may be that the user encounters an obstacle instead of a resource.

The Social Welfare Agency

Social welfare agencies are organizational structures that bring together helping persons, professional and non-professional, in order to provide specific services to identified users. Agencies do such useful things as hire staff, distribute benefits to users of services, and generate community support for social welfare. Like any bureaucratic structure, agencies become obstacles when their concern with organizational procedures disrupts their ability to relate to the users of their services, a point discussed in Chapter 3.

Colleagues in the Helping Effort

We have already seen that professional helpers are resources. However, additional resources are generated when professionals work together to help each other by providing advice and emotional support (Davies, 1981). This is called **teamwork.** We have also seen that formal and informal helping structures work together, so professionals and nonprofessionals are also colleagues. When helping people do not work together, they are likely to be far less effective, and even become obstacles to those they serve by being unaware of services, lacking channels for linking people with needed services and suffering from burnout.

Users of Services

The attributes of users also represent resources and obstacles. Their ability to think, act, relate to each other, ask for help, and care for each other are all important resources. We have already seen that people can also create problems for themselves when they make decisions that are self-destructive, that isolate them from others, and that impede their ability to think and communicate clearly.

Integrating Perspectives

As we have just seen, the resources and obstacles that influence people's need-meeting behavior range from the biological and physiological through the psychological, social, and cultural to the organizational, environmental, and societal. It is important to appreciate the *range* of knowledge that is needed to understand all of these influences. In the next section, we will look at some of the discipline-based concepts that enable us to understand each of them. Now, though, we will address the question of why we need to appreciate the *interaction* and range of these influences.

The **holistic** concept has two significant parts: (1) There are many pieces of which the whole is made. (2) These pieces somehow fit together into a whole, rather than remaining fragments. In terms of human behavior, this means that the various influences noted above— the biological, physiological, psychological, social, cultural, organizational, environmental, and societal—are the pieces making up the whole of human behavior. Each of these pieces is composed of characteristics that themselves cover a wide spectrum. For example, the biological component of human behavior varies greatly. Some people are tall, others short. Some are healthy, others sick. Some are highly intelligent, others less so. Some are disabled, others are not. So, too, for all of the other components—there is much variation within each. For this reason, the concept of **human diversity** is extremely important for understanding the complexity of each component. But the components also have to fit together. The concept of systems enables us to better understand how this happens. In this section, then, we will focus on human diversity and systems as we continue in our effort to acquire a holistic understanding of human need-meeting behavior.

Human Diversity

Human diversity refers to the continuum of differences between people and groups resulting from biological, psychological, cultural, and social factors. Diversity is a major characteristic of any society, but especially of industrialized societies. Any holistic understanding of human and social behavior must be grounded in an awareness and acceptance of how people's diversity affects their behavior. People do, of course, also share many similarities, classically formulated in Towle's "common human needs," Maslow's "hierarchy of developmental needs," and Erickson's theory of "developmental tasks" (Anderson, 1981; Towle, 1952). However, these needs get expressed many different ways because of biological, psychological, cultural, and social diversity. For example, we all have a biological need for food, but it gets satisfied in many different ways. A hospitalized person may have to be fed a glucose solution intravenously. An infant has to suck through a nipple or eat specially processed baby food. Some infants are breast fed, whereas others are fed with a bottle; some get whole milk, whereas others require a milk substitute for proper digestion.

And some adults eat steak and potatoes although others much prefer rice and raw fish, or fried bananas and crocodile meat. Some adults are too poor to eat anything other than bread, gathered-up nuts and shrubs, or whatever can be scavenged in garbage pails. Societies, then, provide a context in which common needs are interpreted within existing value systems and social structures, with the result that people are differentially able to get resources to meet their needs.

Although each person is a unique combination of genetic and environmental characteristics and experiences, people are grouped according to particular characteristics that they share with others. For example, infants are generally defined by their age rather than by their race, ethnicity, hair color, or the wealth of their parents. Adults, on the other hand, are more often grouped according to their ethnicity or wealth. Because each person has many characteristics, people can be grouped in any number of ways. People vary by size, sex, race, ethnicity, intelligence, birth order, the hobbies they enjoy, the types of significant relationships they prefer, wealth, and many other characteristics. Some of these are biologically determined and are called *ascribed*. Sex and race are examples. Others are culturally and socially created, and are more likely to be *achieved*, meaning they are more open to choice and change. Hobbies, occupation, and wealth are examples. Still others, such as ethnicity, are partly ascribed and partly achieved.

As life goals and situations change, some characteristics and group memberships may also change. We all age, changing from children to adults. We may progress from being a high school dropout to holder of a doctorate. And, as a result of a car accident, we may change from able bodied to disabled. As these changes occur, the way we are categorized by society also changes. Each society has its own way of emphasizing categories. In our society, and even more strongly in South Africa, race is a very significant category (*The New York Times,* 1982). Other societies are more interested in family background, wealth, or religion. How people are categorized is likely to have a powerful effect on their experiences and treatment in society, as the tragic example of the Jews in Nazi Germany attests.

As much variation occurs *within* a group as *between* groups, except for the characteristic being used to define the group, and factors related directly to it. Women include those who are rich and poor, lesbian and heterosexual, physically handicapped and not handicapped, those who want to be mothers and those who do not, and those who are of different races and ethnicity. Groups may also change over time.

Understanding how different racial and cultural groups can live together harmoniously and in an environment of equality continues to be a goal for our society. This audience of people from diverse racial and ethnic backgrounds is watching a jazz concert in Boston. (Martha Stewart/The Picture Cube)

The level of income and education of blacks in our society has increased steadily, in spite of continuing prejudice and discrimination (Herbers, 1982).

Groups have roles assigned to their members by society. These roles are frequently based on stereotypes about biological or cultural characteristics—for example, the elderly are forgetful and cannot be trusted with important tasks, or Hispanics cannot speak English and are only suited to farm labor or factory work. These roles can become significant barriers to members of diverse groups, because they affect the kind of training and opportunities people receive. The result may be the perpetuation of stereotypes that in turn further deny members of diverse groups opportunities to act differently. This point is well illustrated in Exhibit 5–1 in the "Reflections on Social Welfare" section at the end of the chapter.

Difference sometimes causes members of a group to be defined as **deviant,** or abnormal. Women who prefer to work rather than marry or have children are sometimes defined as deviant, and subjected to behavior that is harassing and degrading (Miller, 1982). Homosexuals have frequently been defined as abnormal in spite of the lack of scientific data to justify such a stigmatizing label (Plummer, 1975; Bell and Weinberg, 1978). Because working women and homosexuals are living differently from the **norm,** they may become stigmatized with labels that place them outside some of the acceptable bounds of social behavior. This process can make it difficult for stigmatized people to be perceived as anything other than deviant and unacceptable, in spite of their efforts to be productive and healthy. However, the interaction between groups and society is constantly shifting as groups themselves change and as societal values are modified.

In order to understand the behavior of people from diverse groups, a **dual perspective** is needed (Norton, 1978). One perspective is that held by those who belong to the group—their own perspective on what behavior is appropriate and "normal." The other is the perspective of outsiders who evaluate the behavior of members of diverse groups according to their own perceptions and standards. Understanding both views is necessary for understanding why behavior occurs, and why it evokes certain kinds of responses from others. All behavior should be evaluated within the context of a general societal concern with whether it is harmful to others. Even this determination, however, may vary according to the different perspectives of diverse groups.

Systems

In talking about child-care research, Kenneth Kenniston states (Clarke-Stewart, 1978:ix–x):

> First, no isolated type of behavior on the part of caregivers has any invariant effect on children: the consequences of any single kind of action depend on what *else* is happening between parents and children and on what they bring to their interaction . . . The earlier search for simple cause-and-effect relations (e.g., breast feeding produces optimistic children) has increasingly been abandoned for studies of the whole caregiver-child relationship in which each type of caregiver-child relationship is studied in the context of all other interaction patterns . . . The "ecology" of families is exceedingly complex. It includes everything from the quality of family housing to the job (or lack of job) of the parent; from the organization of the neighborhood to the parents' race; from the parents' sense of economic security (or insecurity) to their pride (or discomfort) in their heritage. These extrafamilial factors and forces affect children in two ways. In part, they directly determine the caregivers' behavior . . . And, in part,

they indirectly determine the meaning a child assigns to any given pattern of caregivers' behavior.

Kenniston's statement is an excellent illustration of the meaning and significance of systems for understanding human behavior. Biological and social behaviors occur in internally as well as externally linked systems. Attempts to understand a particular behavior must occur within the context of the systems of which that behavior is a part. We all know, for example, that our bodies are internal systems, so that the actions of our hearts affect the actions of our brains. We also know that what we eat, part of external systems related to food habits and availability of food, affects our hearts through such things as hypertension, cholesterol levels, and so forth. Our social behavior is similar. The reinforcement we receive in our peer group affects what we do, and the peer group is itself affected by societal values relating to age groups, sex-role relationships, leisure activities, and a host of other factors.

Human life, as we have seen, is organized into an interlocking network of structured relationships that begin with the individual and increase in size to the societal and even intersocietal levels. Each can be seen as a separate system. For example, systems of particular importance for social welfare professionals range from the individual to the family, the social welfare organization, and the community. Each of these systems in turn fits together into the whole we call society, also a system. In other words, systems exist and can be analyzed at many levels. We can analyze one system to better understand its functioning, as, for example, when we look at the human body as a biological system. However, when we adopt a holistic perspective, we are also concerned with how the individual systems fit together to form larger systems. A family is composed of individuals; a community of families; and a society of communities. At any given point in the helping process, we can focus on one system or a system comprised of many smaller systems. Whatever our view at a particular point in time, helping professionals must ultimately be concerned with the whole network of systems that influence human behavior.

This is an important point, so let's look at an extended example. In 1982, alarm began to spread about a newly identified disease called AIDS (acquired immune deficiency syndrome) (Marx, 1983). The disease incapacitates the body's immune system, leaving the victim subject to any sort of infection. It has also been especially related to a deadly type of pneumonia and a rare type of cancer. The disease was first found primarily in intravenous drug users, Haitian refugees, people who had had many blood transfusions (especially hemophiliacs), and homosexual men. Gradually, more populations with the disease were identified. The suspected cause is a virus transmitted through the blood or other body fluids, but the cause is not really known.

From a systems perspective, this illness can be understood at many levels. Biologically, the effect of the hypothesized virus can be traced to various organs and bodily functions. Organizationally, the response of specific hospitals to persons with the disease can be studied—an issue of considerable importance because many people with AIDS have been incorrectly diagnosed and treated. The impact on families or loved ones has been substantial, especially because the disease has been linked with stigmatized populations. For example, a man who gets it might be assumed to be either a homosexual or a drug user by family and friends. Whether true or false, these assumptions are going to influence the man's relationships with others. AIDS even affected the societal system. As it spread, the federal Centers for Disease Control became involved, and controversies arose over how research to identify and cure the disease should be funded. Here again, its link to stigmatized groups was significant. As our knowledge of human diversity would suggest, many people felt tax money should not be spent on a disease that primarily affected stigmatized populations. The AIDS epidemic, then, illustrates how all levels of systems have to be understood individually and in interaction to fully understand behavior.

Regardless of the size, a system is defined by four characteristics: boundaries, purpose, exchange, and networks. We will examine each of these characteristics separately, and then use them to illustrate the characteristics and behavior of individual, family, social welfare agency, and community systems. There are many other levels and types of systems. These particular systems have been selected for illustrative purposes because they are so central to the social welfare institution.

BOUNDARIES.   A system is an organized collection of activities and resources that exists within definable social and physical boundaries. For example, the human individual has internal processes that occur within the physically defined entity called the body. Similarly, a community has both physical (geographical) and social (who interacts with whom) boundaries. Boundaries are also important for defining membership, so that it is clear where one system ends and another begins.

PURPOSES.   Systems have procedures that enable them to accomplish their objectives. One purpose is almost always survival, and the concept of *homeostasis* is used to refer to the balance between system components that give it stability. The human body has a state of "health," for example, at which point the body components are stabilized, so that the person is maximally functional. Systems usually have purposes in addition to survival—to become self-actualized for an individual or to deliver helping services for a social welfare agency. These purposes serve to focus the interactions and use of resources within a system, as well as regulating relations between systems.

EXCHANGES.   Although systems have boundaries, they are usually permeable rather than closed. Systems need resources in order to function, and their functioning produces results of some sort (usually relevant to their purposes). Resources may come from within the system, but they often come from outside—these are called *inputs*. For example, people need to ingest food, families need shelter, and social agencies need a societal mandate. Systems *process* inputs in order to produce results of some sort—*output*. Communities, for instance, obtain input (money, food, people, and so forth) that is used to create a living environment for their members (output).

NETWORKS.   The exchanges that systems have occur with other systems, leading to networks of system relationships. This, of course, is why social welfare professionals have to understand human behavior systemically (that is, as part of one or more systems). The lack of availability of inputs from other systems can disrupt a system's homeostasis and lead to altered relationships with other systems. Children whose psychological and social needs are not met (part of the body system) by their family may develop disruptive behaviors (output) as a result. This will in turn alter the input and output of the family system. It is evident, then, that the output of one system has an *impact* on other systems. As each system experiences input-output-impact, it becomes enmeshed in networks of interdependence that relate to the input-output-impact of other systems. Professional helping efforts must reflect these networks so that appropriate and effective points of intervention can be selected.

The preceding material is a very simple systems analysis, but one which has direct applicability to the social welfare institution. Table 5–1

TABLE 5–1   An Illustration of the Systems Approach

	Boundaries	Purposes	Exchanges	Networks
Individuals	The body	Survival Self-actualization Gratification	Input (food, air, nurturance) Output (energy, action) Process (breathing)	Impact (family members, peers, employers) These in turn affect inputs (money for food) and purposes (survival)
Families	Legally defined Kin (blood relatedness) Religiously defined	Preservation of family resources and traditions Socialization Economic	Input (money, societal mandate) Output (nurturance, socialization, work) Process (interactions of family members)	Impact (family members, school, workplace) These in turn affect inputs (decisions about a societal policy for families) and purposes (ability to socialize members)
Social Welfare Agencies	Legally defined	Provision of social welfare services Management of resources	Input (societal mandate, resources) Output (services) Process (employment practices)	Impact (social policy, public opinion) These in turn affect inputs (public support for social welfare) and purposes (resources to use in providing services)
Communities	Legally defined Geographically defined Defined in terms of social identity of its members	Organize economic, spatial and social sub-units	Input (money, media, policy) Output (goods, services) Process (services, social structure)	Impact (families, social agencies) These in turn affect inputs (policy) and purposes (social order)

uses individuals, families, social welfare agencies, and communities to briefly illustrate the systems components discussed above.

An adequate understanding of the situations with which social welfare professionals work requires a systems perspective. Child abuse is closely linked to such group and social problems as feelings of inadequacy as a parent, social isolation, and anxiety that can result from an event such as the loss of employment. The functioning of social welfare agencies may be criticized by users who feel their needs are being met inadequately. At the same time, nonuser groups may feel that too many resources are being used by the agency. In order to survive and function effectively, agencies must be able to understand the social, political, and economic factors impinging on, and motivating the behavior of, both groups. The interaction of systems is complex, yet most problems are created and resolved systemically. Therefore, an understanding of systems must be an integral part of the social welfare professional's holistic view of human behavior. Exhibit 5–2 in the "Reflections on Social Welfare" section at the end of the chapter illustrates this point.

Human diversity and systems are perspectives on human behavior that assist helping professionals in integrating and making use of their biological, psychological, social, and cultural knowledge. Thus to adequately understand human diversity requires examining how the behavior being observed is affected by the interplay of biological, psychological, social, and cultural factors. A systems view examines these same factors as they influence the particular system of primary concern, and the way that system is enmeshed in networks with other systems. In the next section we will survey specific biological, psychological, social, and cultural concepts of particular use in the helping professions. It is important to remember that these concepts must be integrated through the human diversity and systems perspectives, in order to be useful in professional helping. Although particular professions may focus on knowledge in one or two of these areas—medicine emphasizes biological knowledge, for example—*any* profession must use *all* areas to adequately understand human behavior.

Basic Knowledge for Practice

Biological Knowledge

The ultimate limit on human behavior is biological. We can do only what our **genetic potential** makes possible. We will see later in the chapter, however, that environmental conditions are highly significant determinants of how close our actual behavior will be to our genetically established potential. Genetically, we *inherit* from both parents. They in turn carry genetic material from a gene pool going back countless generations (Underwood, 1979). We know that certain characteristics, like eye color and blood type, are directly inherited. It is less clear to what degree other characteristics, such as intelligence and susceptibility to diseases like cancer and schizophrenia, are inherited (Brody, 1982; Mazur and Robertson, 1972). Biotechnology and medical research are making extraordinary advances that are continually changing our knowledge of genetic makeup and the biological basis of human behavior. Nevertheless, we know that there is an important interplay of genetic, biological, and social factors in human behavior, although our knowledge of exactly which factors are involved keeps expanding. But without the biological capacity, behavior—and life itself—is impossible.

Two biological concepts underlie the whole purpose of social welfare—*health* and *growth*. They refer to a genetically based process of increasing complexity, functional capacity, and size. Both have also been applied to psychological and social behavior, but their most fundamental meaning is biological. The *healthy organism* is one in which all bodily systems are functioning properly and in harmony with each other. Health makes *growth* possible, enabling the various parts of the organism to reach their maximum genetically determined size and level of functioning. Health is a variable concept. Because the human organism is composed of many parts (organs, bones, cells, muscles, limbs, glands, and others), some may be healthy and others not. Some may be completely "unhealthy" (that is, unable to function, as occurs in complete paralysis of a nerve), whereas others may be only partially impaired (a bruised arm that hurts but is movable). And, of course, health can be a changing condition. A bruise heals and an infection disappears, but other unhealthy states are permanent or even degenerative—emphysema, for example, is both a chronic and progressive lung disease.

The human organism is characterized by tremendous adaptive capability (Monat and Lazarus, 1977). Unlike most other animals, relatively little human behavior is genetically programmed. We inherit genetic limits but few specific instructions for behavior. These have to be learned through social interaction; indeed, without it, humans cannot survive because the human infant is unable to care for itself for several years and must be nurtured by others. Because we have to *learn* how to behave, the human organism has flexibility built in. Our brains can learn any language, and can organize what we see into learned patterns of meaning. Our stomachs can adapt to many different kinds of food, including grasses, meat, nuts, and fish. Our skeletal structures are very flexible, enabling us to jump, swing, twist, stand, and squat. Because we have the capacity for language, we can create elaborate symbol systems that make language possible, including mathematics and the scientific technology built upon it.

The many ways in which the human organism can be flexible makes possible adaptation to almost any kind of environment and condition. Humans can survive in any climate, and in any geographical area. If they wish, they can coexist with any other forms of animal life and with each other. Alternatively, humans can choose to adapt through dominating and controlling their environment. This ability to control the environment can be used by humans against each other, leading to systems of dominance based on genetic capacity (size, strength, and gender, for example) or on access to resources (being wealthy or having education, for instance).

For all their adaptability, humans inherit a timetable of physical decline that ends in death. Their life span is genetically determined, although it may be influenced substantially by such circumstances as accidents, exposure to illness, and unhealthful living conditions. For example, people whose genetic life-span programming includes Alzheimer's disease, a progressive and fatal deterioration of the brain and loss of control over bodily processes, cannot avoid the inevitable path the disease takes. Still, the care such persons get during the illness can very much influence the impact that the disease has on their daily life and their relations with others (Roach, 1983). As brain deterioration occurs, Alzheimer's disease victims frequently don't know where they are. They are prone to wandering off, and can easily be injured. Being cared for can prevent a premature death from such injury.

When looking at the importance of biological knowledge for social welfare, several points are important:

1. The most basic needs that people seek to fulfill are biological: food, shelter, and nurturance are basic to physical survival and health.
2. Problems in physical functioning create needs. When people are sick, they need help, as they do when they are disabled or facing death.
3. There is a very close and important interaction between the physical and social needs of people. Physical functioning affects social life as, for example, when the pregnant teen is dismissed

from high school. Similarly, social functioning affects biological health, so that drunk drivers are frequently injured or killed in auto accidents.

Because we don't yet know all of the interactions and relationships between physical and social behavior, we need to know as much as possible about both. Chronic headaches can be caused by tension; they may also result from brain tumors. Lethargic behavior can indicate laziness and lack of motivation; it can also indicate mononucleosis, hepatitis, or glandular problems. A holistic view of human behavior demands that we understand how all the significant systems are influencing the behavior at issue. The human body as a system must not be overlooked in this process.

Psychological Knowledge

Psychological behavior is a significant bridge between the biological characteristics of people and their social and physical environments. This bridging function occurs in two important ways.

1. The ability that results from genetic capacities to perceive, experience, and organize stimuli from the environment. These genetic capacities include sight, hearing, feeling, tasting, and sensing through nerve endings throughout the body (when we get a stomach ache, or our knee hurts, and so on). These capacities are basic to our ability to place ourselves in our physical and social environment, and to understand these environments. However, the simple physical experiencing of a stimulus does not automatically lead to our understanding it. We can hear someone speak a language and perceive the sounds but not understand their social meaning if we do not know the language. Similarly, we can experience physical discomfort but not recognize it as a symptom of a particular illness that requires treatment.

Remembering the tremendous flexibility of the human organism, it is easy to understand that our ability to perceive and experience has to be organized into meaningful patterns in order to affect our behavior. The psychological processes of cognition and perception enable this to occur (Hilgard and Bower, 1975; Lidz, 1976). Through our ability to learn, we are taught patterns of perception that enable us to organize the stimuli that we see, hear, feel, and experience. In other words, we learn the particular view of the world and ourselves that our social environment considers important. This enables us to survive in that environment (and, as we will see later, tends to perpetuate the environment itself).

2. Psychological processes also mediate between the biological and environmental aspects of human behavior through the **personality.** Personality refers to the organized and generally consistent ways that particular people act (Tischler, Whitten, and Hunter, 1983). We all know people who tend to be very easygoing and flexible, and others who are generally more formal and less flexible. These are descriptions of personality characteristics, and they enable us to know how to act around different kinds of people. Personality results from the interaction of a person's biological capacity and the demands of the environment (Langer, 1969). In other words, people use their perceptual and cognitive abilities to respond to stimuli from the social and physical environments. People who see well may find the physical world a beautiful and very understandable place. Those who see poorly may experience it as murky and somewhat threatening. People who learn quickly may experience school as stimulating and rewarding, whereas those who learn less quickly may feel frustrated and unrewarded.

At the same time that people are grappling with their environments, they must also cope with demands being placed upon them. Not being able to see a car may result in being hit. Not being able to learn material in school quickly enough may result in failure. Having a disability that makes it impossible to communicate may lead to unemployment and economic poverty. Speaking only a foreign language, or speaking with an accent, may result in ridicule and social isolation. In other words, through efforts to perceive and learn, people are both learning and trying to meet societal expectations. When, because of perceptual and cognitive abilities, they have difficulty meeting societal expectations, part of their learning may be that they are inadequate. This then becomes part of their personality and begins to influence their behavior (White, 1982). When people are able to manage social expectations readily, their personality will probably develop differently and their actions are likely to be far more positive.

Understanding psychological functioning is fundamental to analyzing why people act as they do. Everyone has a particular view of themselves and the world around them, and their behavior reflects that view. Again, behavior is oriented toward meeting needs. People's views of themselves and their environments strongly affect their perceived needs and appropriate ways of meeting them. People who feel weak and helpless are likely to develop personalities that are passive. Those who feel strong and competent are more likely to be active and willing to grapple more assertively with problems. Personalities develop and change throughout the life cycle, although infancy and childhood are periods of especially rapid development. Therefore, an ongoing social welfare goal is to help people better manage the interaction between their own abilities and society's demands. The holistic perspective demands that efforts to do so should consider that the personality is a powerful mediator between the person and the environment. Such a perspective must also maintain a balance between the effects of the biological organism and the environment in understanding how the personality functions. Having considered the biological aspect of the organism, and about psychological processes that mediate between it and the environment, let us now turn to the interaction between the human organism and the society and culture in which it lives.

Social and Cultural Knowledge

We saw earlier that it is impossible to talk about either the biological organism or people's psychological functioning without reference to the social and cultural environment. People do not exist in isolation. From birth they are surrounded by other people—they have to be, or they would not survive. These people teach the new human organism how to survive—what to eat, what not to touch, how to speak, how to act, and so forth. This is necessary because, as we saw earlier, the human being is a remarkably flexible animal, one whose genetic *potential* is enormous, but whose genetic *programming* is rather limited.

The process of learning how to survive and flourish in a particular social and cultural environment is called **socialization** (Federico and Schwartz, 1983). The society into which one is born has particular ways of thinking and acting, called its culture. This is preserved from generation to generation and, although change is a part of every culture, people are expected to act as specified by their culture. Those who do not are likely to be punished through *negative* **sanctions,** while those who act as expected will be rewarded with *positive* ones. We have all experienced this: good grades in school earn praise and gold stars, whereas bad grades result in warnings, scoldings, and being kept in after school. Other sanctions are considerably more intensive: going to jail or being fired from a job (negative sanctions), or getting promoted or being honored with a ticker-tape parade down New York City's Broadway (positive sanctions).

Most societies, especially complex industrial societies like our own, have many subgroups within them. People learn general cultural rules but they also learn the rules of the specific subgroups to which they belong (often called subcultures). For example, a Hispanic person

Ethnic festivals bring people together to reaffirm and share important cultural traditions. This Native American powwow took place in Gallup, New Mexico, in 1980. (Roswell Angier/Archive Pictures, Inc.)

learns certain ways of relating to family members that are somewhat different from, although not necessarily in opposition to, the patterns prevailing in the dominant Anglo culture (Montiel, 1978). Conflict can occur between subgroups when they relate to each other ethnocentrically—that is, when each group thinks of its own way of doing things as superior to those of other groups. In such situations, prejudice (negative attitudes with little basis in fact) and discrimination (hurtful behaviors based on prejudice) are likely to occur (Davis, 1978).

Conflict between groups becomes especially significant when there are significant power differentials between them. When one group has control over resources through the political and economic structures, it is possible for these dominant groups to oppress others, denying them access to resources and limiting their life opportunities as a result. The tragic results of such oppression have been evident in black-white relations in our own society, most recently in the racial unrest in Miami (United States Commission on Civil Rights, 1982). Unfortunately, the problem is worldwide, as recent events in Lebanon, Northern Ireland, Viet Nam, and India have shown. Although oppression is a significant cause of the need for social welfare help, social welfare programs themselves are subject to distortion by the effects of prejudice and discrimination (United States Commission on Civil Rights, 1982a).

Obviously, then, the groups to which people belong influence their behavior. Groups affect what people learn as appropriate behavior, and they have an impact on the way people are treated by others. Members of minority groups may be born with a rich and varied genetic potential, but through oppression may be denied the economic, educational, and social opportunities to develop it. This has been especially true of groups in our society that have been discriminated against because of their race, ethnicity, sex, physical disability, age, or sexual orientation. When people are chronically denied opportunities, their personalities are generally affected: some become hostile and aggressive, others passive and escapist. Furthermore, efforts of social welfare professionals to intervene can become very complicated. As noted earlier, it is necessary to understand the social and cultural environment of the people with which one is working. Because prejudice and discrimination are built into the institutional structure of the society, social change may be a necessary condition for the solution of problems experienced by members of disadvantaged groups.

Because human behavior results from the interaction of biological, psychological, and social/cultural factors, generalizations are always risky. A holistic view of behavior must start with the biological potential of particular people, the realities of the environments they face, and an understanding of how those environments have affected their psychological development. Behavior that may seem illogical on its surface may be much more logical when understood in context, even though the professional helper may still feel that it will be harmful in the long run. Perceiving that people can plan logically shows they have strength, even though they may need help in redirecting their actions in more productive directions. Also, seeing how people can survive very restrictive and oppressive environments increases the helper's appreciation of their adaptive capacity. Finally, understanding how the environment can limit and hurt people should increase the resolve of professional helpers to participate in social-action efforts to create more humane and supportive environments.

Putting It All Together: The Life Cycle

This chapter has attempted to review the major knowledge areas of particular relevance to an understanding of social welfare. It has sought a unified presentation organized around individual development, culture, and the social structure, drawing upon knowledge from the various biological, social, and behavioral sciences as appropriate. To conclude the chapter, the life cycle will be used to illustrate how the knowledge reviewed in the rest of the chapter is pertinent to a systemic, human-diversity, and problem-solving view of human behavior.

The life cycle extends from conception to death and is a mechanism for defining levels of human development according to chronological age. In American society, commonly used life-cycle periods include conception, birth, infancy (0–4 years), childhood (5–11), adolescence (12–15), young adulthood (16–20), adulthood (21–59), retirement and old age (60 to death), and death. Often there are socially structured quasipublic events (sometimes called rites of passage) that signify that an individual has moved from one point in the life cycle to another. For example, entry into school is clear recognition of childhood, and graduation from the primary grades and entry into junior high school is one marker of the transition into adolescence. Marriage is a significant social event acknowledging that the individual is assuming the responsibilities of adulthood, and retirement signifies the passage into old age. Having such social events to mark passage through the life cycle can help people recognize their developing social position. They also help others recognize these changes, enabling them to help in dealing with new situations and responsibilities. Each society has its own ways of defining important stages of the life cycle and its distinctive ways of recognizing their occurrence.

At each point in the life cycle, certain biological, cultural, and social forces come together. We have already seen that society seeks to have the functions performed that have been defined as necessary and desirable for its survival. On the other hand, people are learning how to make use of their genetically transmitted potential through interacting with the environment. The environment is itself culturally defined and operationalized through the social structure (roles, norms, positions, social institutions, and so on). Each of these—genetic inheritance, cultural context, and social structure—provide both resources and obstacles for the individual in the attainment of the societally defined tasks to be accomplished at each life-cycle period. The individual faces a potential crisis when seeking to carry out the appropriate life-cycle tasks—if successful (for example, if the resources are adequate) growth occurs and social dislocations are avoided, but if unsuccessful, growth may be slowed and problems may be experienced in a range of social situations. Because the periods in the life cycle are predictable, the potential crises or periods when the individual is at risk in particu-

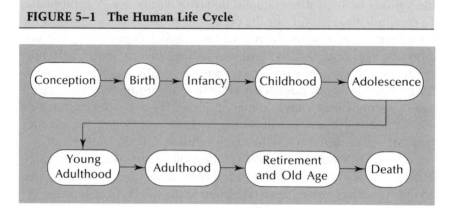

FIGURE 5–1   The Human Life Cycle

lar ways are also predictable. Hence, social welfare services are often structured around the life cycle.

Some examples may help to make this clearer. A diagram of the overall life cycle is shown in Figure 5–1. Each of these life-cycle periods can in turn be pictured as shown in Figure 5–2, which uses adulthood as an example. The sequence of stages shown in Figure 5–1 is self-explanatory. Working through the example in Figure 5–2, the societally defined tasks for adults generally relate to becoming economically self-sufficient, establishing intimate relations with others, living autonomously and in a way that is relatively stable and personally satisfying, having some conceptions of life goals, and using oneself in ways that are productive and consistent with social norms. Common social rituals that provide recognition of having achieved adulthood are graduation from college, marriage, or getting one's own apartment. The genetic and psychological resources for the average adult would include full musculature, fully developed speech and writing ability, mastery of complex cognitive processes, and control over physical functioning and appearance. Cultural resources might include values supporting personal self-reliance, beliefs about desirable jobs and life-styles, and concrete skills such as reading, writing, cooking, and driving. Social-structural resources include the rituals marking passage into adulthood, because they clarify role expectations for the new adult and those who interact with the adult. Social-structural resources could

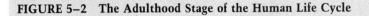

FIGURE 5–2   The Adulthood Stage of the Human Life Cycle

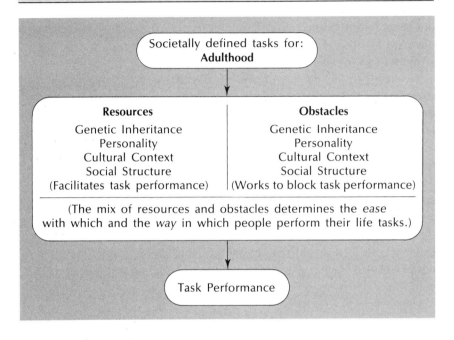

also include family help in finding an apartment, workshops to improve job performance, health-insurance payments in case of illness, and receiving a regular salary. All of these resources would be useful for individuals striving to achieve life-cycle tasks specified for adults in the United States.

Genetic obstacles to adult task performance might be physical handicaps, learning disabilities, or organically caused mental illness. Note that although obstacles may impede task performance, they do not necessarily make such performance impossible, as demonstrated by the many perfectly competent handicapped adults. Psychological obstacles might include the rigid use of inappropriate defense mechanisms or chronic misperception resulting from high levels of anxiety. Cultural obstacles might be values that give interpersonal relations dominance over task performance or beliefs about sexuality and procreation that emphasize supernatural forces rather than biological processes. Social-structural obstacles can include family socialization if, for example, the male role is learned as incorporating spouse or child abuse, or if a homosexual never learns how to constructively manage his or her sexuality. Other obstacles encompass widespread unemployment, a shortage of suitable housing, and lack of adequate day-care facilities for children. All of these factors impede the adult's attempts to function in socially expected ways.

Viewing the life cycle in terms of societal needs and cultural and social-structural obstacles provides an integrated view of experiences, drawing upon a variety of social-, behavioral-, and biological-science knowledge relating to psychological development, biological function-ing, and the social context. It is also consistent with an analytical framework built around systems, human diversity, and problem solv-ing. If all of the periods of the life cycle were to be analyzed using this approach, the web of social relationships would become apparent, as would their effect on each individual, information that would have direct practice relevance. Individual development, the cultural envi-ronment, and the social-structural context are concepts that should be equally useful for integrating specific knowledge in other areas of hu-man life.

SUMMARY

This chapter has focused on the importance of knowledge for profes-sional social welfare helping efforts. Having already looked at the help-ing process in the previous chapter, this one has attempted to show how biological-, social-, and behavioral-science knowledge is the foun-dation for this process. The emphasis has been on holistic knowledge so that the totality of the human functioning can be defined and under-stood. This includes the use of biological, psychological, and social and cultural knowledge to understand the many systems and types of human diversity that influence specific situations in which help is needed. The basic point cannot be emphasized too strongly: no matter how sincere the desire to help, professional helping must be built on a knowledge base that includes biological, psychological, social, and cultural knowledge, which makes possible a holistic understanding of human behavior.

REFLECTIONS ON SOCIAL WELFARE

The following two exhibits provide in-depth examples of how knowledge undergirds the ability of social welfare professionals to understand social welfare in a holistic way.

EXHIBIT 5–1 Agism and Imposed Disability

Our society has often been characterized as a youth-oriented one, in which the elderly are ignored and arbitrarily forced out of productive social roles. This behavior is imposed simply on the basis of age. It frequently has little relationship to the actual abilities of the people involved. The following excerpts illustrate this point, although points are made to show that our present misuse of the elderly need not continue.

The Gray Panthers are a national coalition of old, young and middle-aged activists and advocates working to expose agism's destructive web and to challenge all forms of age discrimination in our society. Agism does not just apply to the elderly. Agism is to see a person's problems as naturalistic and inherent to a chronological age, rather than the consequence of societal arrangements. All too often an individual buys such a belief and constructs a self-fulfilling prophecy of inadequacy.

The issue of agism provides Gray Panthers with the focus of commitment and action. There are four basic dimensions to agism: stereotyping, segregation, paternalism and victim-blaming.

Agism, like racism and sexism, is a method of stereotyping the behavior of certain groups. Society stereotypes the old as "out of date," too slow, sickly, sexless or senile, unchanging, unemployable, etc. Society stereotypes the young as immature, irresponsible, unstable, inexperienced, over-sexed, impatient, etc. These stereotypes provide ready excuses for society not to recognize the individual characteristics, contributions, and needs of the old and young.

Our laws and social structures reflect agism by segregating people from each other in efficient, chronological age categories from nursery school to nursing homes.

Paternalism emerges as a response to the segregation of stereotyped older and younger people. All too often the caretaker is an institution such as a school, retirement community, nursing home or boarding home.

Source: Excerpted from Margaret E. Kuhn, "Gray Panther thoughts on agism, health care and work-life," *The Journal of the Institute for Socioeconomic Studies,* Autumn 1977, pp. 33–42.

Lastly, agism includes victim-blaming, where society's flaws become a social problem as society attempts to absolve itself from the responsibility. Services attempting to blunt pains of the aged seldom empower the victim, but instead reinforce powerlessness.

The Gray Panthers began in 1970 when six of us, friends forced to retire from national religious and social service organizations, decided to pool our efforts and help each other to use our new freedom responsibly. Our initial personal reactions to compulsory retirement were anger, shock, and loss . . . loss of friends, status, income, and purpose in living. We have seen the lives of once vigorous colleagues trivialized and wasted in retirement periods. The course of action we determined for ourselves was to use our knowledge and experience, our network of relationships, and our free time to work for broad-based social change.

Now, for the first time in United States history, the old will soon outnumber the young. Only a radical restucturing of society can solve in a civilized way the enormous problems created by this situation. The 24 million Americans 65 years old and older now comprise about 11 percent of the population. By the year 2010, or even sooner according to present trends, the percentage of older people may double. We see aging as a universalizing force in America—we are all aging. Society's response to these demographic shifts will profoundly affect people of all ages and human conditions. Although many older people need services, we work as advocates to understand and change the societal conditions that have made such services necessary—services which mostly serve to maintain and legitimize existing social structures. What some have described as "the plight of the elderly" will not appreciably improve without basic change in society. What follows are two examples of Gray Panther advocacy which we hope will be instructive to designers of social policy.

Health Care

The health care system gives priority to provider profits rather than user need. Gray Panthers, convinced of the dangers of the medicalization of health, have taken on the formidable task of confronting the medical industry. We have monitored and challenged it on these counts: the concentration of economic power and technology in the medical empires built by the billions of dollars from citizens' taxes and insurance premiums; and the interlocking of interests—the American Medical Association (AMA) with the manufacturers of drugs and hospital equipment, insurance carriers and medical centers with their hospitals, clinics, research laboratories and medical schools. There are artificial shortages of physicians created by the AMA limits on medical school certification and student admissions. We challenge their preoccupation with "sickness" care which treats diseases and grossly neglects prevention and maintenance measures for basic health and well-being. Americans of all ages are the victims of over-specialized services that fragment care and prevent holistic attention to the mental/physical/environmental factors. The neglect of the chronically ill and the disregard of the natural infirmities that come with the fragility of old age enrage us. Our crisis-oriented medical system excludes the old because many physicians do not wish to "waste their time on someone who's going to die anyway." Furthermore, they do not wish to deal with the bureaucratic procedures for Medicare and Medicaid reimbursement. Moreover, our unemployed and underemployed youth simply cannot afford the high cost of insurance premiums. This initial deprivation of health care may be the basis for poor health in old age.

Medical schools teach only the disease treatment model. That eliminates the most basic elements of health care, including nutrition, health education, personal responsibility for one's own health maintenance and awareness of pollutants. Furthermore, the disease treatment model does not provide effective care for the chronic, long-term illness of older people. Gray Panthers have reviewed the curriculum of medical schools and have petitioned at the annual convention of the AMA and the state medical societies to mandate courses in geriatric medicine and gerontology in medical schools. Only a limited portion of courses in family medicine and community health prepare medical students for work with older people. For example, with the omission of geriatric medicine in medical schools, young doctors are poorly equipped to diagnose many physiological conditions which can lead to irreversible mental impairment. Nearly 50 percent of the patients now in nursing homes due to mental impairment need not be there! Furthermore, we have asked the AMA to resume that tradition of house calls and family practice, to include consumer representatives on the various medical society governing boards, and to work with concerned citizens to reform nursing homes. Most of our petitions to the AMA are still disregarded. . . .

Worklife and Mandatory Retirement

The Gray Panthers have chosen the elimination of mandatory retirement as a primary objective because it is a positive step toward the amelioration of the elderly's diminished and degraded status. We have studied the effects of mandatory retirement on the mental and physical health of retired persons. As a result, we have testified at Congressional committee and state legislature hearings, appeared on television, addressed many public gatherings, and joined in class action court suits.

Mandatory retirement is a classic example of agism. It results in and perpetuates negative stereotyping that views old people as unproductive and only capable of rest and play. It creates artificial barriers between age groups and violates the workers' right to choose and to exercise control over their worklife. It forces many to live on reduced and fixed income. This exclusionary policy which arbitrarily views retired people as inadequate and incompetent makes them subject to paternalistic social programs. Economic deprivation and self-devaluation could be less of a problem if society permitted each person the choice either to retire or to continue to work. Hopefully, a change in retirement will impress a sense of empowerment upon the aging worker. If older people can choose to remain as workers in the mainstream of society, then they might more fully realize their ability to control their own lives and influence the direction of society.

The Gray Panthers have never been a "senior power" organization because the most important societal problems have implications that affect many sectors of the population, including the old. Furthermore, we realize that even after abolition of mandatory retirement, a new set of work-related problems may plague the elderly. It may well be that the end of mandatory retirement alone cannot stop stereotyping, segregation, rejection and the elderly's own self-degradation. Yes, elimination of mandatory retirement is important; however, it is just a first step toward a comprehensive reorientation, redirection and reformation of the Social Security system and income transfers . . . If we are to confront the problems of the aged and younger members of society, then we must think of solutions that are systematic and unified in nature.

All too often people confine and relate their thinking on mandatory retirement to the last stage of life. The earlier periods of life set the stage for the difficulties that confront the aged. The combined material of life experiences weaves a composite of personal development and difficulties. Hence, our problem-solving must first ask questions about how societal structure interacts with experiences of personal development. Gray Panthers advocate policies which encourage integrated life cycle experiences, rather than a set of separate, cage-like periods. People of all ages should experience education, work and leisure, rather than the age-segregated stages of school, labor, and retirement. . . .

Rather than seeing the end of mandatory retirement as the solution, we should consider a broad range of options that would make the structure of education, work, and leisure more flexible. A variety of options might include sabbatical leaves, part-time or shared work, and the facilitating of mid-career changes. Retirement could be optional and flexible. We could encourage those who desire to use some of their Social Security benefits before the age of 65 to take a sabbatical leave in search of education, training, and reevaluation of life directions possibly toward new careers. In the long run, we anticipate that workers of various ages will feel empowered by the choice to improve their work style. What will emerge is a new job fluidity and a new consideration of leisure time. They will see the possibility of exercising further control over the administration, organization and structure of the workplace.

EXHIBIT 5–2   The Family Web

The family, as one of the most important social institutions of our society, is a good barometer of societal changes. The systems nature of any society, including our own, is well illustrated in the following comments by Urie Bronfenbrenner, in which he talks about the impact on the American family of several changes in the society external to the family but very much related to its functioning.

Source: "Other things on nation's mind put home in downward spiral," *Greensboro* (North Carolina) *Daily News*, September 4, 1977, Section G, p. 1. © 1977 by The Associated Press. Reprinted by permission.

The family, many experts lament, is dying. And no one cares, says Urie Bronfenbrenner of Cornell University, an expert in child development.

"Family is the primary institution we have," he said in a recent interview. "It certainly is the most effective and most economic system we have for making human beings more human."

"Family is important for nurturing not only the next generation, but everybody. They care for physical and emotional well-being, especially when an individual is young, old, sick, tired, or lonely."

"The number of families doing a good job is decreasing," he said. "What's caused it? An indifference. It's not deliberate, but we've had other things on our minds."

External situations, such as the economy, the increasing population, competition for jobs and a dwindling housing stock, have affected family life as much as changing attitudes and lifestyles.

"There are four principal areas of stress in today's society," Bronfenbrenner said. "They are money, conditions of work, television and the neighborhood."

Single-parent families and blue-collar workers are most affected by money, he said. In those households, employment can cause great tension. Employment also generates stress, particularly in households where both parents work.

"We have finally broken through our stupidities and are admitting that a larger proportion of society is entering the work world, but we've kept the old male work rules—9–5," he said. "We haven't come to terms with the fact that you can't be in two places at once."

Population reports show single parenthood has increased most rapidly among families with children under six, climbing from about 7 percent to 17 percent between 1948 and 1975. The majority of these single parents are in the work force, and most are women.

Bronfenbrenner believes the overwhelming change in family life over the last 30 years is the emergence of the working mother. Government statistics show 37 percent of all married women with children under six were in the labor force in 1975, three times the number in 1948.

And with inadequate and sometimes costly day-care facilities and babysitting services, many youngsters go unattended, Bronfenbrenner said. He calls these young people—with only the television and each other for companionship and guidance—"latch key children." They return from school to empty homes.

"Single parents also use television as a babysitter," he said. "But everyone's upset with what the children see on television and what TV does to them. The bottom line is that no one is home but the TV. Someone has to be home and active."

The fourth stressful area in family—the neighborhood—has fallen apart, he said. "The thing about having young kids is that you need help. And it's not the help you can get by telephone or across the town from a friend or relative," Bronfenbrenner said. "It's a neighborhood, because many of the support systems you need for parenthood have to be close by.". . .

STUDY QUESTIONS

1. Select a life-cycle stage other than the illustration used in the text. Follow the model used in the text, identifying first the major societal tasks for that stage, and then the genetic, psychological, cultural, and social resources and obstacles available in carrying out those tasks.

2. Assume that you are a social worker, and that one of your cases involves a 76-year-old woman whose husband has just died. She is concerned about the adequacy of her income and whether she will be able to keep her six-room home and care for herself. How might you assess her situation, drawing upon biological, psychological, social, and cultural knowledge? What kinds of professional colleagues would you want to involve in this case?

3. Think about the systems in which you are involved. How many can you identify? Try charting them, showing how they relate to each other. Which do you think are especially important? Why? Now compare your chart with that of another student. How might you explain the similarities and differences you see?

4. Undertake next a similar analysis of the kinds of human diversity you represent. What is your sex, ethnicity, race, age, socioeconomic standing, and sexual orientation? How do these characteristics affect your behavior? Which do you think are of particular importance to other people, and thus to the way others treat you? If you could, would you prefer to change any of them? Which ones and why? Even though you might prefer the change, is there anything you would especially miss if you did make any changes?

5. After thinking about the approach to the knowledge base of social welfare taken in this chapter, in what areas do you feel your knowledge is most inadequate? How important do you think these knowledge gaps are for your future development as a professional helping person? What possibilities do you see that could help you to fill in these gaps?

SELECTED READINGS

Berger, Robert, and Ronald Federico (1982). *Human Behavior: A Social Work Perspective*. New York: Longman.

Bernard, Jessie (1981). *The Female World*. New York: Free Press.

Brownlee, Ann Templeton (1978). *Community, Culture, and Care*. St. Louis: C. V. Mosby.

Holler, Ronald, and George M. DeLong (1973). *Human Services Technology.* St. Louis: C. V. Mosby.

Leftwich, Richard, and Ansel M. Sharp (1976). *The Economics of Social Issues.* Dallas: Business Publications.

Morgan, Kathryn L. (1980). *Children of Strangers: The Stories of a Black Family.* Philadelphia: Temple University Press.

Rubin, Lillian (1976). *Worlds of Pain.* New York: Basic Books.

Rogers, Dorothy (1982). *Life-Span Human Development.* Monterey, Ca.: Brooks-Cole.

The Work of Social Welfare

Like any social institution, social welfare is organized into groups of people who have the responsibility of carrying out the many day-to-day activities of the social welfare professions. We have already seen that there are many social welfare professions, each performing specific functions. As society grows and changes, social welfare changes as well. New professions and social welfare services develop in response to new needs, making social welfare both diversified and flexible.

Earlier chapters have looked at various facets of the development and structure of social welfare. In this chapter, we will look at how these forces have shaped the structure of the social welfare professions themselves. We will examine what the social welfare professions are, and who works in them. We will also see some specific examples of what social welfare professionals do day-to-day, including projections about what kinds of new needs seem to be developing. The wide scope of social welfare has created an institutional structure that brings together many different types of professionals, each performing different but highly interrelated tasks. Many find social welfare such an exciting career option because it offers many different work opportunities and possibilities for moving among the many different services.

National Employment Changes

In 1982, the number of people employed in finance, insurance, real estate, and service occupations was greater than those in manufacturing, mining, and construction. For the first time in the nation's history, employment in service fields exceeded that in manufacturing, and this shift was called "an economic milestone" (Stetson, 1982). This trend has pulled more women into the workplace, because the largest occupational group is now composed of service workers rather than factory workers. It has also helped support the ongoing urbanization of America, because these increasingly electronic jobs have been centered in urban areas.

Within this overall context, "The majority of the increases in service and finance employment over (the period April 1981 to April 1982) were in consumer areas such as health and personal services, amusement and recreation, education and social services and nonprofit membership organizations. The employment totals in these rose by 333,000, or 2.7 percent. . . ." (Stetson, 1982). Of these jobs, 235,000 were in health service, clearly the most rapidly growing area. Taking a somewhat longer view, from 1972 to 1981, jobs in social services more than doubled, rising by more than 600,000 (Stetson, 1982).

Projection of this trend into the future shows continued growth in social welfare occupations, but with some interesting variations. Recent data show women moving into occupations previously dominated by men. For example, in 1971, 9 percent of the nation's physicians were women, compared with 22 percent in 1981 (Prial, 1982). Over the same period, women engineers increased from 1 to 4 percent, and by 1981, women comprised 47 percent of all bus drivers and bartenders. Because many social welfare professions like social work and nursing have traditionally been the province of women, opportunities in other areas may reduce the pool of available workers in these fields unless social work and nursing become popular with men, which is not likely.

Other trends are also influencing social welfare careers. The aging of the United States population is creating a growing need for social welfare professionals to work with the elderly. In social work alone, it is estimated that 700,000 jobs will be available for geriatric social workers by 1990 (*NASW News*, 1983). The workplace is also an area in which there will be an increase in the provision of social welfare services. The Renault auto plant in Belgium employs 4,000 industrial workers and ten social workers to help them deal with personal problems that spill over into their work (Alexander, 1983). This pattern of providing medical, mental health, and social-support services in industry is increasing abroad, as well as in this country. During the period 1974–1976, personnel in mental health increased by 21 percent for psychologists, 17 percent for social workers, 16 percent for registered nurses, and 17 percent for other mental health professionals (Kim, Hasan, and Egli,

1981). Present trends indicate that more growth in mental health fields will occur in community-based and outpatient services than in large, residential mental hospitals.

The generalist-versus-specialist issue addressed in Chapter 2 has also created new jobs. The rapidly increasing specialization in the health-services field has created the need for more holistic services. Two examples are the primary nurse and the hospice. The primary nurse must develop a twenty-four-hour plan of nursing care that he or she then supervises. The plan may include such things as altering regular hospital routine, delaying surgery, and accompanying patients through treatments that they fear if the primary nurse feels such actions are indicated (Spingarn, 1982) (see Exhibit 6–4). Hospices return patients who are close to death to environments that emphasize freedom from pain and closeness to significant people and activities in their lives. This procedure contrasts with that of keeping patients in impersonal hospital settings, in which the length of life may be briefly extended but the quality of life greatly reduced. In 1982 there were 800 hospices in the United States, an eightfold increase since 1975 (Brody, 1982).

In social work, cutbacks in federal aid to programs for the poor have encouraged social workers to go into private practice—individual counseling or therapy for which the user (or his or her insurance company) pays. In 1972, 2.9 percent of the members of the National Association of Social Workers were in private practice full time, compared to 7 percent in 1981 (Smothers, 1981).

This overview of some of the helping professions demonstrates how firmly embedded the social welfare institution is in the fabric of the society. Political, economic, and demographic changes must influence the social welfare services provided, how they are provided, and who provides them. The negative attitude toward social welfare projected by the Reagan administration in the 1980s led many to think that social welfare was declining. This has not been the case. It has been changing, but it is still growing. Indeed, many feel that political decisions that increase poverty, unemployment, and inequality cannot help but have the long-range effect of increasing the need for social welfare services.

Working Together and Alone

Much of the work of social welfare is done in teams rather than by professionals working by themselves. This usually reflects two aspects of contemporary helping: the complexity of problems, and the specialization of services. People's problems are rarely simple. Someone who is ill needs medical care, help in carrying on relationships with family, friends, and employers, and assistance in putting together the resources needed to pay for care. The ill person may also need personal help in understanding and accepting his or her illness. No one person can accomplish all these tasks. Therefore, a **team** of professional helpers works together—nurses, doctors, and other medical staff provide health-related services, and social workers, psychologists, human service workers, and volunteers meet social needs. Each tends to perform somewhat specialized activities appropriate to his or her particular profession (Brill, 1976). By communicating among themselves, and coordinating planning and task performance, the total needs of the ill person are met. Konle's description of working with the developmentally disabled in a public school system is a good example of how teams work in social welfare (1982).

The concept of teamwork may also be applied in the sense of collegial interaction. Even groups of helpers with the same professional identity, such as social workers, work as teams. Within the same agency, professionals support each other, providing information, encouragement, and advice as needed. This also occurs among professionals working in different agencies. The member of a mobile geriatric team may call a colleague working in a hospital to explore the availability of a service needed by an elderly person. Colleagues who work in different settings also come together through activities organized by professional associations. These may be focused around political action, social advocacy, or the sharing of knowledge through professional conferences. Exhibit 6–1 in the "Reflections on Social Welfare" section at the end of the chapter uses the National Association of Social Workers (NASW) as an example of services provided to help colleagues throughout a profession work together.

Although social welfare professionals work together in many ways, some also engage in what is called **private practice.** The practitioner has a private office used for helping people. Most people are familiar with the private practitioner physician. Private practice allows helping people to organize services in the manner they consider most useful. Services are paid for directly by the user or indirectly by insurance plans that cover medical treatment or counseling services. These indirect payments are called **third party payments,** because payment is from a source outside of the professional-user combination. An example of a third party payment would be when Blue Cross pays a medical bill.

In some respects the concept of private practice is inaccurate, because no professional works in true isolation. Even though the professional may be free to establish a private office and conditions of work, helping cannot be isolated from its environment. Professionals depend on a network of colleagues for consultation, referrals, and personal support. Because the private practitioner does not usually interact with other professionals on a daily basis in an agency, other opportunities—such as regularly scheduled meetings, informal contacts, and associating with colleagues through activities sponsored by professional associations—have to be found.

Working in Agencies

Most social welfare professionals work in social agencies of some sort. These agencies vary in the way they are organized. Some of these variations were explored in Chapter 2 when issues related to bureaucratization and professionalization were explored. Here we will focus on how the ways agencies are organized affect the work experience of the social welfare professionals within them. Four areas of agency organization will be discussed, each of which represents a continuum. That is, agencies will vary in the degree to which they approximate one of the two extreme approaches in each area. The four areas, each of which will be analyzed in turn, are:

- host agencies versus those dominated by one profession
- public versus private auspices
- accessibility to the community
- focus on specified users or specified problems

Host Agencies Versus Those Dominated by One Profession

Agencies vary in the degree to which they are primarily one profession or multiprofession agencies. A hospital is generally multiprofession, having a range of medical personnel and others who provide therapy, counseling, and help with financial needs. A Department of Social Services (Public Welfare) is generally much more of a one-profession agency, dominated by social work. However, even here, other professionals may be involved—home health aides, psychologists for administering psychological tests, psychiatrists with whom to consult

*Day-care workers provide valuable educational experiences for chil-
dren. They may also be an important part of a family's efforts to
care for its children while also meeting its economic needs.
(Elizabeth Hamlin/Stock, Boston)*

when serious mental illness is suspected, and others. Multiprofession
agencies are frequently dominated by one of the professions. Hospitals are dominated by physicians, and schools by teachers. Obviously,
the agency whose workers are primarily from one profession will more
likely be dominated by the values and procedures of that profession.

Multiprofession agencies offer rich opportunities for teamwork,
because they utilize the expertise and perspectives of many professions. As noted earlier, teamwork is often extremely useful when dealing with problems in a holistic manner. However, sometimes the dominant profession functions to restrict the input of the others. Some
social workers complain, for example, that doctors discharge patients

when medical treatment is completed, but without consideration for other kinds of helping plans that may not yet be completed. The single-profession agency is more likely to become somewhat isolated from input from other professions. This is sometimes easier for the helpers, because they don't have to negotiate so much with those having different perspectives. In the long run, however, having such control may not result in optimal service delivery. It can also prevent the continuing growth and stimulation of the workers themselves.

Public Versus Private Auspices

Many have pointed out that it is becoming increasingly difficult to define agencies as public or private (Kamerman, 1983). Increasingly complex interrelationships are developing between agencies traditionally supported by private funds, such as the Red Cross, and public agencies that contract with them for specific services. In addition, more and more government grants are awarded to private agencies to fund specifically desired services. In spite of these developments, agencies can still be categorized as primarily supported by either private or public funds, and administered by regulations developed under public law or according to the wishes of nongovernmental groups.

The shift of responsibility for essential social welfare services to the public realm increased the size and complexity of public agencies. Many of them are complex bureaucracies enmeshed in inflexible civil service procedures that sometimes give minimal recognition to professional training. In addition, public agencies focus many services on the most needy, who are often also the most difficult to serve. Along with poverty sometimes comes little education, housing that makes bathing difficult, anger, and hopelessness. As a result, work in public agencies can be fraught with voluminous paper work, colleagues who may have had little, if any, professional education, and users who may resist attempts to serve them. On the other hand, public agencies offer a wide range of service delivery opportunities. They also offer the satisfaction of knowing that their users depend on the services they receive from the public agency for their very survival, and for whatever opportunity to grow and develop they may have.

Private agencies often avoid many of the problems of public agencies but exhibit other shortcomings. Private agencies are frequently smaller, hire better trained personnel, and have less cumbersome procedures. Because they are thus potentially more flexible, it is easier for them (and they are more *likely*) to experiment with new and innovative programs. Because these agencies often charge fees, users tend to be better educated, better dressed, and to have better developed social skills. On the other hand, private agencies rarely provide services of last resort. People who use private agencies usually have other resources to work with. Indeed, private agencies frequently work closely with public agencies, which address basic life-sustaining needs like income and housing. Also, the smaller resources of many private agencies limit the range and duration of services they can provide.

The whole issue of private versus public services is very much in transition. Let us use a Women's Shelter as an example. The Shelter is probably funded by fees, private contributions, and grants from the local and state governments. It has its own staff of counselors but works closely with the Police Department in identifying and protecting battered women and rape victims. It provides short-term shelter for women and their children who have escaped from abusive situations, but long-term housing needs have to be referred to the Department of Social Services. Support groups are provided by the Shelter's staff, as is personal and employment counseling. However, financial needs are referred to the Department of Social Services. This example shows how public and private agencies are becoming increasingly inter-related and interdependent. Nevertheless, these agencies do provide somewhat different environments for their workers.

Access to the Community

Agencies vary in how accessible they are to members of a community. At the most open end of the spectrum would be a drop-in center or a telephone hotline, accessible to members of the community at their own initiative. At the opposite extreme would be a maximum-security prison or a mental hospital with locked wards. These agencies, sometimes called **total institutions,** closely control movements into, out of, and within the agency. Most agencies, of course, fall somewhere in between these extremes. Hospitals with emergency rooms are very accessible, although the rest of the hospital has much more limited access, which is regulated by such practices as visiting hours. Many residential facilities are geographically located in areas that limit accessibility. Other agencies may be very accessible geographically but have such unattractive surroundings and such demeaning procedures that users are reluctant to enter. And some agencies, like halfway houses, help people who have been in total institutions or other types of isolated helping settings become reintegrated into the community.

Sometimes isolation is needed to protect the user or the community from potentially harmful behavior. However, controlling behavior violates basic professional helping values about self-determination. Also, because the modern approach to helping is based on mutuality of interest (that is, the helping person and the user being equals), controlling the user's behavior gives the helper most of the power in the relationship and makes problem solving more difficult. On the other hand, removing people from protected environments and placing them back in the community is not necessarily helpful. Many people wandering the streets of large American cities were turned out of mental hospitals or other kinds of residential facilities. They are unable to maintain themselves in a healthy way in the community, and they need some type of protected environment to spare them the abuse and suffering they encounter on the streets.

Professional roles in agencies with little community accessibility can

The police provide a range of helping services wherever the need for help occurs. This officer is helping a young woman involved in an auto accident. (Jill Freedman/Archive Pictures, Inc.)

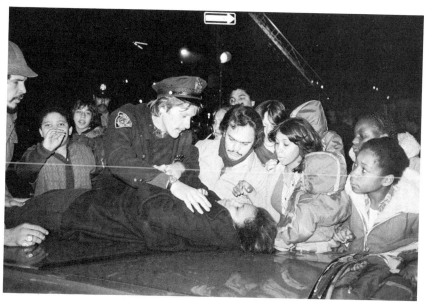

be rewarding if the isolation enables more effective helping to occur. This is the case in hospitals, where patients need to be protected from infection, or in residential homes for the elderly, who might hurt themselves if left unattended. However, functioning as a professional helping person in an environment in which users are forcibly restrained for punitive rather than rehabilitative purposes, such as prisons and some mental hospitals, is often a frustrating experience. When users of services do not want the services, and do not see their value, it is unlikely that they will invest the necessary energy in cooperating with a professional helping person. Also, community-based programs have a much wider network of resources to use in the helping process. Family, friends, employers, and other agencies are more accessible to programs that are community based. This generally helps professionals to address the totality of the problems with which they are working.

Focusing on Users Versus Focusing on Needs

Any agency has the organizational need to identify its objectives (you will recall our earlier discussion of system boundaries and purposes). One approach is to focus on meeting one or more particular needs, serving whatever user group might have the needs. For example, the police will intervene in any situation in which people are fighting or otherwise being harmed. It doesn't matter if the people are men or women, adults or children. A different approach is to focus on providing for the needs of a particular group, regardless of what those needs might be. A Women's Center serves women in whatever way they need assistance, although obviously it will draw upon other agencies when needed. Similarly, a Senior Citizen's Center serves the elderly, a Lesbian and Gay Community Center serves gays and lesbians, and Catholic Social Services has mostly Catholics as users.

The focus on user group or need relates to the issue of specialization and generalist practice. Focusing on particular *needs* makes it easier to specialize. Addressing the range of needs of a particular user *group* usually requires a broader approach, and thus may require the use of specialists and generalists. From the professional's standpoint, some prefer to work with only certain needs, enjoying the opportunity to develop specialized expertise. Others enjoy the challenge and range of activities that are associated with meeting the varied needs of a particular group. Of course there are also agencies that are general service agencies, providing a range of services to a range of users. Departments of Social Services are examples, providing a variety of financial and social services to children, adults, and the elderly.

Professional Education as a Base for Practice

Chapter 2 explained that specialized knowledge is a part of any helping profession, and Chapter 5 discussed some of the components of the knowledge base of the helping professions. Here we will look at yet another aspect of professional education as a base for practice: credentialing. Many states have laws that control who can practice as helping professionals. For example, all states control the practice of psychiatry, medicine, and nursing. Many others control the practice of social work, marriage counseling, and teaching in day-care centers. This is **legal credentialing,** meaning the legal control of practice in a helping profession to those meeting certain standards. Some professions also have **professional credentialing,** credentials established by a profession that indicate that practitioners have met criteria established by that group's professional association. For example, social work has both kinds of credentialing in New York state. There is legal certification, requiring a Master of Social Work degree and passage of a test in order to call oneself a Certified Social Worker. There is also professional certification, the Academy of Certified Social Workers, that requires the Master of Social Work degree, passing a test, a certain amount of experience, and letters of reference.

Credentialing serves several important functions:

- It is a type of assurance to the public that the person involved has met certain competency-based criteria. Obviously some people occasionally become credentialed who are not competent, but the profession must monitor its own membership to control this problem.
- It clarifies which profession will provide what services. As various professional groups attempt to get legislation passed to certify their members, they have to demonstrate what services their members provide and why there is a need for those services. This helps to clarify the boundaries between professions.
- It helps to organize third-party payments, which are usually restricted to people who are credentialed in specified professions. Not just anyone can file a claim for medical reimbursement from Blue Cross; only credentialed medical personnel can do so.

Social Welfare Professionals at Work

This chapter will conclude with three descriptions of social welfare professionals at work in the "Reflections on Social Welfare" section that follows. Exhibit 6-2 describes the work of human-service workers who deliver services to the developmentally disabled. Exhibit 6-3 focuses on the work of generalist social workers, using as an example a social worker practicing in a hospital setting. Exhibit 6-4 looks at the work of a different kind of social welfare professional who works in a hospital—the primary nurse. This chapter cannot provide detailed descriptions of the work of all the many kinds of helping professionals. However, the three that are presented should give you a good idea of the kinds of work involved—as well as the kinds of rewards.

SUMMARY

The work of social welfare takes place in many different kinds of agencies by a variety of helping professionals working with and on behalf of many kinds of people. The work of social welfare takes place in a cooperative environment that enables professionals to use their specialized expertise in conjunction with that of others. All helping professionals work from a grounding in professional education, through which many become credentialed in order to assure the highest level of competence possible. Nevertheless, analyzing the work of social welfare cannot capture its excitement and diversity. Nor can it capture the very special rewards derived from seeing someone grow stronger and happier or find more effective solutions to problems that trouble them. As Exhibit 6–4 suggests, social welfare cannot always extend life, but it can improve the quality of life. That in itself is a worthy gift for one human being to offer another.

REFLECTIONS ON SOCIAL WELFARE

The exhibits in this section focus on what social welfare professions and professionals do. The first looks at the functions of a social welfare professional association, and the remaining three examine the specific kinds of activities performed by three different types of helping professionals.

EXHIBIT 6–1   Social Workers Together

The National Association of Social Workers, like all professional social welfare associations, engages in a number of activities to help its members work together for the growth of the profession and themselves.

Political Action

NASW's activities in the political arena include:

- research and legislative analysis, human services, public welfare and other issues of concern to professional social workers and their clients;
- lobbying and advocacy for responsible public social policy legislation; and
- mobilizing and educating members on how to influence the political scene.

NASW's national political action committee (PACE) and its counterparts in each state support pro-human service candidates and encourage the joint participation of social workers and elected officials in social policy development. An education legislative action network (ELAN) informs social workers on political issues. NASW's leaders are increasingly involved in advocacy with Members of Congress.

Source: Setting a Standard of Excellence, pp. 5–9. Reprinted by permission of the National Association of Social Workers, 7981 Eastern Avenue, Silver Spring, MD. 20910.

Social Advocacy

NASW is a progressive organization that responds to contemporary issues as they affect the welfare of society. NASW advocates for the poor and recent legislative activities include organized opposition to the Administration's weakening of the human service delivery system, a block grant analysis program, federal budget studies and concerted activities to rescue public welfare programs.

Other NASW responses include support for the ERA, addressing gay and lesbian issues, enforcing a strong affirmative action program and, most recently, organizing opposition to nuclear proliferation.

Conferences

NASW organizes a number of national conferences each year on a variety of topics of interest to the profession. The largest is the Symposium which brings more than 3,000 social workers together around a wide range of professional issues.

Each spring, social workers from around the U.S. gather in Washington, D.C. for a political action conference—Social Workers in Politics—to develop political strategies and meet members of Congress.

Minority affairs, clinical practice, women's issues and social work services in schools have been the topics of other recent national conferences. In addition, chapters sponsor state conferences throughout the year.

Professional Issues

NASW serves as the nation's primary source of information on professional social work issues, including labor force data, job development for the profession, the enhancement of professional practice. NASW works closely with the Council on Social Work Education to promote contemporary social work education and to link education with social work jobs.

Publications

NASW's extensive publications operation, with offices in New York City, is the nation's primary source for professional social work books and journals. Included are:

- *Social Work* . . . the major journal in social work, published bi-monthly;
- *Health and Social Work* . . . the comprehensive journal for helping professionals, quarterly;
- *Research and Abstracts* . . . the standard reference journal for the profession, quarterly;

- *Social Work in Education* . . . a primary source for school social workers, quarterly;
- *Practice Digest* . . . a quarterly magazine for practitioners.

NASW also publishes such basic reference tools of the profession as:

- *Encyclopedia of Social Work;*
- *NASW Register of Clinical Social Workers;*
- *Professional Social Workers Directory;* and
- *Directory of Agencies.*

Membership Services

NASW provides a variety of important benefits to its members such as group health and life insurance, professional and liability insurance, accident and disability insurance benefits. Also, a legal defense service, travel/study programs, the monthly *NASW NEWS*, employment exchange and specialized information. NASW also serves its members with activities to achieve wider recognition in the profession, expanded employment opportunities and protection against unfair employment practices.

EXHIBIT 6–2   Working with People Having Developmental Disabilities

The following is a description of the helping activities of human service workers who work with the developmentally disabled.

Human service workers play a vital role in the delivery of services to individuals who are developmentally disabled (DD). In many DD agencies, it is the human service worker who has the most direct and constant contact with clients. HSWs provide this direct treatment in a wide range of institutions from schools to state hospitals. They work with adults, adolescents, children, and the aged, with people whose levels of functioning vary according to the severity of their developmental disability.

The most widely accepted definition of a developmental disability is that of the American Association on Mental Deficiency: "a handicapping condition evident in the developmental period which results in mental retardation, cerebral palsy, autism, epilepsy, or other neurological impairments which limit an individual's adaptive abilities." The developmental period is usually considered to be from conception to age 18, the time period when the person is

Source: NCHSW Worker Forum, Vol. 1, No. 2, January/February 1983, p. 3, published by the National Commission for Human Service Workers, 1710 Gervais St., Suite 205, Columbia, S.C. 29201.

growing physically, mentally, and emotionally. A developmental disability generally cannot be cured, but services can be provided which assist the DD person to maximize his or her human potential.

Workers who specialize in developmental disabilities work in programs which focus on early prevention and diagnosis, special education, parent training and education, day care, respite care, and vocational training. In the past, the emphasis for treatment of people with DD was in institutional settings, but today care is given in sheltered workshops and training centers, advocacy groups, community living apartments and halfway houses, recreational programs, and pre-schools, as well as in residential training centers and other long-term health care facilities. . . .

Human service workers in the DD field function in a variety of roles. They perform evaluations, carry out therapeutic activities, document progress and perform other record-keeping tasks, participate in planning, teach skills, work with parents and community agents, and provide outreach and follow-up as well as advocacy support. A small number function as administrators, program managers, or team leaders.

Human service workers who provide services to DD clients would probably describe their primary duties as providing education and rehabilitation for clients, for this is often the greatest overall need of the clients—to learn. There are many care-giving responsibilities as well, particularly in residential settings. However, human service workers appropriately see their role as teaching clients how to provide for their own needs to the fullest extent of their ability.

Human service workers are also concerned with creating normal environments for their clients and serving as advocates for clients who are inexperienced or unable to provide totally for themselves. They are particularly careful to protect clients from the harmful effects of being "labeled" so that society will not reject them and/or lower its expectations of them.

Teaching adaptive behaviors and communication skills, planning for client growth, facilitating clients' acceptance into communities, and keeping a secure environment in which individuals can develop their potential for growth are the major activities of human service workers who work in DD settings. Because many DD people have special health care needs, many human service workers work in health-related facilities where they apply physical care skills.

EXHIBIT 6–3   The Generalist Social Worker at Work

The following is a description of the work of a baccalaureate-level, generalist, professional social worker. Although this social worker worked in health care, other social workers work in child welfare, public welfare, drug- and alcohol-

Source: Copyright 1983, National Association of Social Workers, Inc. Reprinted, with permission, from *NASW News*, Vol. 28, No. 3, March 1983, p. 9. Excerpts. Also by permission of Elaine M. Kurosky Olin, BSW, LSWA Medical Social Worker, Sinai Hospital, Baltimore, MD, and Marywood College, Scranton, PA.

abuse settings, mental health, family service, with the developmentally dis-
abled (like the human-service worker described in the preceding exhibit),
industry, business and labor, schools, with youth, and with the aged.

Elaine Kurosky Olin . . . works in Baltimore's Sinai Hospital Department of
Social Work . . . Olin, along with her team leader, an MSW, works three
nursing units at Sinai with a total of 80 beds. One of those units is the oncology
ward where she provides services to cancer patients and their families.

Olin and other social workers at Sinai help patients and their families understand their illness, become adjusted to hospitalization, and ease their way back
into the community through discharge planning. . . .

On two of the three units, Olin does rounds with multidisciplinary teams,
including physicians, nurses, physical therapists, and other health professionals. She participates in weekly team conferences in which the care of each
patient is reviewed.

Olin is also assigned on rotation to the emergency room. She and her colleagues have to be prepared to be pulled from their daily rounds to handle
emergency cases.

"These are anxiety producing for the social worker as well as the client,"
says Olin, "because the social worker has had no time to plan, because the
patient and family are more distraught than those who have time to prepare
themselves for hospital admission, and because of the pressure to dispose of
the case quickly."

"Most emergency room cases," she says, "don't need to be admitted for
medical reasons, but many have no place to go once they leave the emergency
room. That is why hospitals have a lot of 'social admissions.' There's no way
you can get patients into a nursing home or a boarding home in two hours."

"But some of the most difficult cases, "says Olin," are those in which the
patient has multiple problems, e.g., social, financial, medical, etc. For instance," she says, "an alcoholic patient might come in who, in addition to his
medical problem, not necessarily related to the alcoholism, may have no home
or live in inadequate housing. In those families there are often family problems
as well."

"In cases like these, you can't just deal with one problem and ignore the
other three. Many times the treatment of the medical problem can't begin or
be done appropriately until you alleviate the financial or social problems. You
can't expect a person to pay for eight kinds of medication if they don't have
enough money to buy them, or to follow a specific diet if they can't buy the
food they need, or don't have a stove to prepare it on because their gas or
electricity has been cut off."

Olin says work with cancer patients is equally difficult, but not for the same
reasons. "The problem with working in an oncology unit," she says, "is that
you only get to see the people who are really sick or dying. We don't generally
see the more healthy patients, those coming in for outpatient services, going
into remission, or who have another five or ten years of quality life. The people
we work with are usually end-stage, terminal patients."

EXHIBIT 6–4   New Vistas in Social Welfare: The Primary Nurse

The role of the primary nurse has developed to help ensure coordinated and humane care for patients being treated in a medical-care system that is built around specialized services. The following description of the work of the primary nurse illustrates how specialized and generalist services can be used together to improve the quality of social welfare services.

Josephine Cordischi proudly displays the chart she was given during her previous stay at Beth Israel Hospital in Boston: down the left side, a long list of medicines, along with the dosage and time she was to take them; down the right side, check marks showing that the directions had been followed.

Susan E. Johnson, in white pants and striped shirt, who comes into Mrs. Cordischi's room to adjust her intravenous tubes, is a far cry from the traditional white-capped nurse. Not only does she administer to her patient, who suffers from chronic asthma, but she also draws up a 24-hour plan of nursing care that she supervises while she herself is on duty and that other nurses follow in her absence.

Miss Johnson, 24 years old, is a "primary nurse," one of a new breed of medical professionals who have come into being to offset the increasing fragmentation of patient care and nursing accountability. Contributing to the need were several factors: the spread of team nursing, wherein each nurse does only one task during an entire shift, the rapid advance of medical technology and the continuing shortage of nurses resulting from fewer people being attracted to or staying in a profession which, they feel, does not let them fully practice the healing arts they acquired at nursing school.

While the basics of primary nursing are as old as the nursing profession itself, only recently have they come to be applied on an appreciable scale. In primary nursing, the ideal one-on-one nurse-patient relationship has been broadened to include a considerable amount of decision making and has been extended beyond individual working shifts. . . .

Some traditionalists in the medical profession have trouble dealing with the "decentralized decision-making" aspect of primary nursing, which cuts across established medical-care lines. If, for example, a primary nurse feels that a patient still reeling from a bolt-from-the-blue diagnosis of cancer needs more time to adjust to the reality of his situation before facing surgery, she will serve as his advocate with his doctors and, unless his condition is critical, the operation will be delayed. Or if a patient is unduly worried about even a simple procedure, his primary nurse can arrange to accompany him to the treatment room. On a more mundane level, if a patient would rather watch the "Donahue" show in the morning and postpone his bath to the afternoon, and

Source: "Primary nurses bring back one-on-one care," by Natalie Davis Spingarn, *The New York Times Magazine*, December 26, 1982, pp. 26ff. © 1982 by The New York Times Company. Reprinted by permission.

the primary nurse decides there is no reason for him not to, she does not have to ask a superior for permission to flout hospital routine.

Nor is primary-nursing care confined within hospital walls. For a limited period after patients are discharged, primary nurses remain available, either by phone or through home visits, to help with whatever problems may arise. And before patients are released from the hospital, primary nurses show them how to avoid tensions that can aggravate their conditions, and may teach them how to walk, climb stairs or lift grocery bags without exerting undue strain on mending limbs and organs.

Primaries, who at Beth Israel are paid no more than other registered nurses, an average of $20,000 a year, also are available to accompany patients going from hospital to nursing home, to ease their way into a new environment and to consult informally with the new caretakers. . . .

Clearly, Josephine Cordischi, 48 years old, is delighted with the primary-nursing system, and so is Susan Johnson, who came to Beth Israel in 1980 directly from Massachusetts's Fitchburg State College. There are many more rewards in primary nursing than in the more prevalent system of team nursing. "It's much better," Miss Johnson says, "to know a whole patient and his family than to know him only as the man down the hall who gets digoxin for cardiac disease. You can find out what his special needs are, and while you treat him physiologically, you get to help him adjust psychologically to meeting any restriction his illness may place on him."

Her hospital's hierarchy seems pleased, too. Nurses are leaving every three to five years instead of every three to six months, as they had been before the introduction of primary nursing at Beth Israel.

Elsewhere, nurses seem to be displaying their discontent with their traditional handmaiden roles by continually moving from hospital to hospital or dropping out of the profession entirely, creating troublesome shortages—about 80,000 hospital staff positions for nurses are currently going begging.

STUDY QUESTIONS

1. Visit a social welfare agency that interests you in your community. What kinds of programs does it offer? What kinds of people use its services? What kinds of professional and paraprofessional staff does it employ? Would you enjoy working there? Why or why not?

2. Interview a social welfare professional in your community. What frustrations and rewards has this worker experienced? Would you find these frustrations tolerable? Would the rewards be adequate?

3. Make a list of the characteristics you would want in your ideal social welfare job. Then organize them in terms of the criteria used to analyze agencies in this chapter. For example, if you listed "working with children" you would put that under an agency that is focused on users. Remember that the criteria are not mutually exclusive, so one of your characteristics might fit under more than one criterion. After doing this, what kind of agency seems ideal for you? Is there such an agency in your community? If not, what compromises might you have to make to find a satisfying job?

4. Identify the social welfare profession of most interest to you. Research job opportunities in that field, using Department of Labor statistics and getting information from the professional association in that field. If you don't know how to find occupational data published by the Department of Labor or the name and address of the relevant professional association, speak with your instructor or reference librarian.

5. How important is credentialing to you? Would the existence of credentialing influence your choice of a social welfare profession? Why or why not? Can you see any negative aspects to credentialing for a profession, its members, and those it serves?

SELECTED READINGS

Konle, Carolyn (1982). *Social Work Day-to-Day*. New York: Longman.

Lauffer, Armand, with Lynn Nybell, Carla Overberger, Beth Reed, and Lawrence Zeff (1977). *Understanding Your Social Agency*. Beverly Hills, Ca.: Sage Publishers.

Lipsky, Michael (1980). *Street-Level Bureaucracy*. New York: Russell Sage Foundation.

Rudestam, Kjell Erik, and Mark Frankel (1983). *Treating the Multiproblem Family: A Casebook*. Monterey, Ca.: Brooks-Cole.

Sheehan, Susan (1978). *A Prison and a Prisoner*. Boston: Houghton-Mifflin.

Social Welfare's Role in Shaping the Future

Alvin Toffler, a sociologist who has specialized in looking at the social processes that are likely to affect the future of societies, has recently talked about what he calls the "third wave." He summarizes his ideas in the following way (Toffler, 1982):

> The agricultural revolution of 10,000 years ago launched the first great wave of change on the planet; the industrial revolution triggered the second. The demassification process occurring today is part of the Third Wave of global change.
>
> The worldwide transformation is marked by the decline of "Second Wave" industries like auto, textile, or steel, and the rise of "Third Wave" industries based on information, the biological revolution, space, ocean and environmental technologies, new forms of agriculture and new services. It involves the transfer of certain jobs out of the office and into homes equipped with personal computers, cheap video equipment and the like—the spread of electronic cottage industry. Also important is the rise of "prosuming"—self-help and do-it-yourself activities. . . .
>
> For those concerned with civil rights, this massive economic restructuring presents enormous problems. The emerging industries need highly skilled

workers. But because of the heritage of discrimination, and for other reasons, job skills are not evenly distributed in society. Thus blacks, Hispanics, and other minorities are least prepared to take advantage of the new opportunities. Most non-whites are employed in declining Second Wave occupations, rather than the Third Wave growth sectors.

In addition, millions of chronically unemployed and underemployed members of minority groups have never cut loose from their First Wave, rural origins. They have never successfully become part of the urban industrial culture. Yet we already face the need to adapt to something dramatically different from both.*

Toffler's analysis is at once exciting and disturbing. The lives of most people have been physically improved by being spared much of the heavy, dirty, often dangerous agricultural and industrial work of the past. Yet the new technologies of the "third wave" have brought with them problems of pollution, boredom, unemployment, and a greater likelihood that disadvantaged members of society will be forced even farther outside the mainstream.

What does all of this mean for social welfare? One thing is obvious—the problems people face are changing, rather than disappearing. Although some problems have been solved or greatly reduced, others appear and cry out for solution. The need for humane and adequate social welfare programs continues, and there is little reason to believe that this need will disappear in the near future. However, it is equally clear that the social welfare structure of the past is not likely to be adequate to address the problems of the future. New problems will call for new solutions. This chapter, then, will look at how social welfare can play its rightful role in building on the past and the present to help shape a just and humane future.

Social Welfare and Social Change**

To talk about the future role of social welfare in society is to talk about social change. Everywhere we look we see change taking place. Some concern people's rights, such as the right to choose to die (Schmeck, 1983) or the rights of women and other minorities to have access to employment (Pear, 1983a). Others address the changing conditions under which people live that affect the adequacy of their housing

---

*Copyright © by Alvin Toffler. Reprinted by permission of the author.
**Special thanks to Dean Pierce, DSW for his help in conceptualizing this section.

(Rule, 1983) or their need for legal help to manage daily transactions that have become so complex and costly that many cannot understand them (Severo, 1983). Still other changes affect the relationships between the economic, political, and social welfare institutions. The rapid growth of private, for-profit hospitals is an example: ". . . their tilt toward people who can pay to be mended and their avoidance of the utterly poor, nonwelfare patient may be undercutting the assumption that everyone has a right to decent medical services" (Kleinfield, 1983). Such changes inevitably affect the ability of people to live satisfying lives. Therefore, these changes must be of concern to social welfare professionals.

The role of social welfare in social change falls into two major arenas:

- influencing those who make the decisions that lead to social change
- working with members of society to understand changes, to participate in decision-making processes that affect change, and to become linked to the resources needed to continue to function effectively in a changing world

Let us begin in the first arena, influencing people's decisions that lead to change. Germain (1982:27) suggests that the task of social welfare is to help others to make decisions that will reduce:

1. the technological pollution of our physical environment that affects the physical and mental health of all people.
2. the social pollution of poor housing, education, and health care in urban and rural life.
3. the cultural pollution of racism, sexism, agism, speciesism, and other forms of injustice that create noxious environments.

Decisions are made in all the eight systems discussed in Chapter 5. For example, with more women deciding to marry later and have fewer children, there is a cumulative effect on the size and composition of the population. The decision of social welfare agencies not to appeal changes in government regulations that reduce services to users increases the likelihood that similar changes will occur in the future. The task for social welfare professionals is to help decision makers in all of the eight systems to consider the impact of their decisions. Quoting René Dubos, Germain (1982:27) notes, "we must think globally but act locally." Throughout this chapter, we will highlight specific issues to show how this can be done.

The second area in which the social welfare institution functions is to help people respond to change. First, they must understand changes that are occurring, or that are being proposed. This is critical if they are to participate in the change process described above—they must know why it is in their own best interest to try to affect decision making, and how to do so. Once change has occurred, they need to understand how it will affect them. This means knowing what new resources are available and how to obtain them. If the changes have reduced resources, people need to be supported as they find whatever alternatives may exist, or as they develop organized efforts to adjust to the changes. If resources have been increased, people should learn how to use them most effectively to attain their life goals. This may also entail helping people to understand why they should support changes that increase resources, even if the resources are more immediately useful for others than for themselves.

The rest of this chapter will explore five areas in which social change is occurring: poverty, immigration and population changes, life-style changes, regional relationships, and the accountability of social welfare to society. Let's now look at each in turn.

The Issue of Poverty and the Underclass

In one form or another, poverty has always been an issue in American society. It has moved from one group to another and been associated with different social conditions at different times, but it has always existed. As we saw in Chapter 3, the Kennedy and Johnson presidencies tried to develop social programs that would finally eradicate poverty as a way of life for millions of Americans. The programs they initiated started to advance society in this direction. Unfortunately, by 1980 these gains had been reversed. The median family income for 1980 was 5.5 percent *below* that of the year before (Herbers, 1982), and the number of people living below the poverty level increased from 11.6 to 13 percent. By 1981, the poverty rate was up to 14 percent, based on an official poverty income of $9,287 for an urban family of four (Herbers, 1982a).

The policies of the Reagan administration consistently attacked programs that benefited the poor. The 1981 Omnibus Budget Reconciliation Act enacted changes in the Aid to Families with Dependent Children program that were expected to eliminate benefits for 20.5 percent of the caseload, and reduce benefits for an additional 7.5 percent (*Washington Social Legislation Bulletin*, 1983). Economic problems became evident in a number of ways. Unemployment hit a post-

Devastated neighborhoods and damaged lives are indeed broken promises. They are one of the results of population and geographical changes occurring in the United States. (Barbara Alper/Stock, Boston)

war high at the end of 1982, reaching 10.8 percent, dropping only slightly to 10.4 percent early in 1983. Sustained unemployment created a "new poor," those who had previously worked regularly, owned homes that they had then lost through foreclosure, and who had always considered themselves middle class. Having lost their roots, thousands of people took to moving from place to place in search of work and an income, often living in their cars in the process (Cummings, 1982). Others simply became homeless where they were, straining community resources and community tolerance (Cummings, 1982a). Inevitably, some are destroyed as psychological and biological correlates of poverty erode their ability to cope.

Poverty has many effects that go well beyond the immediate lack of money. The recent rise in joblessness and the consequent increase in financial stress demonstrated once again that people experiencing financial stress may also become depressed, passive, and angry (Clymer, 1983; *Washington Social Legislation Bulletin,* 1983). When poverty continues for extended periods, what has been called an **underclass** is created. These are people cut off from society and lacking "the education and the skills and other personality traits they need in order to become effectively in demand in the modern economy" (Gunnar Myrdal, quoted in Auletta, 1981). Auletta estimates that one-third of those in poverty are in the underclass (Auletta, 1982). Auletta sees four distinct groups making up the underclass: hostile street criminals, hustlers who earn their living in the underground economy, mothers with a long-term dependence on welfare, and what he calls the "traumatized," such as homeless former mental patients (Auletta, 1981:95).

Not everyone in the underclass is poor—some hustlers and criminals make out fairly well, for example. Most, however, live in poverty, and all share a sense of isolation from the mainstream society. Access to money on a regular and legitimate basis enables people to buy not only food and shelter but also provides access to benefits like education that in turn help when seeking employment and social respectability. When money is lacking, it is increasingly difficult to maintain stable social networks that provide a personal sense of well-being (Wiseman, 1970). Finding ways to steal or hustle for money does little to bring people back into the economic or social mainstream, although it may enable them to be more physically comfortable in their day-to-day living.

The continuation of poverty poses several problems for society. Poverty is costly, both in terms of welfare payments and in terms of lost human resources. Long-term poverty increases these costs and at the same time creates the potential for social conflict. When people feel that they have nothing to gain from existing social arrangements, they may allow them to deteriorate or even attack them (Toffler, 1982). America has always been proud of the way its middle class has prevented the polarization of classes into two isolated groups, the "haves" and the "have nots." The continued existence of an extensive underclass could create such a division. If some middle-class people continue to slide into poverty because of widespread unemployment, they will add to this economically deprived and socially alienated group.

The Contribution of Social Welfare

Social welfare has traditionally worked to prevent poverty and the costs associated with it. Many of the programs studied in earlier chapters have sought to attain this goal. This function of social welfare is as necessary as ever, and some of the strategies used earlier continue to be useful. America has to hear about, *and see*, its poor. In a media world, the poor have to be shown on TV. Society has to know that poverty is clearly tied to social conditions. For example, America needs to know that minorities are much more likely to be poor than whites, and that women suffer in poverty far more than men (*Statistical Abstract,* 1981:433, 444, 447). The reasons for these differences have to be recognized and addressed. Myths that attribute poverty primarily to laziness and lack of motivation need to be challenged with facts. In other words, social welfare professionals should seek to influence public opinion and public policy.

Organized social welfare reform efforts must also include specific proposals for programs and procedures. A number of program areas cry out for reform based on accurate data and creative thinking. The Social Security retirement program (OASDI) is one. It has been experiencing problems because the American population is aging. More and more people are receiving benefits and proportionately fewer and fewer people are working, people whose contributions to Social Security support the program (see Figures 7–1 and 3–2).

The Social Security Act Amendments of 1983 attempted to address these problems. They mandated the inclusion of workers not presently in OASDI (new federal employees, state and local employees now outside the system, and workers in nonprofit organizations), changing the computation of cost-of-living increases, increasing the payroll taxes that support the system, and increasing the retirement age (*Washington Social Legislation Bulletin,* 1983a). These changes modify the existing program rather than reform it in any fundamental way. They also shift a greater burden to the elderly by reducing or postponing their benefits in spite of proposed higher taxes, which would be borne disproportionately by those with lower incomes. Using general tax revenues to help support OASDI would be a reform (see Exhibit 7–1 in the "Reflections on Social Welfare" section at the end of the chapter). This, of course, raises the value issues discussed in Chapter 2 regarding social insurances versus grant programs.

Social Security is not the only program for aiding the poor or dealing with poverty that desperately needs creative thinking and reform. Medicare appears to be rapidly approaching a bankruptcy situation similar to that of OASDI. During 1981, outlays exceeded income, and this situation will worsen in the coming years (Pear, 1983). This is in part because the nation's health-care bill has been growing faster than the economy. Indeed, in 1980 national health expenditures reached $247 billion—an average of $1,067 per person (*Washington Social Legislation Bulletin,* 1982). Yet with health insurance most often tied to employment, larger numbers of people are finding themselves both unemployed and without health insurance at the same time that health costs are escalating and federal health insurance programs are faltering. And health care is not the only problem; housing is also critical. We have already discussed the plight of the homeless, but we could also explore the problems of abandoned housing, gentrification of low-cost rental areas by high-cost cooperative and condominium housing, and the failure of much public housing. We will see later in the

FIGURE 7–1   Demography and Social Security

The following charts show that because the U. S. population is aging, there are proportionately fewer employed persons to support the elderly through the OASDI program.

America Is Getting Older

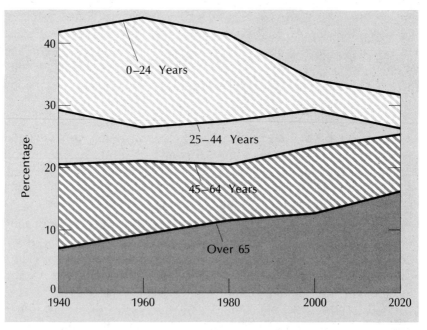

Source: The New York Times, February 4, 1983, p. A12. © 1983 by The New York Times Company. Reprinted by permission.

People Holding Jobs Per Beneficiary

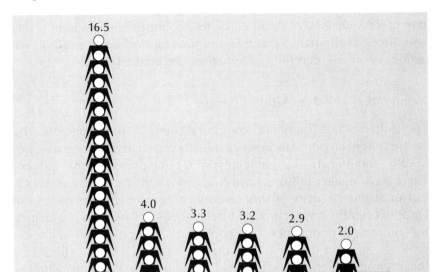

Numbers for each calendar year.
Figures for 1995 and beyond are projections.
Source: The New York Times, February 4, 1983, p. A12. © 1983 by The New York Times Company.
Reprinted by permission.

chapter that minorities of all kinds are having their rights and their quality of life eroded. In addition, public education is struggling to maintain itself. The list of problems goes on and on.

The Reagan administration's approach focused on balancing the national budget and cutting social welfare costs while increasing the military budget. This is hardly reform; it is simply reducing social programs. This strategy cannot address the complex problems involved in designing programs that meet people's needs more effectively and efficiently. Social welfare professionals must join forces to generate alternative approaches. Creative thinking is critical—we need national health insurance, even though it might require restructuring and limiting growth in the nation's free-enterprise system of health care (Kleinfield, 1983). We also need cost-efficient social welfare, even though that might rule out $90-per-hour fees for therapists and a similar amount for an eight-hour shift by a private-duty nurse. Mostly, though, we need creative thinking and concerted action. Social welfare professionals have to be in the forefront of *thinking* about viable and effective alternatives, and in the forefront of social and political *action*, to ensure that these alternatives are implemented.

Immigration and Population Changes

The United States is a nation composed primarily of immigrants. The Native American population was gradually dominated numerically, politically, and militarily by immigrants who came primarily from Europe. There were smaller influxes from Asia and South and Central America, but until the last half of this century, most immigrants came from Europe. Even the importation of black people as slaves did not change the numerical dominance of people with European cultural backgrounds, nor did it change the shaping of United States culture by those groups. Being non-European in cultural background, whether Native American, African, Asian, or Hispanic, has always meant being a member of a minority group.

This country has traditionally been a haven for people from other societies seeking a refuge from some type of persecution or economic disaster. Although some immigrants came to increase their wealth, most came to survive. Irish and Italian immigrants fled agricultural conditions that promised slow starvation; Jews and other religious groups fled persecution; Mexicans sought opportunities in lands that had once been dominated by Spanish culture. These same push-and-pull migratory processes continue today, but for different groups. There is still some immigration from Europe because of persecution, most recently by Soviet Jews, over 66,000 of which immigrated to the United States between 1978 and 1982 (Schwamm et. al., 1982). However, most recent immigration has come from other parts of the world, and the effect of this immigration on the American populaton has been substantial. This, in turn, has affected questions of social, political, and economic power.

The 1980 Census showed that Asians were the fastest-growing ethnic group in the United States during the 1970s, a growth rate expected to increase even further during the 1980s (Lindsey, 1982). Political and racial oppression motivated hundreds of thousands of Koreans, Chinese, Thais, Japanese, Vietnamese, Cambodians, and other Asians to seek a better life here. Asian-Americans have traditionally done very well in this country: in 1980 they had the highest median family income in the United States, and 75 percent were high school graduates, compared with 69 percent of whites. Although Asian-Americans make up only about 1.5 percent of the national population, they are overrepresented in many of the most prestigious schools and in the arts and the sciences. This has been attributed to their culture and support from close-knit family groups (Lindsey, 1982:28).

However, newer immigrants from Asia and elsewhere have some different characteristics from those who arrived earlier. At the end of 1980, there were over 444,000 refugees from Vietnam, Cambodia, and Laos in the U. S. (Schwamm et al., 1982). The "boat people" from Cambodia, Laos, and rural Vietnam are often poorly educated, unskilled, and lacking any knowledge of English. This is also true of refugees from China, in contrast to earlier Chinese immigrants from Taiwan and Hong Kong. Their efforts to settle into communities are often painful. Orange County, California, has had a very large influx of Vietnamese, Laotians, and Cambodians, causing the public schools and medical facilities to become overloaded. Competition with existing minority groups has also increased (Lindsey, 1982:33). Similar groups settling in other communities encountered similar problems (Hornblower, 1980). Problems have also arisen with the most recent immigrants from Cuba and Haiti, many of whom lacked the level of education and job preparation needed for our "third wave" economic system. The effects of new immigrant groups have been even more noticeable because over 70 percent have settled in only six states— California, New York, Florida, New Jersey, Illinois, and Texas (Schwamm et al., 1982).

Population also grows as a result of birth. In 1979, the highest birth rate in the United States was among Hispanic women (25.5 percent versus 14.7 percent for non-Hispanic women), leading to the prediction that people of Hispanic origin will outnumber American blacks, currently the largest racial minority group, before the end of the century (*The New York Times*, 1982). Yet we saw earlier in this book that Hispanics generally have lower incomes and lower levels of education than other groups, so their need for social welfare services may increase in the future. Census data also show that the population as a whole is aging, and that families maintained by women with no husbands present are increasing (Herbers, 1982b). We have already seen that both the elderly and women who are single parents are economically very vulnerable.

The Contribution of Social Welfare

This society values freedom and opportunity, so it has tended to welcome immigrants. However, poor economic conditions increase competition and especially affect the poorly educated and the least skilled. As competition becomes severe, resentment often results. People begin to feel that immigrants are taking jobs away from "Americans" and they may encourage the imposition of stricter immigration quotas. They may also discriminate against, and even physically harm, those they resent.

The changes in our population are widespread and complex. Some changes, such as increasing numbers of the elderly, affect everyone and are more readily accepted as legitimate concerns for society. Others may elicit very different kinds of societal responses. Minority populations experiencing high birth rates may have income-support programs reduced in order to discourage additional children. Immigrant groups may be subject to exclusionary legislation to prevent their immigration or even to force their return to their homelands. These responses are likely to harm the people involved and damage the ability of the society as a whole to adapt to social change.

There are a number of approaches that social welfare professionals can take to these issues. One approach is to develop competence in other languages and to learn about other cultures. It is impossible to provide the kinds of services needed if communication is impossible, and if services are not delivered in ways that are consistent with the culture of the recipients. Service delivery has to be organized in ways that encourage the participation of users, especially when those users are members of a minority group. The elderly best understand their own needs, as do Asians, Hispanics, and others. Better communication will also help to avoid stereotyping and insensitivity. Although the dominant culture may think in terms of global concepts, such as Asians and Hispanics, the many separate cultures that comprise these groupings are distinct and must be understood and worked with individually. The same is increasingly true of blacks, whose cultural roots may be in Haiti, Jamaica, Barbados, Nigeria, Liberia, or other Caribbean and African cultures.

Understanding and appreciating diverse groups is a task faced by the whole society. Social welfare professionals should work to increase the media coverage of these groups and their participation in planning for such coverage (O'Connor, 1982). Legislators must understand the needs of different groups and appreciate the contribution they make to our society. Even social welfare agencies have to reexamine their policies and their attitudes (Brownlee, 1978). As with any type of discrimination, the daily conversations overheard by social welfare professionals that perpetuate myths have to be challenged with accurate data.

The problems caused by immigration and a changing population are in part economic, so strategies to address poverty discussed in the preceding section are also relevant. All poor people, whether native born or from abroad, face a similar problem—how to gain access to needed resources. When people consider underlying economic issues, they will not blame members of minority groups so frequently for the poverty that victimizes them. People will not worry that minorities are taking away jobs or threatening the quality of school systems or neighborhoods. Opportunity is a basic value in the United States. When it is available equally to everyone, unrestricted by racist attitudes and practices, the new immigrants will find their own way into the social structure, just as immigrant groups did in the past.

Changing Life Styles

A recent article ended with the author stating, "Even as I write, I know this way of life is fragile and will one day pass from the world" (Colony, 1981:134). The author was not talking about rapid developments in technology affecting behavior; she was talking about being a housewife. To be sure, technological changes have had a profound impact on who works, where they work, and how they work, to say nothing of how we shop, pay our bills, travel, and use our leisure time. However, many changes reflect other things: cultural differences brought by various immigrant groups, changing values about freedom of choice, and the emergence of self-help groups that have supported people in their efforts to live as they wish or must.

The family has been a focal point for identifying many changes in life styles. The divorce rate, which doubled between 1966 and 1976, now shows that roughly half of those who marry will divorce (Dullea, 1983; *Statistical Abstract*, 1981:80). Divorce has brought a number of life-style alternatives. Because close to 75 percent of divorced women and 83 percent of divorced men remarry, about one in five households with married couples have at least one partner who has been divorced (Collins, 1982). This high rate of remarriage creates what has been called **binuclear families**—those linked together through divorced and remarried spouses. Recent research shows that a number of patterns are emerging that enable divorced adults to maintain cordial, working relationships, so that they can cooperate in caring for their children (Collins, 1982). Divorce has also, of course, created significant problems for adults and the children who depend on them.

Divorce has also greatly increased single-parent families. Between 1970 and 1980, the number of female-headed, single-parent family households increased 55.3 percent; male-headed, single-parent families increased 38.9 percent (*Statistical Abstract*, 1981:42). Although divorce is an important cause of single parenthood, some single parents have never been married and never intend to do so. Artificial insemination, surrogate parenting, changed attitudes, and adoption help make single parenthood a viable choice. It is estimated that by 1990 about half the children in America will have lived with a single parent for some period (Collins, 1982).

Another trend clearly visible in the United States is the number of people choosing to live alone. In 1960, 17.3 percent of men and 11.9 percent of women eighteen and over were single. By 1980 these figures had jumped to 23.5 and 17.0 percent, respectively. Figures like the above can be misleading, however, because they do not necessarily reflect various kinds of alternative life styles, such as people in committed relationships who choose not to live together. These arrangements may exist among homosexuals or heterosexuals, but in either case create emotional ties and social relationships that more closely resemble family life than they do single life.

Other life-style changes are also visible. Interracial married couples nearly doubled from 1970 to 1980 (*Statistical Abstract*, 1981:40). The number of couples in which both partners work has also been increasing, partly in response to economic pressures (*Statistical Abstract*, 1981:383). Self-help and support groups have developed to enable people to lead life styles that would have been extremely difficult in the past. Lesbians and gay men especially have been able to relate to each other more openly. They have also asserted their right to be parents, either as divorced spouses, as single parents, or as gay or lesbian couples (Lewin and Lyons, 1982).

The Contribution of Social Welfare

Changing life styles sometimes bring new needs. Divorce, and adjustment to the new permutations of family units that result from it, often bring pain and confusion. Social welfare professionals need to be flexible enough to develop new services to meet emerging needs that do not necessarily spring from traditional patterns of behavior. Living alone can be lonely, and requires that people be able to perform major life chores for themselves, rather than relying on a spouse (Bernikow, 1982). Many youngsters whose parents both work have to be more self-reliant (remember Bronfenbrenner's "latch key children" in Exhibit 5–2). It is not always easy to think beyond the familiar, and to lay aside one's own values in order to recognize and accept new life styles. Yet carrying out social welfare's commitment to society demands such responses from social welfare professionals.

Changing life styles can have considerable social repercussions. Falling birth rates have made some grade schools superfluous in many communities. Singles have different housing needs than do families. Less enduring family units may need a more highly developed support structure to provide counseling, income maintenance, and child-care services. Legal changes may be needed to protect people as they enter into new types of relationships and new kinds of contracts: "palimony," negotiating leases among two unmarried people living together, child custody and visitation arrangements, and the rights of partners in committed relationships outside of marriage are all examples. These kinds of issues touch the very heart of society's basic social institutions and can be expected to generate anxiety and hostility until they are better understood. It is the task of social welfare professionals to ensure that this interpretation process continues.

In a society that believes that people have the right to select their own life styles as long as they do not hurt others, social welfare must continue to advocate freedom of choice. Social welfare professionals need not endorse the choices people make in order to support their right to make them. The more societal change occurs on a planned basis, the more likely it will be that individuals will have fewer problems adjusting. As we have already seen, social welfare can help generate planned-change efforts and help people understand and respond to them.

Changing Regional Relationships

Try answering the following questions:

1. What metropolitan area in the United States has the highest per-capita income?
2. What metropolitan area has the highest per-capita local government expenditures?

3. What metropolitan area has the highest percentage of its population on welfare (defined as AFDC and SSI)?
4. What metropolitan area has the highest percentage of blacks in its population?

You may be surprised at the answers. In order, they are Casper, Wyoming, resulting from mineral wealth ($12,842, compared with $7,330 for the nation as a whole); New York City ($1,535, versus $778 for the nation); Visalia, California (15.9 percent, versus 6.4 percent for the nation); and Albany, Georgia (40.8 percent, versus 11.7 percent for the nation) (Herbers, 1982b). Although Albany has the highest percentage of blacks, the New York City area has the largest number (almost 2 million), along with the second-largest number of Hispanic people (Los Angeles has the largest number). Sarasota, Florida, has the largest percentage of people sixty-five or older (30 percent), whereas in Anchorage, Alaska, the percentage was the lowest (2 percent). Alaska has the highest average pay at $25,350, whereas Vermont and Maine had among the lowest, at $12,000–13,000 (*The New York Times*, 1982a).

These data, supported by much more from the 1980 Census, demonstrate that the nation is becoming more diverse (Herbers, 1982c). As we already saw, immigrant populations have tended to cluster in certain cities. The elderly have drifted toward Florida and the Southwest. Young people have moved out of depressed industrial areas of the Northeast and the Midwest and moved to California and the Southwest, where they hope there will be more economic opportunity. Table 7-1 summarizes some of these regional differences.

The result has been shifting needs and resources that are addressed differently in different regions. The Reagan administration's efforts to shift decision making and financial responsibility to the states has reduced the federal role in smoothing out regional differences. The issue of responsibility is an important one. The growth of the role of the federal government in social welfare occurred in part because of significant regional differences in services. Regional differences often reflected regional values. For example, the Southern states were least responsive to the needs of blacks, and the Southwest has tended to have minimal standards for social welfare benefits (King, 1982). As the nation becomes more diverse, the need continues for some type of system to ensure that citizens are treated fairly, regardless of where they live. Unfortunately, the actions of the Reagan administration retreated from this goal.

TABLE 7–1   The New Face of Regionalism

The 1980 Census showed that major cities in the South and West were doing significantly better than cities in the North, as measured by such indicators as income, employment, and racial patterns. The data also showed that suburbs throughout the country continue to grow and prosper at the cost of central cities.

The State of the Cities: 22 Major Metropolitan Areas

| | % change in pop., 1970–80 | RACIAL COMPOSITION (Percentage of population) | | | Median annual household income | % of pop. aged 65 or older | Married couples with children as a % of all households |
		White	Black	Hispanic			
THE NORTH							
New York	−10.4%	60.7%	25.2%	19.9%	$13,855	13.5%	18.6%
Suburbs	−1.4	89.0	7.6	0.4	23,740	12.2	31.1
Chicago	−10.8	49.6	39.8	14.0	15,301	11.4	20.3
Suburbs	+13.6	90.8	5.6	3.9	24,811	8.7	23.5
Philadelphia	−13.4	58.2	37.8	3.7	13,169	14.0	19.5
Suburbs	+5.4	89.8	8.1	1.7	20,940	10.4	33.0
Detroit	−20.5	34.3	63.0	0.2	13,981	11.7	18.7
Suburbs	+7.8	94.1	4.2	0.1	24,038	8.7	34.8
Baltimore	−13.1	43.9	54.8	1.0	12,811	12.8	17.8
Suburbs	+19.1	89.2	9.0	1.0	22,272	8.6	34.0
Indianapolis	−4.9	77.1	21.8	0.9	17,279	10.3	26.5
Suburbs	+24.5	98.3	1.0	0.5	26,854	9.0	39.2

TABLE 7-1 (Cont.)

	% change in pop., 1970–80	RACIAL COMPOSITION (Percentage of population)			Median annual household income	% of pop. aged 65 or older	Married couples with children as a % of all households
		White	Black	Hispanic			
THE NORTH (cont.)							
Washington	−15.7	26.8	70.3	2.7	16,211	11.6	11.8
Suburbs	+12.5	78.5	16.7	3.1	25,728	6.4	32.4
Milwaukee	−11.3	73.3	23.1	4.1	16,061	12.4	21.5
Suburbs	+10.8	98.4	0.5	1.0	23,805	10.0	37.5
Cleveland	−23.6	53.6	43.8	2.9	12,277	12.9	19.7
Suburbs	+0.9	91.8	7.1	0.6	22,024	11.2	31.3
Columbus, Ohio	+4.6	76.2	22.1	0.8	14,834	8.8	22.6
Suburbs	+10.6	97.4	1.9	0.5	20,604	8.7	37.8
Boston	−12.2	69.9	22.4	6.4	12,500	12.6	14.6
Suburbs	−2.6	96.6	1.6	1.5	20,469	11.9	30.3
THE SOUTH AND WEST							
Los Angeles	+5.5	61.2	17.0	27.5	15,746	10.6	21.1
Suburbs	+7.2	71.9	9.6	28.9	19,410	9.1	33.4
Houston	+29.2	61.3	27.6	17.6	18,474	6.9	26.1
Suburbs	+71.2	86.3	6.7	10.9	24,847	5.4	44.1

Dallas	+ 7.1	61.4	29.4	12.3	16,227	9.5	21.9
Suburbs	+47.9	92.2	3.9	5.3	21,301	6.9	39.2
San Diego	+25.5	75.4	8.9	14.8	16,409	9.7	23.1
Suburbs	+49.4	85.9	2.6	14.6	17,808	10.7	29.2
San Antonio	+20.1	78.6	7.3	53.6	13,775	9.6	32.0
Suburbs	+22.4	88.1	5.2	23.4	19,452	7.7	41.0
Phoenix	+30.9	84.0	4.9	15.1	17,419	9.6	29.1
Suburbs	+92.1	89.4	1.4	11.2	18,085	13.6	28.8
San Francisco	– 5.1	58.3	12.7	12.2	15,867	9.2	13.0
Suburbs	+10.0	81.1	6.5	10.6	22,375	14.1	27.0
Memphis	+ 3.6	51.6	47.6	—	14,040	10.4	23.4
Suburbs	+26.9	77.8	21.0	1.0	18,753	6.8	43.2
San Jose, Calif.	+38.4	73.9	4.6	22.0	22,886	6.1	35.2
Suburbs	+ 8.8	83.1	2.1	13.0	23,832	8.8	26.5
New Orleans	– 6.1	46.2	55.3	—	11,834	11.7	19.4
Suburbs	+38.9	85.4	12.6	—	19,678	7.1	36.8
Jacksonville, Fla.	+ 7.3	73.0	25.4	—	14,426	9.6	27.4
Suburbs	+67.2	88.3	10.7	—	16,084	9.6	34.3

Source: "The state of the cities: 22 major metropolitan areas," *The New York Times*, February 28, 1983. © 1983 by The New York Times Company. Reprinted by permission.
Selected characteristics from census reports. Median household income is for 1979.

The Contribution of Social Welfare

If people had perfect freedom of movement, and if the land held uniform resources, perhaps regional differences could be allowed to flourish unimpeded. If people were unhappy, they could move easily, and every geographical area would offer equal opportunities for development. Neither condition is true, however. People cannot move at will—many cannot afford it, or they have family or job ties. And there are considerable geographical differences. Some communities are struggling with the problems associated with becoming boom towns because of their wealth of mineral resources. Others face severe problems associated with climate, pollution, and lack of water that may leave them ghost towns; an example is the fate of Times Beach, Missouri, whose land was poisoned by the chemical Dioxin. Having become uninhabitable, the entire town had to be bought by the federal government and its inhabitants relocated. Allowing individual communities to struggle alone with these problems is not likely to produce solutions. It is very likely, however, to create competition among communities and increase the human suffering of their residents. We also have to acknowledge that when problems arise in individual communities or regions they eventually affect the whole society. For example, problems encountered by Cuban and Haitian refugees in southern Florida created nationwide efforts to help resettle them. Experience has also shown that civil rights issues can only be successfully addressed at the national level (see Exhibit 7–2 in the "Reflections on Social Welfare" section at the end of the chapter).

Regions cannot prosper at the expense of each other. A national economy cannot be strong if part of it is crippled, no matter how strong the other parts may be. Moreover, just as *international* migration occurs as people try to escape misery and seek opportunity, so does *internal* migration. People move from region to region in search of jobs and opportunities (King, 1982). This movement has drained resources from regions that need them to rebuild, while flooding other regions beyond their capacity to provide jobs or social welfare help. As a result, many people have become stranded and homeless.

Social welfare professionals have to continue their traditional efforts to improve social welfare services in each state so that regional disparities are minimized. We must develop services and provide for *all* citizens, regardless of minority status. At the same time, the federal government must reassert itself and vigorously enforce fairness in

Our technology sometimes creates more problems than solutions.
These researchers found such high levels of the toxic chemical
dioxin in the soil of Times Beach, Missouri, that the entire town
had to be evacuated. (Owen Franken/Sygma)

every state and every region. We must resist, as vigorously as possible, efforts to weaken laws and the regulations that implement them. This nation must create a social welfare system, with as much uniformity as possible, that protects everyone equally from the ravages of destructive social forces.

Beyond these activities focused on issues of service delivery, social welfare professionals should resist myths that glorify some regions over others. Climate is only one factor in assessing attractiveness. Pollution, overcrowding, adequate housing and transportation, safe and plentiful water, and closeness to loved ones are also considerations. No region of the United States has everything. Instead, each region has a unique combination of climate, resources, and opportunities, as well as cultural riches contributed by the ethnic and racial groups that live there. When people can see the nation as a patchwork of different but equally valuable and equally appealing regions, the cooperation that is badly needed may finally replace the competition that recent federal government policies have encouraged.

Issues of Accountability

Social welfare as an institution depends on a societal mandate. Unless society believes that social welfare services are effective, it is not likely to support them. This need for support calls for ways of demonstrating efficiency and effectiveness of services in order to justify their continued existence. However, the need for accountability goes well beyond satisfying society's decision makers. The very heart of professionalism is the commitment to quality service delivery and the responsibility to monitor procedures within each social welfare profession, in order to assure competent practice (MacNair et al., 1982).

Accountability became a particularly serious issue during the Reagan administration. The administration threatened to reduce federal funds in proportion to the number of claims paid in error by states in the Aid to Families with Dependent Children, Food Stamp, and Medicaid programs (*Washington Social Legislation Bulletin*, 1982a). Even before Reagan, erroneous welfare payments had been an issue, and in 1980 regulations were issued to force states to reduce errors or lose some of the federal monies that they received for the programs. Although error rates were not high (see Table 7–2), there has been a steady push to reduce them, with little recognition of the difficulty of doing so. In part, this reflects the myth that most people who receive financial aid are cheaters. The truth is that most errors result from rapid changes in the programs themselves, the inability of many recipients to speak English fluently or to understand the technicalities of the programs, or the fact that "some recipients are already overwhelmed with trying to deal with children and poverty" (*Washington Social Legislation Bulletin*, 1982a:154).

The issue of accountability has taken a different path in the medical-care field. There the concern is with quality assurance, meaning the adequacy of the staff and program structures providing services, the quality of the methods used to provide services, the effectiveness of services, the quantity of services in relationship to the needs, and the availability of services to those needing them (Coulton, 1982). In the medical-care field, the creation of Professional Standards Review Organizations (PSROs) and the activities of the Joint Commission on the Accreditation of Hospitals have been significant for quality-assurance efforts. Title XX of the Social Security Act emphasized accountability in the mental-health field, and service providers who seek third-party reimbursement also have to demonstrate effectiveness in some way. Unfortunately, there has been little effort to coordinate or standardize accountability efforts among these various groups, regulations, and pieces of legislation (Coulton, 1982).

Focusing on error rates rather than quality assurance is a very different approach to accountability. Indeed, the issue of accountability has been an extremely difficult one because of the many ways it can be approached:

> During the last decade the dual pressures on the human service administrator to provide an atmosphere for (the professional's) professional autonomy while at the same time documenting the outcome of services have become increasingly evident. These pressures have increased the number and the degree of conflicts between the administrators and clinical workers. The foci of the conflicts are: the (professional)/client relationship, which is governed by professional values, such as autonomy, confidentiality, dignity, and respect for the client; techniques of practice; and the administrator's need to monitor the quality and quantity of services rendered (MacNair et al., 1982).

The potential for conflict between those who provide services and those who administer the service agencies is evident. Administrators must meet criteria established by outside funding agencies, usually by providing data about service delivery. Although they recognize the importance of continued funding, those providing services often feel overwhelmed by the techniques used to collect data, believing that these mandatory procedures reduce the time they have to spend with users of services. Also, their concern is more likely to be assessing their own service delivery effectiveness rather than the number of cases opened or closed during some period of time. Thus, although everyone seems to agree that accountability is important, little agreement exists on how to measure effectiveness. The need to effectively address the different aspects of social welfare services and service delivery of primary concern to funding sources, agency administrators, practitioners, and users of services is a still-elusive goal.

A hidden factor in issues of accountability is the impact of values. Decisions about criteria to use in determining successful service delivery reflect value judgments about what is important and how it can be measured. If success is defined as a closed case rather than as people improving their resources, a value judgment is being made about *what* is more important. When professional people themselves decide about the adequacy of a given service and end intervention on that basis, rather than according to the user's perceptions, a value judgment is made about *how* to determine service adequacy and accountability. Exhibit 7–3 in the "Reflections on Social Welfare" section at the

TABLE 7–2   Welfare Fraud

Although error rates for AFDC, food stamps, and Medicaid have been low, the federal government has continued to push states to lower them even further. Failure to do so results in loss of some federal matching monies. The error rates shown here are for the period April–September 1980.

Error Rates
[In percentages]

State	AFDC	Medicaid	Food stamps
Alabama	7.6	6.5	7.9
Alaska	14.4	9.6	13.3
Arizona	9.5	N.A.	10.7
Arkansas	6.1	4.4	6.5
California	5.1	N.A.	7.8
Colorado	13.3	10.3	8.8
Connecticut	6.2	6.7	10.3
Delaware	7.9	5.9	7.5
District of Columbia	10.5	13.3	11.5
Florida	5.8	8.1	8.6
Georgia	7.8	9.5	8.8
Hawaii	9.2	5.4	4.2
Idaho	11.8	4.7	10.0
Illinois	6.9	3.2	7.9
Indiana	4.6	1.7	6.8
Iowa	3.8	5.9	8.1
Kansas	7.4	3.4	9.2
Kentucky	4.7	3.2	6.3
Louisiana	7.2	3.5	7.6
Maine	7.3	9.8	8.0
Maryland	12.7	2.4	14.5
Massachusetts	8.2	9.5	9.9
Michigan	7.3	4.5	10.1
Minnesota	2.3	2.3	6.3
Mississippi	6.9	1.8	10.6
Missouri	5.9	4.5	8.0
Montana	11.2	12.7	10.2
Nebraska	4.3	4.8	10.1
Nevada	2.3	2.6	3.1

TABLE 7-2 *(Cont.)*

State	Error Rates [In percentages]		
	AFDC	Medicaid	Food stamps
New Hampshire	11.1	7.6	8.4
New Jersey	9.3	3.1	7.5
New Mexico	8.2	4.2	12.5
New York	9.7	4.1	14.8
North Carolina	4.8	7.2	9.3
North Dakota	4.7	2.6	7.9
Ohio	8.7	4.2	9.1
Oklahoma	4.8	2.5	6.4
Oregon	4.0	3.0	9.1
Pennsylvania	8.0	N.A.	6.4
Rhode Island	9.7	4.4	12.3
South Carolina	6.9	5.9	9.5
South Dakota	6.8	1.9	8.3
Tennessee	7.0	2.7	10.5
Texas	7.8	3.1	7.2
Utah	5.5	7.0	11.5
Vermont	11.4	8.0	8.9
Virginia	4.7	2.4	8.1
Washington	9.1	1.6	7.9
West Virginia	6.9	2.0	7.3
Wisconsin	7.6	N.A.	8.6
Wyoming	16.4	N.A.	10.0
Guam	N.A.	N.A.	8.4
Puerto Rico	10.3	N.A.	7.6
Virgin Islands	5.4	N.A.	12.2
Total (weighted average)	7.3	4.7	8.9

Source: House Ways and Means Committee Data. These data appeared in the *Washington Social Legislation Bulletin*, Volume 27, Issue 39 (August 9, 1982), p. 155.

end of the chapter illustrates the impact of values on what and how accountability is determined. In evaluating the effectiveness of services to Native American families, removing the child is seen by the service-delivery network as successful intervention (the how), and the number of children so removed as an indicator of success (the what). Therefore, from the service-delivery network's point of view, these services are successful, even though the Indian children and families may evaluate them quite differently. Only if the users of services are the ultimate evaluators of services can this situation be changed, but this method is itself value related. Service users will not be involved in evaluation and accountability procedures if the users are seen as ignorant, demanding, or strange. When the diversity of human experience is recognized and valued, accountability may take on new meaning in social welfare.

The Contribution of Social Welfare

The contemporary thrust toward efficiency and effectiveness is good. If social welfare professionals seek to improve social functioning and minimize suffering, they must have some techniques to measure whether or not their actions are accomplishing these goals. If they are not, they will have to find new ways of dealing with people's needs. With limited resources available to the social welfare institution, professionals must use these resources in the most effective manner. The accusation that there has been too much emphasis on process (what was done) rather than results (what was accomplished) is a valid one. Yet the fact remains that it is very difficult to measure effectiveness in many cases, and more efficient alternatives are often unknown. Sometimes the professional simply has to rely on the best-known treatment, whether in microsurgery, treating mental illness with medication, or selecting counseling techniques. Much more scientifically validated research needs to be done before we know whether artificial hearts will work, whether the death penalty controls crime, whether psychotherapy prevents suicide, and how much impact government policy has on poverty and related social problems.

Another strategy for improving accountability while linking it more closely to professional goals and values is to involve users of service. Participation can occur on at least two levels. The first is participation in planning, something that is rarely done. The hierarchical and specialized nature of bureaucracies makes it difficult for users of services to have input into the service-delivery structure. Bureaucracies that operate within a market system are presumed to permit user feedback through decisions to use or not use the service offered. However, many social welfare service areas are not provided in a market system. Children needing foster homes cannot choose the agency that will place them, nor can patients with a life-threatening medical emergency choose the hospital that will care for them. For this reason, many kinds of social welfare services are called monopolies.

Social welfare monopolies have several problems (Reid, 1972:47):

1. Organizations not accountable to consumers often define service goals vaguely or not at all. When the goals are unclear the means to attain them cannot be precisely defined and often change.
2. Lacking accountability to consumers, organizations may allocate energy and resources in a way that is not consistent with the needs of service users. Because the organization is presumed to be worth preserving, it spends an inordinate amount of energy preserving itself rather than serving its users.
3. Clients (users) tend to be defined as irresponsible. With the emphasis of the organization so clearly internal, the demands of users are seen as threats to the organization's goals, and therefore tend to be resisted. One way to do this is to rationalize user demands as irresponsible.
4. Workers get caught between their professional values, client demands, and organizational structure, becoming alienated from the agency and seen as adversaries by clients.

Reid goes on to suggest some strategies for the reform of the social welfare monopoly:

1. *Strengthen the influence of professionals within the organization and in service-planning contexts.* This strategy encounters one of the problems with professions themselves. Chapter 2 noted that they are built on a specialized knowledge base, and are characterized by professional autonomy and self-regulation. This can result in professionals being detached from the people they serve, because by definition users lack the specialized knowledge with which to evaluate the service they are receiving from the professional. This potential for professional isolation from its users can serve to reinforce the monopolistic tendencies with social welfare delivery systems.

2. *Develop countervailing power, that is, develop power structures that clients can use to have an impact on social welfare delivery systems.* An example would be the National Welfare Rights Organization.

There are obvious problems in the development of countervailing power. Users run the risk that they will be excluded from the services they may desperately need, and frequently educational and financial resources with which to develop viable countervailing power structures are inadequate. An additional problem with the use of this strategy is the possibility that clients may use their power unwisely in terms of selecting services. However, as in all aspects of the helping situation, sometimes the right to assume responsibility for one's own life entails making mistakes as part of the growth process.

3. *Create competing services, thereby allowing users to have an impact on the service-delivery system by selecting the services they feel are most helpful.* This is the last strategy discussed by Reid and would most directly strike at the monopolistic character of the social welfare delivery system. It could be operated through a system of vouchers that clients could use in whatever agency they wished. Because any agency, public or private, must at some point justify its existence in order to obtain resources, lack of selection by users would presumably seriously undermine an agency's ability to justify itself. This strategy would require that there be a meaningful choice of services for each need, so that someone needing income maintenance would be able to select from two or more agencies. This could result in a proliferation of agencies, and raises interesting possibilities for the use of advertising by social welfare agencies in order to attract users. Were this to be the case, the problems an uninformed consumer has in selecting wisely among alternative and highly advertised commercial products could invade the social welfare field. Obviously, any strategy to reduce the disadvantages of a monopolistic social welfare delivery system will have its own set of problems and disadvantages, but they are worth thinking about in the quest for more efficient and effective services.

The Future of the Social Welfare Professions

Obviously, the social welfare institution is shaped by policy decisions made in political structures and in private-agency board rooms. Yet the social welfare professions themselves also have a significant impact on the structure of social welfare. They train their members and develop standards for evaluating their work. They develop and support values that they seek to implement in the larger societal decision-making arena. They provide daily, concrete, social welfare services in ways that either help or do not help those in need. They interact with other social institutions and nonwelfare professionals to generate support for their goals. In a complex, competitive society, social welfare professions are responsible for fighting for more adequate attainment of social welfare objectives. In order to carry out all of these functions, the social welfare professions themselves must be strong and must have clearly defined objectives and methods. The future of social welfare includes the future of the social welfare professions. Let us now examine several issues that will have an impact on the future of these professions.

Changing Models of Professionalism

In the past, increasing professionalism was thought to lead to better professional service, but that assumption is now being questioned (Galper, 1974). Professions have always claimed the right to be relatively autonomous. Working from the assumption that they were dedicated to public service, they claimed the right to formalize their own values, to identify their own objectives based on these values, to codify a specialized knowledge base, and to translate this knowledge into specialized practice principles and techniques. These principles emphasized the profession as a self-monitoring one, thereby protecting it from intervention by outsiders not oriented toward public service or not knowledgeable about the complexities of providing helping services. By creating a group of cohesive, organized professionals, professions could become countervailing forces to work for changes in social policy that would improve the quality of life for America's citizens. The American Medical Association is often used as a model professional organization—strong, politically active, and effective in controlling standards of medical training and practice.

Against these advantages, some significant disadvantages of the professional model must be weighed. Highly organized professions can become elite groups with the power to protect their own interests. The same countervailing power that can be used to fight for needed social change can also be used to resist it if it threatens the profession's power. The American Medical Association has been heavily criticized for resisting national health insurance, for example. The Association argues that it will reduce the quality of medical service. Others argue that it may weaken the Association's power over what is currently a virtual medical monopoly, thereby improving service but weakening the organization. The point is that professional power can be used in many ways. If the assumption of public service turns out to be incorrect, professional power may be used to generate or perpetuate professional and personal privilege rather than improved social welfare services. Even the assumption of a public-service function has been questioned. Who should have the right to decide what is "public service"? Should a public assistance recipient decide what services he or she needs, or should a skilled professional make that decision? Should the medical profession decide that life should always be preserved as long as possible, or should each individual decide that for oneself? Should psychiatrists decide when a person is mentally healthy, or should the individual have some say in the determination? The power vested in professions to make very important decisions about what people ought or ought not do, what services ought or ought not be available, what groups should receive services or should be excluded, obviously affects the access that people have to social welfare services. If powerful professions are trying to protect themselves rather than concentrating at all times on service to the public, then their right to make these decisions should be questioned.

Even the professional's right to select knowledge and develop interventive methods based on that knowledge has been questioned. Some would question the validity of social science as a basis for understanding human behavior, for example. Movies portraying scientifically grounded behavior modification as an uncontrollable monster with inhuman effects raise this point. Being "objective" in dealing with people's problems has also been criticized as being a dehumanizing approach to helping. Providing helping services in large, centralized bureaucratic settings has generated resistance and resentment. Most important of all, accusations have been made that social welfare professions simply attempt to control people so that they will accept the existing social system, rather than attempting to change it to make it more responsive to human needs (Piven and Cloward, 1971; Bell, 1983). Here again, professional autonomy is at issue: Should people participate in decisions about the kinds of service they are to receive? Should there be free clinics and neighborhood service centers rather than huge, isolated service structures? Should social welfare professionals be avowedly in the business of societal reform? Who controls the social welfare professions, and whose interest do they really represent? Exhibit 7–4 in the "Reflections on Social Welfare" at the end of the chapter illustrates some of these issues.

The issues are reasonably clear, but the solutions are much less so. The historical development of social welfare has shown that providing helping services to people requires much more than good intentions.

It requires training, resources, and societal support. It also requires a commitment to helping, and a set of values that supports this commitment in practice. Professions are structures for providing such training, for obtaining and effectively using resources, and for developing ways of operationalizing commitment effectively. A profession must have some degree of self-protection simply because there are many competing structures in society fighting for the same social resources. The question becomes one of finding a level at which the profession can protect itself and still be open to input from the users of its services. It must not become so preoccupied with its own interests that it becomes disengaged from the needs of those it serves.

It is naive to want professions and professional organizations to be totally responsive to users, and to have as their primary mission the reform of society. The professions and their users are much too dependent on society's mandate and resources to be able to challenge directly the existing social structure. However, professional commitment requires a more just society. This suggests that the professionals of the future must be astute political actors who can work within the existing social structure to use available resources and yet still find and use opportunities to affect social policy. They must also live by their democratic values and involve the users of services in decision making about those services. Yet they must continue to use their specialized training, in order to have their own input into decision making. As has been said many times earlier in this book, the social welfare professional of the future will have to be involved in far more than a peaceful nine-to-five schedule.

Specialization and Integration

Two trends seem to emerge from current thinking about the future of social welfare practice. The changing shape of society itself has created an increasing need for integrative kinds of services. Society has become so complex and is changing so quickly that people can easily become lost. At the same time, many kinds of specialized services help people function more effectively. The task is to help people find the services they need, and to help them understand the procedures necessary for obtaining these services. This calls for an integrative function within social welfare, including outreach, brokerage, mobilization, advocacy, and supportive activities. All help to individualize social welfare services, making them more accessible to those who need them.

Kahn and Kamerman conclude, after an extensive study of the social-service systems of eight countries,

> There also may be evidence of convergence on the need for a "generalist" practitioner or team at the core of the local service system. The picture remains mixed, but some countries do not see the possibility of a comprehensive and universal program unless there is at the front line, offering the core service, a person or unit with scope and range, not too tied to one intervention strategy or one type of response to need (Kahn and Kamerman, 1976:368).

They define as follows the minimal baseline social-services functions that such a generalist worker would perform in the course of serving all population groups (Kahn and Kamerman, 1976:369):

1. Giving information and advice and making referrals about all of the social sector (human services, in the broadest sense).

2. Giving access to a range of social-care services which enable handicapped, frail elderly, and disturbed people to remain in community living under some protection and with needed services and resources.

3. Providing front-line counseling, if only on a simple level.

4. Coping with emergency daytime, afterhour, and weekend needs for housing, food, protection, institutionalization for the vulnerable aged, children, the mentally ill, and others—whether directly or by access to other community service personnel.

5. Carrying out appropriate ongoing treatment, including efforts in individualized, group and residential contexts to bring about changes in adjustment, functioning, view of self or others.

6. Providing case integration, assuring that sequential service . . . or work with different family members within the personal-general social services or between programs in different systems . . . is mutually supportive and properly meshed.

A recent baccalaureate social-work curriculum development project in this country reached similar conclusions about the functions of the entry-level professional practitioner in social work (Baer and Federico, 1978), and the concept of holistic medicine captures the same idea.

The generalist is well suited to perform integrating functions as described in the previous paragraph, and is therefore a vital member of the professional team. However, as medicine discovered some time ago, a need also exists for specialists to deal with certain kinds of especially difficult and complex problems. Social-work education appears to be moving in this direction by beginning to identify two levels of training: generalist training at the bachelor's level, and specialized training at the graduate level. A specialist might deal with something like services to the deaf, in which the ability to sign (that is, use manual symbols in place of speech) must be learned, as well as a great deal of highly technical knowledge about the causes of deafness, levels of deafness, and the relationship between levels of deafness and levels of social functioning. A generalist might assist a specialist in making use of the range of services available to a deaf family in a community (schooling, recreational services, vocational rehabilitation, and so on), and might make contact with significant nondeaf persons, such as teachers and neighbors. The specialist would provide the major ongoing service to the deaf person or family being helped.

The issue of specialized and integrated services can be related to the earlier discussion of models of professionalism. Service structures that combine generalists and specialists may maximize the professional's specialized training at the same time that it maximizes professional involvement in and awareness of user needs. As generalists seek to identify and develop services to meet needs, and deal with the problems of co-ordinating many kinds of services in a community, they are sensitized to issues in service delivery and have contact with a range of user groups. They can provide a valuable mechanism for organizing users so that they can participate in professional decision making. At the same time, the specialist draws upon knowledge and skills identified by the profession as appropriate for specific problem areas.

Professional Priority Setting

However the issue of professional autonomy versus user input is resolved, the professions must not lose their ability to affect social policy. The social welfare professions are intimately acquainted with human need and problems in the structures developed to meet those needs. They must constantly provide data to support the need for more adequate services, and participate in the political processes out of which societal decisions emerge. America can become a welfare state in the best sense of that term—a society in which all members have opportunities to develop fully and function effectively, with services available to assist them when needed and desired. It is a basic responsibility of the helping professions to make sure that America's priorities are humane priorities. Society's primary function is to provide services and resources for its members. Society must serve, and social welfare professionals must help it to understand and achieve the most effective ways of serving. This can occur only if they participate in decision making at the national, state, county, city, neighborhood, and organizational levels. Without a societal decision to give priority to social welfare needs, the social welfare professions will not be able to function effectively. In this basic sense, the future of social welfare must lie in societal priorities that make comprehensive social welfare services possible.

SUMMARY

Achieving changes in social values sometimes seems a hopeless task. Although there is no question that the social welfare structure is solidly institutionalized in the United States, this book points out that adequate services are still needed in many areas. Certain basic social values must be changed if these needed services are ever to be feasible. The perspective of history is encouraging. When one thinks of the centuries it took to achieve the breakthrough of the Social Security Act, the lesson is clear—social change is slow and tedious. This country has made progress in social welfare. We do care for others in ways and at levels unthinkable not too many years ago. Yet we as a society still value individualism, discrimination, and laissez-faire capitalism, and these values often conflict with social welfare goals. Any projection that attempts to predict the resolution of this conflict would require a prediction about the future of the society. This is an impossible and perhaps sterile task. What the issue of value change in the future does suggest in a practical way is that all of us, as citizens, will affect the values of the future. Values are made and can be changed. If we as human beings, citizens, and social welfare practitioners believe in certain values, we must fight for their adoption. It is a worthwhile project for the future, for each of us.

It always comes down to us. *We* are "society." We are the social welfare system. We are human beings. We make our own decisions. The study of social welfare is so inspiring because it calls on us to assume the responsibility of our human heritage by using ourselves to make the life of everyone better. It involves us totally: our feelings, our values, our ability to think, learn, and reason. It can be a life-encompassing task, or a part of other tasks. But it is there. The future? I hope that here, at the end of this book, the future presents itself to you in a different way from before. I hope that you see it as rich with many opportunities, theoretical and practical. Most of all, I hope you see it as an active challenge to assume the responsibility for making everyone's social welfare a part of your life.

REFLECTIONS ON SOCIAL WELFARE

This section contains four exhibits, each of which addresses issues related to the contemporary needs of one of four groups: retired or disabled workers and their families, minorities of color, Native Americans, and gay men. Together they provide thoughtful perspectives on some of the future social welfare needs of members of our society.

EXHIBIT 7–1　A Different Approach to Reforming Social Security

The following essay was written by John F. O'Neill, Dean of Eastern Washington University's Inland Empire School of Social Work and Human Services. It looks at a possible strategy for reforming the OASDI program rather than simply revising various tax or benefit levels.

The debate over means to save the Social Security system has focused on strategies for implementing two alternatives: 1) reducing the benefits and 2) increasing the Social Security tax. A third alternative has received little discussion or attention: using general tax funds to meet the cost of benefits.

Strategies under the first alternative include eliminating the cost of living increases, linking cost of living increases to wage levels rather than the consumer price index, raising the retirement age, and adding a means test. The second alternative can be achieved by increasing the Social Security tax rate and/or by raising the level of taxable income. Former Social Security Administrator, Robert Ball, suggests income tax credits might be allowed to cushion the impact of payroll tax increases on workers' spendable income (a step in the right direction).

Arguments for alternative three, using general tax funds to finance Social Security benefits, are made by economists such as The Brookings Institute's John A. Brittain. Their concerns are tax equity; contribution to economic stability; and factors of efficiency, incentives, and growth. Another rationale for alternative three is that the Social Security Trust Fund has been used for

John F. O'Neill, "Saving Social Security," *Newsletter* of the Inland Empire School of Social Work and Human Services (Cheney, Wash.: Eastern Washington University), Vol. 6, No. 1 (Fall 1982).

welfare purposes, i.e., it has been used to avoid meeting certain welfare needs through public assistance programs, financed through general tax funds. Repeatedly, the Social Security Trust Fund has been raided, its integrity impaired by providing benefits to retirees, survivors, and dependents who had contributed to it only minimally. Now that the program is maturing, the benefits of workers who will have contributed for 40, 50, or more years are threatened as a result of political decisions made almost annually since 1938.

On Franklin D. Roosevelt's insistence, the 1935 Social Security Act provided for a "fully funded reserve." That is, the trust fund would at all times have sufficient resources to pay all contracted claims, like fully funded private endowment or life insurance. FDR wanted to establish the *right* to benefits so that "no damn politician" in the future could deprive workers of their benefits.

The plan for a fully funded reserve was controversial from the start. Opponents feared it would create a trust fund too large for the government or the economy to handle. The transformation from a fully funded reserve to pay-as-you-go system occurred over a period of several years, sometimes purposely and sometimes serendipitously.

In 1937 Senator Vandenberg (R-Michigan) introduced a resolution calling for abandonment of the fully funded reserve. The first steps in this direction were taken in the 1939 amendments which changed the Social Security program from one aimed at replacing part of the wage loss occurring through retirement at old age, to a family security program—it added survivors and dependents. In this and subsequent amendments the program was broadened in coverage and increased in benefits without raising the tax rate. Scheduled increases of the payroll tax on employees and employers were repeatedly postponed from 1939 to 1950, when the tax was increased from 1% to 1½%. By that time prospects for a fully funded reserve were gone forever.

The integrity of the trust fund as the sole source for benefit payments has been weakened by paying benefits to many who have not "earned" benefits through lifelong contributions. Changes in the Social Security Act contributing to this include: liberalization of the retirement test; liberalization of requirements for attachment to the labor force; allowing credits for military service; provisions for benefits for survivors of certain WW II veterans; reduction in the benefit age for dependent wives, retirees, and widows; special benefits for persons over age 72; lower tax rates for the self-employed than that paid by employer and employee; and others. As the law has been amended to bring new groups into coverage, provisions have been made to cover even those who were near retirement. Most notable was the 1950 "new start," which changed the system for computing entitlement. Full retirement benefits are, and have been, paid to many people who contributed to the trust fund as few as six quarters (1½ years).

Liberalization of the Social Security Act has made it unnecessary for many retirees, disabled workers, dependents, and survivors to apply for public assistance. They were not pauperized by the poor-law provisions of P.A.; they received benefits to which they *felt* they had a right. The fiscal effect was to save general tax funds and to deplete the Social Security Trust Funds. Viewed more harshly, the effect was to transfer responsibility of the general welfare of society to the backs of workers who contributed to the Social Security Trust Fund.

Using general tax funds to pay Social Security benefits is not a new idea. In 1938 the Social Security Advisory Committee recommended that as coverage was broadened, financing of the system should be borne by approximately equal contributions from employers, employees, and the general fund. Recognizing that the expansion of the program might place an inordinate drain on the reserve funds, Congress authorized appropriations to the trust fund from the general treasury in 1944. No funds were ever appropriated under this provision; the authorization was repealed in 1950. Small sums have been transferred from the general fund to the Social Security Trust Fund to reimburse for some special benefits to persons over age 72 who did not contribute to the program.

It may be hoped that the National Commission on Social Security Reform, the Congress, and the President will take a step now which was recognized as desirable 35 years ago and by so doing avoid further tax and benefit inequity.

EXHIBIT 7–2   Civil Rights: A National Issue

Regionalism often breeds its own particular brand of prejudice and discrimination. The South historically discriminated against blacks, feelings against Mexicans and Asians surfaced in parts of California, Puerto Ricans encountered discrimination in New York, and Cubans faced hostility in Southern Florida. Experience has shown that leadership from the federal government has been critical for overcoming these regional prejudices. In the quotes that follow, leaders of various minority groups express their opinions about the current state of federal enforcement of civil rights legislation.

John E. Jacob, President of the National Urban League:

Because full equality of opportunity is still far from being reached, the frozen nature of civil rights progress is disturbing. It is puzzling to many Americans that back in 1957 a President who never once spoke out in favor of desegregating the schools sent soldiers to enforce desegregation at the point of bayonets, while in 1982 a President pays a humane visit to the victims of Klan cross-burners but also helps the notorious segregation academies get tax-exemptions. . . .

Affirmative action . . . has been twisted and distorted out of all recognition by its opponents, who now include the Federal department (Justice) responsible for protecting the constitutional rights of minorities.

Virtually all civil rights actions of the past have been subjected to neglect and to pressures to dilute their effect; housing discrimination is still rampant, absent amendments enforcing the law, affirmative action programs are dor-

Source: Perspectives: The Civil Rights Quarterly (Summer 1982), pp. 42–46, published by the U. S. Commission on Civil Rights.

mant, absent strong enforcement measures, school desegregation is still far from a reality in many parts of the country. . . .

Raul Yzaguirre, President of the National Council of La Raza:

For those who have been involved in civil rights activism for the past 25 years, it appears that everything has stopped abruptly in mid-movement, like a film stopped in mid-frame. Suddenly, priorities have changed. We used to talk about improvement, about filling the gap between the guarantees expounded in the Constitution and the actuality of discrimination. We used to say that the foundation for protecting basic civil rights is already in place in existing legal statutes; the question was how these rights could be enforced. The answer, we thought, was to strengthen the Federal government, which we as citizens believe is an entity designed to assure the compliance of the individual states to the will of the country as a whole. And for 25 years, the Federal government has strongly supported almost all basic civil rights.

Today the Federal government can no longer be counted on to stand on the side of civil rights. This fact has been made obvious in many ways: attempts to dismantle the most important of the civil rights agencies; attempts to name persons to head these organizations whose commitment to the concept of affirmative action and equal opportunity is questionable, if not nonexistent; and a noticeable reluctance on the part of the Federal government to take a stand in legal discussions of civil rights issues.

Marian Wright Edelman, President of the Children's Defense Fund:

. . . we are now confronting a government that blames society's victims . . . for society's ills, and is conducting an all-out assault on their civil rights.

The assault is coming on a variety of fronts. Much public attention has focused on attempts to weaken school desegregation, affirmative action and voting rights efforts. Less attention has been paid to the government's virtual cessation of enforcement of the less visible civil rights laws. . . .

Even less attention is being paid to the setback that civil rights have suffered by the erosion of Federal standards in programs that have served minorities, women and the handicapped. Hundreds of laws that protect against the arbitrary or discriminatory administration of public benefit programs are being eliminated. Explicit Federal substantive standards—that programs be run statewide; that states give poor people a specified share of benefits; or that states objectively define eligibility and priorities of need—have been essential in entitling minorities . . . to a minimal share of governmental benefits. By repealing such requirements, or by converting mandated benefits for people into block grants to states, the Federal government is subjecting the subsistence benefits of minorities to the unregulated actions of state and local officials or private providers of health care and social services. . . . A child's ability to obtain decent health care, nutritious food, a quality education and adequate housing should not have to depend on where he or she lives.

EXHIBIT 7–3   American Indian Child Removal

The following account of child removal practices with American Indian families raises a number of questions about values and their impact on service delivery. However, it is also a good illustration of how questions of accountability may be seen very differently by professional helpers and those they serve. After reading these excerpts, to whom do you think professionals are ultimately accountable: funding sources, the profession's values, or consumers? Why? How are value conflicts to be resolved?

Surveys of states with large Indian populations conducted by the Association on American Indian Affairs (AAIA) in 1969 and again in 1974 indicate that approximately 25–35 percent of all Indian children are separated from their families and placed in foster homes, adoptive homes, or worse . . . The disparity in placement rates for Indians and non-Indians is shocking. In Minnesota, Indian children are placed in foster care or in adoptive homes at a per capita rate five times greater than non-Indian children. In Montana, the ratio of Indian foster care placement is at least 13 times greater . . . In Wisconsin, the risk run by Indian children of being separated from their parents is nearly 1600 percent greater than it is for non-Indian children.

The Federal boarding school and dormitory programs also contribute to the destruction of Indian and community life. The Bureau of Indian Affairs (BIA), in its school census for 1971, indicates that 34,538 children live in its institutional facilities rather than at home. . . .

In addition to the trauma of separation from their families, most Indian children in placement or in institutions have to cope with the problems of adjusting to a social and cultural environment much different from their own. In 16 states surveyed in 1969, approximately 85 percent of all Indian children in foster care were living in non-Indian homes. In Minnesota today, according to State figures, more than 90 percent of non-related adoptions of Indian children are made by non-Indian couples. Few states keep as careful or complete child welfare statistics as Minnesota does, but informed estimates by welfare officials elsewhere suggest that this rate is the norm. In most Federal and mission boarding schools, a majority of the personnel is non-Indian.

It is clear then that the Indian child welfare crisis is of massive proportions and that Indian families face vastly greater risks of involuntary separation than are typical of our society as a whole. . . .

In judging the fitness of a particular family, many social workers, ignorant of Indian cultural values and social norms, make decisions that are wholly inappropriate in the context of Indian family life and so they frequently discover neglect or abandonment where none exists.

For example, the dynamics of Indian extended families are largely misunderstood. An Indian child may have scores of, perhaps more than a hundred,

Source: Excerpted from William Byler, "Removing children," *Civil Rights Digest,* Summer, 1977, pp. 19–24.

relatives who are counted as close, responsible members of the family. Many social workers, untutored in the ways of Indian family life or assuming them to be socially irresponsible, consider leaving the child with persons outside the nuclear family as neglect and thus as grounds for terminating parental rights.

In the DeCoteau case, the South Dakota Department of Public Welfare petitioned a State court to terminate the rights of a Sisseton-Wahpeton Sioux mother to one of her two children on the grounds that he was sometimes left with his 69-year-old great-grandmother. In response to questioning by the attorney who represented the mother, the social worker admitted that Mrs. DeCoteau's 4-year-old son, John, was well cared for, but added that the great-grandmother "is worried at times."

Because in some communities the social workers have, in a sense, become a part of the extended family, parents will sometimes turn to the welfare department for temporary care of their children, failing to realize that their action is perceived quite differently by non-Indians.

Indian child-rearing practices are also misinterpreted in evaluating a child's behavior and parental concern. It may appear that the child is running wild and that the parents do not care. What is labelled "permissiveness" may often, in fact, simply be a different but effective way of disciplining children. BIA boarding schools are full of children with such spurious "behavioral problems."

Poverty, poor housing, lack of modern plumbing, and overcrowding are often cited by social workers as proof of parental neglect and are used as grounds for beginning custody proceedings. In a recent California case, the State tried to apply poverty as a standard against a Rosebud Sioux mother and child. At the mother's bidding, the child's aunt took 3-year-old Blossom Lavone from the Rosebud Reservation in South Dakota to California. The mother was to follow. By the time she arrived one week later, the child had been placed in a pre-adoptive home by California social workers. The social workers asserted that, although they had no evidence that the mother was unfit, it was their belief that an Indian reservation is an unsuitable environment for a child and that the pre-adoptive parents were financially able to provide a home and a way of life superior to the one furnished by the natural mother. Counsel was successful in returning the child to her mother.

Ironically, tribes that were forced into reservations at gun-point and prohibited from leaving without a permit are now being told that they live in a place unfit for raising their children.

One of the grounds most frequently advanced for taking Indian children from their parents is the abuse of alcohol. However, this standard is applied unequally. In areas where rates of problem drinking among Indians and non-Indians are the same, it is rarely applied against non-Indian parents. Once again cultural biases frequently affect decisionmaking. The late Dr. Edward P. Dozier of Santa Clara Pueblo and other observers have argued that there are important cultural differences in the use of alcohol. Yet, by and large, non-Indian social workers draw conclusions about the meaning of acts or conduct in ignorance of these distinctions. . . .

The decision to take Indian children from their natural homes is, in most cases, carried out without due process of law. For example, it is rare for either Indian children or their parents to be represented by counsel or to have the supporting testimony of expert witnesses.

Many cases do not go through an adjudicatory process at all, since the voluntary waiver of parental rights is a device widely employed by social workers to gain custody of children. Because of the availability of the waiver and because a great number of Indian parents depend on welfare payments for survival, they are exposed to the sometimes coercive arguments of welfare departments. In a current South Dakota entrapment case, an Indian parent in a time of trouble was persuaded to sign a waiver granting temporary custody to the State, only to find that this is now being advanced as evidence of neglect and grounds for the permanent termination of parental rights. It is an unfortunate fact of life for many Indian parents that the primary service agency to which they must turn for financial help also exercises police powers over their family life and is, most frequently, the agency that initiates custody proceedings.

The conflict between Indian and non-Indian social systems operates to defeat due process. The extended family provides an example. By sharing the responsibility of child-rearing, the extended family tends to strengthen the community's commitment to the child. At the same time, however, it diminishes the possibility that the nuclear family will be able to mobilize itself quickly enough when an outside agency acts to assume custody. Because it is not unusual for Indian children to spend considerable time away with other relatives, there is no immediate realization of what is happening—possibly not until the opportunity for due process has slipped away.

There are the simple abductions. Benita Rowland was taken by two Wisconsin women with the collusion of a local missionary after her Oglala Sioux mother was tricked into signing a form purportedly granting them permission to take the child on a short visit, but in fact, agreeing to her adoption. It was months before Mrs. Rowland could obtain counsel and regain her daughter.

It appears that custody proceedings against Indian people are also sometimes begun, not to rescue the children from dangerous circumstances, but to punish parents and children unjustly for conduct that is disapproved of. In a recent Nevada case, a Paiute mother had to go to court to recover her children following her arrest for a motor-vehicle violation. Parents of Nevada's Duckwater Bank of Paiutes were threatened with the loss of their chidren when they sought to open their own school under an approved Federal grant and refused to send their children to a county-run school.

A few years ago, South Dakota tried to send an Oglala Sioux child to a State training school simply because she changed boarding schools twice in two months. In a report sent to us by a Minnesota social worker, she unashamedly recounts threatening her Indian client with the loss of her children if she is "indiscreet."

And it can be so casual—sometimes just a telephone call from an attorney or even the mere rumor that there is an attorney in the offing is enough to persuade a welfare department to drop the case. Sometimes it can be desperate. Ivan Brown was saved because the sheriff, the social worker, and the prospective foster parent fled when the tribal chairman ran to get a camera to photograph their efforts to wrest the child from his Indian guardian's arms.

In some instances, financial considerations contribute to the crisis. For example, agencies established to place children have an incentive to find children to place. In towns with large Federal boarding facilities, merchants may fight to prevent their closing. Not long ago, in response to political intervention, one boarding school in the Great Plains was being phased out as unnecessary because the children could do better at home. The merchants complained and, again as a result of political pressure, the full school enrollment was restored. Very recently merchants protested the proposed closing of Intermountain School with its large Navajo enrollment, despite the fact that closing was advocated by the Navajo tribe.

EXHIBIT 7–4   Kick, Kill, or Cure

Moral issues related to trying to help others have been and will continue to be important in the social welfare professions. They are closely tied to the knowledge available for use in understanding behavior and developing change strategies—knowledge shapes moral values and vice versa. Social welfare professionals cannot be totally blamed for the effects that the imposition of moral values have on people, because they act within social standards as do most others in a society. Yet helping people do have a special responsibility to respect and understand diverse behaviors beyond that of nonprofessionals; it is part of their advocacy for others. This will become an increasingly important but difficult task in the future as our society struggles with attempts to guarantee social justice and human rights for all people as well as the backlash that such efforts seem to produce. The following account of a homosexual man's treatment illustrates the difficulties social welfare professionals face in meeting these challenges—it also illustrates why such efforts are so important.

Thanks to the gay liberation movement and the confidence and courage it has inspired, there is more of the "live and let live" attitude to homosexuals these days than there is of the old "kick, kill, or cure."

But it's important to remember that not long ago (and perhaps even today) the importance of being a "healthy heterosexual" was so great that some homosexuals sought a "cure" and some psychiatrists* reckoned they could do the job. . . .

The Programme of Treatment

The treatment consisted of two five-day sessions of drug therapy separated by nearly three months, and one out-patient session of electric shock therapy.

The idea is to put the patient off his "antisocial" ways by "conditioning"

Source: Excerpted from Ralph Knowles, "Kick, kill, or cure," *Aequus,* May 1976 (Gay Liberation Front. Christchurch, New Zealand), pp. 10–12.

* The American Psychiatric Association no longer considers homosexuality an illness, although psychiatrists still treat homosexuals. Most do not use the aversion therapy described here.

him. This involves encouraging him to think about men and sex while making him violently sick, so that subconsciously his mind will connect homosexual activities with feeling ill and, therefore, avoid them.

First Drug Therapy Session

The stimulus used was erotic pictures provided by me and a tape recording based on incidents I had related. The tape began in a calm, neutral fashion, then concentrated on disgust and revulsion ending with the triumphant announcement that I was feeling sick—which was not surprising since at each session I was given an injection of a nausea-producing drug together with a measure of whiskey just to help things along. The combination certainly worked, as I was violently ill on every occasion—though I suspect they had to use increasingly large doses to produce the desired effect.

If you've ever been sick time and time again through the night until you can only dry retch and drool all over your clothes, you'll have some idea of what it's like.

I presume the conditions were usual—the room was bare of ornaments and colour, and the window was blacked out. No clean clothes or bed linen. No food. And no visitors other than the administering orderlies and the psychiatrist.

There was a pause of several hours after the first dose because, I gather, my blood pressure dropped dramatically; but, after that these little sessions continued every two hours day and night, with glucose and lime to prevent dehydration every other hour.

After about four days I begged the doctor to stop, but he asked me to continue, and when I eventually agreed, his manner changed and he announced that that was "it"! Apparently my agreement to go on meant that my will had been broken or, at least, that my determination to go through any kind of hell to be "normal" was now sufficiently strong.

The male orderlies suddenly disappeared. I was bathed and given clean pyjamas and linen. Flowers and curtains were provided by attractive female nurses, and my parents and friends were allowed to visit.

The Interim

The months that followed were University holidays during which all my friends, male and female, were away; and a gradually growing feeling of loneliness and desperation led to my spending a night on a coastal ship in port. Any port in a storm, they say, and it had certainly been a rough trip. That night remains in my memory bathed in a golden light (actually, the light came from a little radio in the steward's cabin; but let's go lyrical). I should have felt ill, I should have been disgusted and guilty, but, instead, I felt the relief of being back to normal, my normal.

Second Drug Therapy Session

The doctor didn't share my point of view, and a second session was suggested as a result.

One of the weaknesses of the first session was that it was aimed at deorientation rather than reorientation. The whole purpose was to put me off homosexual encounters, and nothing had been done to spur me on to heterosexual endeavours. It didn't work. The second session was modified accordingly. After it had finished I was given a hormone shot, an alluring heterosexual tape narrated by a husky-voiced woman, and some rather crude nudie picture books (this was before the more attractive *Playboy*-type literature was available).

Electric Shock Therapy

A few weeks later I visited outpatients for a short follow-up session using electric shock. Electrodes were applied to my hand, and when I conjured up an interesting thought or two I signalled the doctor, who promptly closed the circuit. An electric current running through you does not help sexual daydreaming!

After a number of repeats, the doctor did not close the circuit, but the pictures in my mind vanished nevertheless in expectation of the shock. It is probably true to say that had this treatment continued, volts might have proved more effective than vomiting, and I might have been a sexless wonder today (or even "straight"!!).

However, we didn't persist with the attempt, and in spite of dire warnings about the disasters which lay ahead, I soon began a relationship that has now lasted eleven years . . .

Outcome (Positive)

It would be unfair to finish without making it clear that the experience wasn't all bad. First, I discussed my homosexuality with my parents for the first time on the eve of going into the hospital, and have kept it quietly in the open since, to everyone's obvious advantage. It was, then, the occasion of my "coming out."

And second, after the failure of the treatment I took stock of my situation and came to terms with myself and society calmly and finally, and have since been able to organize my life both in terms of career and relationships on a stable base of honest and welcome acceptance of being gay.

Conclusion

I would certainly never approach a psychiatrist again for similar or related treatment, nor would I advise anyone else to, regardless of how desperately they wanted to "change."

I consider this treatment psychiatrically crude and physically barbaric—not to mention medically ineffective, morally wrong, and socially outrageous.

The programme was outlined clearly to me, and I undertook it voluntarily; but I would be very angry if I learnt that someone more desperate to change, or more confused in his identity, was persuaded or encouraged to undergo it. I am pleased that there are signs that not all the psychiatric profession shares this doctor's views about homosexuality, heterosexuality, and the desirability of being "straight."

STUDY QUESTIONS

1. This chapter talked about five aspects of contemporary society that are likely to influence the future of our social welfare institution: poverty, immigration and population changes, life-style changes, regionalism, and demands for accountability. Which one of these do you personally believe will have the most profound effect on social welfare? Be sure to explain the reasons for your choice, using material that you have read or learned through the media as well as your own personal experiences. Try to think through the kinds of impact that your choice is likely to have on the future of social welfare.

2. Let us assume that you do not go into a social welfare profession, either because you choose to do something else or because circumstances make it impossible. What career do you think you will enter? How could you work to affect the future of social welfare in that career, and as a citizen of the United States?

3. The average college student will have an active work life of approximately 40 years. How do you assess the kinds of changes that seem likely in the social welfare professions over this span of time? Do these make social welfare a more or a less attractive career option for you? Explain the reasons for your decision.

4. Make a list of what you think the major problems facing American society will be in the next ten years. For each, list the social welfare services currently available to meet these needs. What areas of need remain unmet, if any? What predictions could you make about the future of the social welfare institution on the basis of this exercise?

5. Interview an elected official at either the city, county, state, or national level. Ask them to address future needs for which they feel the government should be preparing. Ask them whether, to the best of their knowledge, such preparations are under way. Then ask how they have tried to work toward the provision of resources required to meet the needs they foresee.

SELECTED READINGS

Dalphin, John (1981). *The Persistence of Social Inequality in America.* Cambridge, Mass.: Schenkman Publishers.

Freire, Paulo (1970). *Pedagogy of the Oppressed.* New York: Seabury Press.

Kahn, Alfred J., and Sheila Kamerman (1976). *Social Services in International Perspective*. Washington, D. C.: U. S. Government Printing Office.

The New York Times. Newspaper published daily by The New York Times Company, 229 West 43rd St., New York, N. Y. 10036.

Sheehan, Susan (1975). *A Welfare Mother*. Boston: Houghton-Mifflin.

Toffler, Alvin (1980). *The Third Wave*. New York: Telecom Library.

APPENDIX: SUMMING UP

Many strands weave together to make up the social welfare institution. In this book, we have explored them and tried to illustrate them through the Exhibits, Tables, Charts, and Figures in each chapter. Now, however, it may be helpful to see the complexity of social welfare as it affects the daily life of real people. With your knowledge of social welfare, you can analyze each case to see which parts of the social welfare institution are of particular significance.

Four cases will be presented, each tied specifically to one aspect of social welfare that you have studied in the text. The first is about Antonio Lopez-Olano, and illustrates points about values, identifying needs, and providing services in ways acceptable to the recipients of them. These aspects of social welfare were discussed in Chapters 1 and 2. The second case is about the life of the Hunt family, and shows how the structural characteristics of social welfare addressed in Chapter 2 affect service delivery. The Babekuhl family is discussed in the third case. It shows how the recent changes in social welfare analyzed in Chapter 3 have interacted with some of the societal changes discussed in Chapter 7, and the resulting effects on people's lives. The fourth case is a fairly lengthy presentation of the use of professional helping skills to help the residents of an apartment building obtain better housing and other needed services. It illustrates how the helping process presented in Chapter 4 is used, and it shows the wide range of systems that are involved in professional helping efforts.

The purpose of this appendix, then, is to help you to review and integrate the content that you have learned about the social welfare institution. It is always more interesting to read about real people than to simply study concepts and facts, and it is hoped that you will enjoy reading these cases. However, remember that your ultimate purpose is to better understand how a knowledge of social welfare helps you to see how social welfare affects people's lives. You will also gain a richer appreciation of the issues involved in creating social welfare systems that are humane, just, and effective. Let's now turn to each case in turn.

The Case of Antonio Lopez-Olano

This case raises some painful dilemmas about social welfare. Mr. Lopez-Olano has lived a life with few financial and other concrete resources but with a sense of independence and a loving relationship with a woman, which are very meaningful to him. When he became involved in the formal social welfare system, which he was reluctant to do, his life seemed to disintegrate. His physical environment and resources were much improved, but his sense of control over his own life seemed to be diminished.

Reading about the improvements in his living environment is encouraging— who wants to think of an old man living alone in an abandoned building? Yet because of his particular set of values, he has difficulty accepting and adjusting to his new life. What most people might consider an improvement he considers interference. His resulting loss of spirit and motivation then becomes a serious problem for the social welfare system, because his ability to survive physically depends on his will to live. When, at the end of the case, Mr. Lopez-Olano talks about the professional helper as having done something to him, it is hard not to be both angry and sad.

This case is an excellent illustration of the impact of values on social welfare, as well as some of the difficulties encountered in trying to identify needs and respond to them. Sometimes what seems to be the most sensible actions to those within the social welfare system are perceived as intrusive and even destructive by those being served. This is an ongoing dilemma with no easy answer. Finding a balance between what our training tells us people need, and what their values and life experiences lead them to want is a difficult and sensitive task.

Source: From Anna Quindlen, "An old man who fears too much care," *The New York Times,* April 14, 1982, p. B1. © 1982 by The New York Times Company. Reprinted by permission.

It is only in this, the latter part of his life, that Antonio Lopez-Olano has been discovered by social welfare agencies. In theory, his lot has improved enormously: the government benefits, the neat apartment in the housing complex for the elderly, the medical care. In practice, he says he wishes everyone would just leave him alone.

Sometimes he means it, railing against well-wishers and do-gooders and old age from a position of weakness in a narrow single bed; sometimes he does not, and grouses only in that sharp, constant way that some people—particularly those who have been alone much of the time—seem to take such pleasure in.

Now he is in the hospital, and this is the final straw. For all of his life, he was unknown to and uncared for by the government, and lived in a tenement building where the tenants could tell time by the whoosh of the passing trains.

Now he has been subsidized and relocated, and for the first time in his life he is ill. This proves conclusively to Antonio that government aid means sickness, even death. None of this could have happened while his Jacquelina was alive.

"I'll tell you, lady, I am sick of money," he said the other day. "The government sends me these checks. What do I do with them—I put them away. Before, when I was young, I take money and go crazy, go up to 142d Street, dance, carry on. Now, I don't know, my life is like they say in the movies—cut."

No one is exactly sure how old Antonio is, and no one much cared until a little over a year ago, when Raphael Flores began to visit him. Mr. Flores is the executive director of Hot Line Cares, which is on Third Avenue in East Harlem. Its mission is to help the people of that area in a variety of ways.

Antonio was living in a building on Park Avenue near 116th Street, in a railroad flat with sheets of ice on the floors, and cold so pervasive that two of his toes had turned black. He had lived there for 46 years with Jacquelina, and the two of them had filled the place with odd collections of books and knickknacks—a set of encyclopedias Antonio had constructed himself out of National Geographics, dozens of china Dutch boys and girls with little peaked caps, volumes on contract law, imitation Dresden shepherdesses.

While Antonio had to spend last winter under a half-dozen blankets in the living room, and Jacquelina was in the hospital, it was still home, even if everyone but the superintendent had abandoned the building, and the hallways stank of urine.

Antonio was living on the money in a big porcelain piggy bank he had cherished for many years; he had never cared for ordinary banks since one lost $30 he had in a savings account during the dark days of 1929. Jacquelina always asked him to open an account for her, just in case he abandoned her, but he never would put the money in the bank, and he never would abandon her.

Raphael brought him coffee, and cigarettes, and discussed the possibility of moving to a place with heat and running water. He investigated Antonio's age. A traffic ticket given him in New Orleans indicated that he was 102 years old, and suddenly everyone was asking him the secret of a century of life.

"I can't tell you, lady, because I thought I was 92," he said, shrugging. Recently, however, Raphael found a chauffeur's license that suggested that Antonio is indeed 92. This reinforces Antonio's suspicion that Raphael doesn't know what he is doing.

"I'm the bad person and the good person," said Raphael. "He says, 'Ralph, before I met you I had no problems.' "

This is exactly what Antonio does say. Raphael helped him apply for welfare benefits and moved him out of the old apartment and into a place in the Corsi Houses only two blocks away, with a little yellow kitchen and a subsidized rent of $72. Raphael tried to arrange the furniture just like the living room in the old apartment. Antonio seems to hate the place. He thinks his Jacquelina would not have approved.

"I kind of have mixed emotions about it," said Lenora Jones, the aide at the James Weldon Johnson Senior Citizens Center who found the new apartment early this year. "When he was in that terrible place, I used to think oh that poor old man—I don't know if he'll live until tomorrow. But now it seems like since he moved, he's gone downhill."

In fact, the new apartment has become a metaphor for what Antonio has lost. "I'm thinking about what you did to me, Ralph," he said, waiting to go to the hospital. "What you did when you brought me out of my house and brought me in here. I was a man. Now I am a boy. You try to do good things, but no good. I don't want to be here. All my things—I don't want them anymore. I used to love my books—now I don't want them anymore. Nothing. I'm going to the hospital to die, Ralph."

If Antonio does die in the hospital, where he is losing weight, and the will to live, there could be any number of clinical causes. No matter what his exact age, he is an old man, a lithe boy faded to a wraith. But in truth, he probably will have died of a broken heart.

More than a half century ago, Antonio met a girl with wavy hair, and together they later found a pleasant apartment with small square rooms, and they furnished it. She worked as a maid, he as a laborer, and the years slipped by, and the apartment building went to ruin, and the girl grew old, and last year she died.

Antonio loves Raphael because Raphael helped him bury Jacquelina, and because he knows deep inside that Raphael is trying to help him. But sometimes he hates him, too.

"He can talk," Antonio said scornfully. "He's all right—healthy! If I live, I'm going to tell him off. He'll be sorry he did this to me."

The Case of the Hunt Family

The Hunt family has to depend on welfare to survive. Its efforts to attain its life goals within the complex network of programs that comprise "welfare" illustrate many of the concepts discussed in Chapter 2. This case provides an excellent basis for assessing the strengths and weaknesses of many of the structural characteristics of social welfare programs.

When studying this case, a number of issues come to mind. The manifest purpose of social welfare is to help people to function more effectively. But the sacrifices and compromises that Sharon Hunt has to make to survive on the money she receives raises questions about whether this purpose, helping people to function more effectively, is being attained. Does making a "welfare mother" do what Sharon Hunt has to do instead focus on the attainment of other objectives, both manifest and latent? Values are also addressed, because it becomes clear that the Hunt family is working hard to use its resources most effectively, and to achieve independence (note that the oldest son is in college and is completely self-supporting). This is hardly a family of "welfare cheats," yet the programs available to them still encourage survival rather than long-term independence. The family, then, seems to have internalized American values of thrift, caring for each other, and seeking self-sufficiency, but the structure of the programs available to them do not really help family members operationalize these values.

The Hunt family also illustrates the interplay between formal and informal helping, because family and friends are emergency resources when the few dollars simply cannot be stretched further to cover unanticipated needs. This relationship is also shown in Sharon Hunt's talking about her welfare-rights activities. She participates in a statewide poor people's organization, which is a voluntary effort by concerned poor people to improve their lives. It is not part of the formal social welfare organization, although it attempts to influence what happens within that formal system. This is also an interesting example of the concept of self-help activities in Chapter 4. Helping people to organize on their own behalf is an important strategy for change. People can achieve things in groups that they cannot achieve individually. In Sharon Hunt's case this would probably include political action. But when people work together to solve common problems they also become supports for each other, helping one another in ways that are rarely possible for professional helping people.

As you read the Hunt case, keep searching for the interplay of the structural characteristics of social welfare, value issues, and strategies for solving problems. You might also want to reflect on the strength and motivation of Sharon Hunt, and consider whether these qualities might be better reinforced by other

Source: From Sheila Rule, "Family tries with welfare to 'make do,' " *The New York Times,* March 23, 1982, pp. B-1ff. © 1982 by The New York Times Company. Reprinted by permission.

types of social welfare structures. Finally, take a moment to think about whether you could survive in her circumstances. And what do you think happens to people "on welfare" who are not as strong and well-educated as she is?

After buying necessities and paying bills, Sharon Hunt had $11 left from her welfare check. But there was an unexpected expense for her baby, Tanya.

Miss Hunt said the 13-month-old child's synthetic-blend pajamas, purchased as "great bargains," were causing a rash. "I'm going to have to break down and buy her some cotton nightgowns even though we'll have less money to last until the next check comes in about two weeks," she said.

Miss Hunt said she went back on welfare about five months ago for the first time in 10 years after Federal budget cuts eliminated her job at New York Community Advocacy Research and Development, a food and nutrition program.

A Painful Choice

As is generally the case for welfare recipients and other poor people, narrow choices and hidden costs of poverty have been insistent bullies in the lives of Miss Hunt and her children. Even after developing a spiritual armor that helped them through tough times, she said, it is still painful to have to decide between the lesser of two evils.

Martin Burdick, acting deputy administrator of the city's income maintenance programs, says that because of the effect that inflation has had on public-assistance grants, making do is more difficult for the poor these days. And difficult decisions are more plentiful.

"I have to give my kids more than hard times for a diet," Miss Hunt said.

Several social-service and welfare groups were asked to recommend a welfare recipient who would be willing to discuss the family's budget and its strategy for living on public assistance. Miss Hunt, a short woman with electric energy, is a welfare-rights activist who agreed to discuss her finances in detail.

She allowed a reporter to accompany her to a welfare center, where she was required to establish her eligibility for continued public assistance. She must go through this procedure three times a year. There was no way to verify independently that she had no other sources of income. It also could not be determined whether she might have been able to find a job that would pay enough to get off welfare.

Over several recent days in her Manhattan apartment and on shopping trips, Miss Hunt had to decide between a cold child and a rash, between buying what was on sale and what her family actually needed, between not meeting her family's needs and going deeper into debt.

The 40-year-old mother scoured advertisements for the coupons she clips, picked through bins of damaged goods at bargain stores for clothing for her children and walked more than a mile for a bargain on a detergent.

Miss Hunt said she avoids public transportation unless it is absolutely necessary. She also is unable to budget for entertainment nor does she have a reserve for emergencies.

"Sharon really does the best she can for her family, probably better than I could do," said Mary Bighorse, program director of the American Indian Community House, a multiservice center in New York City. She has known Miss Hunt for about five years. "Considering her circumstances, it's a miracle that she makes it," she said.

Two Checks a Month

Miss Hunt receives a monthly welfare grant of $340 in two separate $170 checks, one at the beginning of the month and one in the middle, for herself, Tanya and a 10-year-old daughter, Kayla.

After $110 is deducted to pay the rent for her public-housing apartment on the Lower East Side, Miss Hunt's total welfare grant leaves about $2.55 in cash a day for each member of the family. Her food-stamp allotment is $115 a month, or about $1.28 a day for each family member, amounting to about 43 cents for each of three meals.

After receiving her first $170 check and the food stamps one week, she went about juggling them and her stamina in an effort to survive. She gathered the check, stamps and supermarket coupons, bundled up Tanya in the stroller she had borrowed money to buy, and prepared to walk from her home on Franklin D. Roosevelt Drive at East Houston Street to a supermarket on Avenue A and Fourth Street that was advertising specials.

Twice as Expensive

As is generally the case in most poor neighborhoods, she said, nearby corner markets offered goods that were twice as expensive and of lesser quality than those she could find outside her immediate area.

Miss Hunt had $1 in cash the day the welfare check arrived. The family had only a few cans of tuna, some boxes of instant macaroni and cheese, some beef pot pies, spinach and eggs. There were also the ever-present canisters of rice and beans, which Miss Hunt calls her "safety net" against hunger.

On this cold day, Kayla had worn to school the pair of boots she shares with her mother. So Miss Hunt put on a pair of thin, cloth-topped shoes she had bought for $1 at a bargain shop.

Along the route to the supermarket, which took her and her baby past knots of drug addicts, abandoned and graffiti-scarred buildings and vacant lots, Miss Hunt stopped at a storefront check-cashing business and paid $1.38 to cash her welfare check and an additional 95 cents for a $110 money order for her rent. She said grocery stores would not cash her welfare check.

She was then left with $57.67 in cash and the food stamps.

In the supermarket, she rolled her shopping cart past fresh vegetables and meats and loaded it with canned tuna and vegetables, cereal, baby food, bread and other items on sale.

Miss Hunt said she checks advertised specials and clips coupons before going to the supermarket. Once there, she said, she usually selects items on sale that are rich in protein, nonperishable and inexpensive.

Experience and Necessity

She purchases fresh vegetables and fruits only "when there is a really good buy," she said. While her former job in the nutrition program reinforced her knowledge of what constitutes a good diet, she said, it was "practical experience and absolute necessity" that shaped her current shopping habits.

She paused at the poultry section and thought for a while before putting two chickens into her basket.

"Darwin is coming home from college this weekend, so maybe I can fix chicken for him on Sunday," she said. Darwin, who at 20 is her oldest child, is a student at the State University College at Old Westbury, L.I. He works and receives Federal and state grants to pay for his education and living expenses.

Another son, Maurice, is a dishwasher and security guard in Atlantic City.

After the cashier rang up the bill, Miss Hunt handed over $53.62 in food stamps and $2.33 in cash for items that the stamps did not cover. She was left with $61.38 in food stamps and $55.34 in cash.

Surplus Cheese and a Hat

On the way home, she stopped at a community center to sign up for the state program for the distribution of cheese from the Federal Government's surplus and at a Salvation Army store, where she bought a hat for 49 cents and a cooking pot for $1.29. This left her with $53.56 in cash.

Miss Hunt looked briefly at a small coat and hat that cost $4.05.

"That would fit the baby next year, but I don't have money to spend on something for next year," she said.

The next day she walked an even greater distance, to 14th Street near the Avenue of the Americas, to buy a detergent on sale at $1.56. And after paying $20 on a $350 debt and about $21 for her telephone bill, she had $11 in cash.

"I've lived without a telephone in the past and there have been times when I didn't have a dime to call somebody when my babies and I needed help," Miss Hunt said, explaining why she spends money for a telephone.

She also bought milk, juice, applesauce and other foods at a cost of $14.38 in food stamps, leaving her with $47 in stamps for the next two weeks.

In Debt to a Friend

Not unlike other welfare recipients, who often have to find additional means of support through family and friends, she is in debt to a friend.

The friend, who helped her when she had no income for seven weeks while applying for welfare, continues to help when she is in financial trouble.

But Miss Hunt says she still has difficulty adjusting to the anxiety that hits her when one of her sons visits and in one day drinks the juice that was meant to last for five, or when the baby screams in the night and there is no money for emergencies.

"It shouldn't hurt to be born in America," Miss Hunt observed. "It does, though. My salvation has been my children and my activities as a welfare-rights activist."

"Able to Fight" for Rights

"Welfare mothers have to organize," she said. "I've been able to fight for my rights through the help of the Redistribute America Movement." The group is a statewide poor people's organization.

"My life," Miss Hunt added, "has been hard, but my stuff is light compared to some people's stuff."

Kayla, whose youthful energy seems tempered by a sense of responsibility, says she enjoys having her mother at home rather than out working when she returns from school. But the family's financial situation has sometimes made Kayla the target of other children's insensitive comments.

"Sometimes the kids at school tease me," she said softly. "They ask me why I wear the same pants all the time or why I never have money for candy when we go to the store.

"I tell them if you don't like me the way I am, then we just can't be friends. A lot of the kids ask, 'Why are you on welfare?' And they say that we're living off the government. But I tell them we're just trying to survive, that's all."

How One Family Spent Its Welfare Allotment

Sharon Hunt receives a monthly welfare grant of $340 in two separate $170 checks, one at the beginning and one in the middle of each month. She also gets a monthly food stamp allotment of $115. Expenditures below show what she paid in the first half month.

Rent	$110.00
Check-cashing fee	1.38
Money order to pay rent	0.95
Groceries not covered by food stamps	2.33
Hat	0.49
Cooking pot	1.29
Detergent	1.56
Personal debt	20.00
Telephone bill	21.00
Cash after expenses	11.00
CHECK TOTAL	**$170.00**

The Case of the Babekuhl Family

Unlike the Hunt family, the Babekuhls are not "on welfare." They are, however, struggling to make ends meet as hard as is the Hunt family. Their efforts to attain their life goals illustrate a whole other aspect of social welfare—the way in which social welfare decisions affect everyone in society, even those who are not receiving "welfare."

The Babekuhl family illustrates historical developments of several kinds discussed in Chapters 3 and 7. It is a family that has been modified by divorce, resulting in it being female-headed. This is a rapidly growing segment of the American population, and is one that is very vulnerable economically (see the graph that is part of the case)—Joan Babekuhl is not unusual in struggling to find work that will enable her to support her family. The combined ravages of inflation, unemployment, and cutbacks in welfare programs (especially at the federal level) have increased the pressure on single-parent families, especially female-headed families, to remain independent financially. If Joan Babekuhl

Source: Nathaniel Sheppard, Jr., "Single parent finds inflation and aid cuts are economic stumbling block," *The New York Times,* October 14, 1982, p. A20. © 1982 by The New York Times Company. Reprinted by permission.

should fail in this effort, she will face the conditions with which Sharon Hunt is struggling.

This case provides an interesting perspective on the patchwork-quilt characteristic of the structure of social welfare. Joan Babekuhl has tried to tap into individual programs that could help her in some way, but there was no overall program that could serve her needs. In addition, individual programs are very susceptible to being modified or eliminated one by one, leaving gaps in services that are not covered by other programs. Also, even if a particular program remains, the eligibility standards for receiving it may be changed, again throwing the total helping plan out of balance. This happened, for example, with respect to food stamps.

This family falls into what is sometimes called the "working poor." These are people who are working but cannot earn enough to be financially independent. Yet because they do have some income, they may not be eligible for financial aid programs. As a result, they may be as poor as people who do not work and receive all of their income from financial aid programs. The effect on people's motivation can be devastating, as Joan Babekuhl shows. Here again we confront a structural problem: How can services be developed in some sort of a comprehensive way so that efforts to be self-sufficient are rewarded, while also stimulating those who do not work but who have the ability to do so to work toward greater financial independence?

Finally, the Babekuhl family demonstrates an often-overlooked form of social welfare—child support and alimony payments. These are essentially income transfer programs to redistribute money from those in a dissolved family who have more to those who have less. Given the sexist nature of our society, this has generally meant from men to women, although in principle the person with more pays the person with less. As in the case of Joan Babekuhl, child-support payments can be a significant source of income for a single parent. However, in the majority of cases, these payments are made erratically or not at all. This, of course, creates hardship for the single parent dependent on this money.

As you read this case, keep in mind that the Babekuhl family lives in Minneapolis. Social welfare pervades our society—it is not limited to the slums of New York, Chicago, or Los Angeles. Everyday families confront problems with which they need various kinds of help, and it is the manifest function of social welfare to help them meet their needs. Hopefully, these cases enable you to assess their success in doing so.

Once a month, when dinners of chicken, hot dogs or hamburger-and-noodle casseroles had become overwhelmingly monotonous, Joan Babekuhl would load her five children into her 1974 station wagon and treat them to a meal at the Ponderosa Steak House.

That was two years ago, when times for the Babekuhls were tough and the low-cost steak dinners were affordable only with discount coupons clipped from newspapers. Today, however, things are even tougher and such splurges are out of the question.

Mrs. Babekuhl is a single woman, and her family is one of a growing number of families around the nation headed by divorced, unmarried and widowed women. About half the families in poverty are in this category. While the Babekuhl family is not officially on the poverty rolls, Mrs. Babekuhl says she is having financial trouble because of continued inflation and cuts in Federal benefits.

In 1978, Mrs. Babekuhl earned about $2,000 and received about $10,000 in child support and Federal aid, not including the free school lunches her children received and other assistance. This year she expects to earn about $11,790 and get $5,000 in child support, but no Federal aid. As a result, she says her family's life continues to be difficult.

Trouble for a Single Parents

"Judging by the many bills I am falling behind on and all the things we can no longer do, like go to the steak house once a month, I would say that our situation is much worse now than ever before," she said.

According to the Census Bureau, the number of families headed by single women grew to 3.23 million in 1981 from 2.56 million in 1979, especially in large and moderate-sized cities, such as Minneapolis. Typically, the women are 45 years old or younger, and their families have $1 to spend on basic needs, including food, utilities and clothing, for every $2 available to families in general. Seventy percent of the families are white.

In 1979, the poverty rate for families headed by single women was 30.1 percent, as against 5.3 percent for all families and 10.1 percent for families headed by men. By 1981, the figures were 34.6 percent for families headed by women, 11.2 percent overall and 10.3 percent for families headed by men.

The $8,600 earned by Mrs. Babekuhl in 1981 and $5,500 in child support payments put the family $3,140 above the median income of $10,960 for families headed by single women and $1,651 over the poverty level for a family of six. However, they were left well below the $22,390 median income for families in general.

In 1978, Mrs. Babekuhl earned $2.65 an hour at a bakery, where she worked 15 hours a week, and she received $150 a week in child support payments. The family was also aided by Federal day care, food stamp and infant nutrition programs. In her current 35-hour-a-week job as a secretary-bookkeeper for an electrician's training center, she earns $6.20 an hour and takes home about $400 in pay every two weeks.

"I had been able to make ends meet because the food stamps, day care and the infant care programs helped stretch my budget," said Mrs. Babekuhl, who is now 40 years old. "But now that we are ineligible for these programs, I have to pay those expenses out of my pocket, along with the house note and utility bills. As a result, I am falling farther and farther behind on my bills."

Median Income: Families Headed by Women Vs. All Families

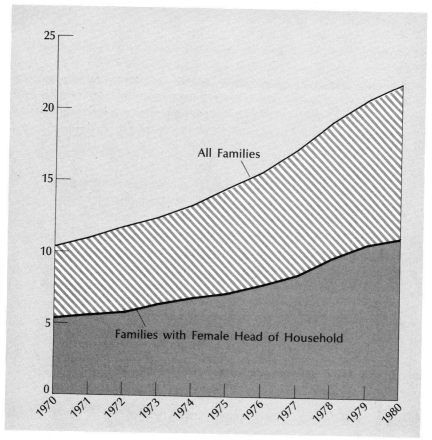

Median annual income in thousands of dollars.
Source: Census Bureau

Effects of Inflation

"It seems," she continued, "that the more you try to improve yourself, like my finding a better paying job that will help you catch up with your bills, the more the Government kicks you in the pants by cutting back aid so that you can never catch up."

Mrs. Babekuhl said that she voted for the Democratic ticket in the 1980 Presidential election and that she planned to do so in November. She said she was displeased with the Reagan Administration "mainly because of budget cuts in social programs which hurt children and individuals who can't fight back."

For the Babekuhl family, times got harder when they entered the ranks of single-parent households in 1978, after Mrs. Babekuhl divorced her husband.

The family qualified for $130 worth of food stamps a month and her 4-year-old daughter, Joy, was eligible under the Special Supplemental Food Program for Women, Infants and Children to get $30 a month for milk and other dairy products.

Her other four children—Paul, 16, Mary, 15, Donna, 14, Barbara, 12, Federick, 11—were in the free lunch program at school and got small jobs through the Neighborhood Youth Corps, she said. A friend minded her youngest child, freeing her to work part-time. In the winters, a Federal fuel assistance program kept the family's furnace burning.

"These programs helped tremendously," she said, "because I was only earning $2.65 per hour and working 25 hours a week. I had monthly payments of $325 for the house, $50 for gas, $35 for electricity, $15 for water, $10 for braces for one of my daughter's teeth and $10 for the children's tuition at parochial school."

Mrs. Babekuhl, who became a grandmother in early August, speaks both with pride in her family's resourcefulness and with frustration at its plight when describing the various ways she and her children economized and kept their expenses down at that time: They bought their clothes at second-hand stores and got $4 haircuts at barber schools at five-week intervals. They lowered the thermostat on the water heater and dried their clothes outside. They went to free concerts and plays in city parks for entertainment.

Lost Aid from Government

But the family's expenses still outstripped its income. As they lost eligibility for one assistance program after another, their indebtedness grew. In February 1980, Mrs. Babekuhl quit the bakery, where she was earning $3.50 an hour and working 25 hours a week, to become an office manager at $4.50 an hour, 20 hours a week. By 1981, the increases in her salary and revisions in eligibility guidelines had forced the family out of Federal assistance programs.

"Last spring, I took on a part-time job to make up some of the lost aid," Mrs. Babekuhl said, referring to a $2.65-an-hour job at a concession stand at the domed sports stadium downtown. "In a way it seems that I am being punished for the improvements I have made in my situation. The more I made, the more aid was taken away, never mind that costs were rising, too."

"My house payments have increased by $100 a month because taxes and insurance went up. My water bill has doubled to about $33 a month, and my gas bill has increased from $72 a month to $84 a month."

The family, Mrs. Babekuhl said, also washes its clothes less, takes fewer baths, gets fewer haircuts and uses regular instead of premium gas in the station wagon. She said she had also accepted $20 gifts from her mother.

The predicament, Mrs. Babekuhl said, has left her somewhat "doubtful of whether it is worth it to try to improve yourself."

"I would like to become self-sufficient and sever all ties with aid programs," she said, "but the odds are stacked against me."

"I try to look at it philosophically though. I tell myself that there are people out there who need help much more than I, and I tell myself that maybe there is even something in the loss of these programs for me—perhaps inner growth and spiritual strength that will help me make it."

The Case of the Building on Howell Street

The following case is a lengthy analysis of efforts to help residents of an apartment building improve their living conditions. Although this was the principal purpose of the helping effort, many other objectives were included. In order for the residents to get help, they had to learn how to work together as an organized unit. This was necessary in order for them to agree on goals, and to act in unison when dealing with outside social welfare agencies. The process of developing as a group in turn entailed a considerable amount of individual and family counseling. In the past, the problems faced by individuals and families had been major obstacles to enabling the residents to communicate and relate effectively with each other.

The Howell Street case illustrates many aspects of the helping process discussed in Chapter 4. The problem-solving process and the systems approach are especially clearly evident, and you might want to review each in order to follow how they are used in this case. This case also shows the use of a generic approach to helping. The many dimensions of the needs of the residents are identified and dealt with, using a wide range of specific helping techniques in the process. For example, meetings are held with social welfare personnel, from agencies providing services to residents of the building (financial assistance agencies, housing departments, legal aid offices, and so on), and with related service providers like the landlord and building manager. Counseling sessions are held with individuals and families. Group meetings are held with residents to help them learn about and use the group process and social-action techniques. Throughout, it is easy to see how the professional helpers responsible for this case collected data and engaged in evaluation as part of their ongoing efforts to find the most successful strategies available.

The Howell Street case demonstrates the way in which all the social institutions of society work together to both create problems and solve them. Resi-

Source: Louis Lowy, Leonard M. Bloksberg, and Herbert J. Walberg, *Teaching Records: Integrative Learning and Teaching Project* (New York: Council on Social Work Education, 1973), pp. 85–107. Reprinted by permission of the Council on Social Work Education.

dents faced economic problems, family problems, education limitations, and a feeling of political powerlessness. On the other hand, family members often supported each other, residents were able to share financial and educational resources, they developed some skill in acting effectively in the political system, and their religion was sometimes a resource. This shows how important a holistic approach is, as discussed in Chapter 5. Human life is a totality, and its many pieces have to be understood in order to address the whole. The holistic approach even included the biological limitations, which some members of the Howell Street building faced, such as alcoholism and heart trouble.

A final component of this case is the insight that it provides into the nature of professional helping, a topic addressed in Chapter 6. At times, the professional helpers in the case get discouraged, are worried whether a strategy will work, and are elated on experiencing some degree of success. Professional helping does involve all of these feelings, some of which are very pleasant indeed, and others of which are painful and depressing. The important point illustrated by the workers in the case is that persistence is critical. They kept going even when discouraged, trying to figure out what other approaches they might take that would be more successful. They also did not expect total success. They were able to partialize situations and work them through in a systematic way, enjoying each little victory and then moving on to try for another. The conditions of the residents at Howell Street will never be perfect, but they will be far better because of the efforts of the helping professionals in this case.

This last case is extensive enough to allow you to pull together all of the strands of this book. It shows how values, the structure of programs, professional helping techniques, the use of knowledge, and the legacy of historical events all make social welfare what it is. For this reason, it ought to enable you to sum up what you have learned in this book. Good luck!

Part 1: Introduction

The Project

The [Adelphi University] School of Social Work received a training grant from a federal agency and, in cooperation with the Southside Community House, assigned six graduate social work students to service tenement dwellers in the area. The tenements to be serviced were selected on the basis of past tenant participation in agency programs; this is not to say, though, that all tenants had a past relationship with the Community House. The number of tenants who had a past relationship varied from building to building. One of the selected buildings had been serviced in like manner for a few years previous to the initiation of this project by the agency itself, and its experience and interest were important to the decision as to which agency the school would cooperate with in the implementation of the proposal.

Though the original plan was to have one first-year student and one second-year student service a particular building, prior to the commencement of the work a decision was made to extend the service to six dwellings; and therefore, each of the six students was assigned to a separate dwelling. The basis for each tenement assignment was unknown to me; that is, I do not know why I was assigned the tenement I worked in rather than one of the other five.

Other factors were also important in the selection of these six from the many tenements that existed in the area. In each there were recognized multiple and complex social problems. These included poverty, overcrowding, discrimination, family disorganization, out-of-wedlock children, poor and deteriorating health, and emotional disturbance. In most of those selected there also were problems of mental illness and narcotics addiction, but I did not find such to be extensive in my tenement.

Social-work servicing was to take the form of a generic approach with particular emphasis upon developing a tenant group in each building. Participation of all tenants was to be striven for, but this objective or goal would be subject to modification after more was learned about the building and the tenant system. Specific goals could not be formulated until more was learned about each tenement complex, but basic or broad goals were formulated prior to the initiation of service. The tenants in these buildings were recognized as having experienced oppression, defeat, disillusionment, and despair. They were therefore in need of assistance in learning how to negotiate the complex bureaucratic structures which influenced them, in need of developing a stronger sense of community, in need of recognizing their true worth and abilities, in need of personal enhancement and development, and in need of developing a more positive image of the wider community and realizing their place in it.

The Agency

As previously mentioned, the Southside Community House, an established agency with a long history of service to the community, embarked on such a program six years before this program began when it recognized that several disturbed youngsters using its program resided in the same building. The idea of working with all the families as a tenement social system was explored as an alternative to the more traditional plan of trying to work with each family as an isolated unit. Though the tenement program was funded from outside sources, the original program was undertaken at agency expense. Since the inception of this plan, graduate social work students have serviced the one particular building selected.

The Tenement

The building was a five-story walkup with three apartments on each floor except the ground floor, which had two. All apartments facing front had three rooms, while those in the rear had five. Three years earlier, title of the building was transferred to the City Department of Real Estate, and at that time the building was partially renovated. Cockroaches were to be found in abundance throughout the building. Rats showed themselves infrequently. There was usually garbage in the halls, but not to any great degree.

The exterior and halls, though in need of paint and plaster, were in fairly good order. The complaints usually involved poor plumbing, holes in the floors and walls, defective utilities, and difficulty in getting anything fixed—from the front door lock to the rear room window sashes.

The Group

One must understand that all the tenants were viewed as the client system to be serviced. The group which was formed not only was used to enhance the lives of those who actively participated, but was the vehicle used for reaching out to the others. Hopefully, the development of the group would have a positive effect on even those who were not participating members. Therefore, the group was not closed or limited; it was open to "other members." I personally preferred to view those adult tenants who had yet to participate, as members who would one day become active participants, rather than as possible members. This must be clearly understood, for it was important in my approach at all times. I have lost sight of the children, teenagers, or "visiting" adult males, but a focus was necessary and I decided to work with the strongest and most influential members of the entire client system: the mothers. For the purpose of this discussion, then, "the group" refers to only those who actively participated in group sessions.

Most of the members were there because of urban renewal and felt cheated that they had been displaced because of the building of housing projects and yet had been rejected in their many attempts to gain admittance to one. The large majority were dependent on the Department of Social Services for their economic needs, and all were dependent on the Department of Real Estate for their housing needs. In the tenement they had to cope with the lack of concern of the building agent; they had to watch what they said and did that might come to the attention of the DSS caseworker; they had to worry about what to do when someone became ill. The tenement is where they were, but all felt despair and defeat in being there.

The stresses which they had to endure came from almost anywhere. They could come from a large complex bureaucracy or from one's own child. They could come from inorganic as well as organic sources. Each tenant learned to deal with these stresses in his own way, but no one seemed to be able to get out from under. Seemingly, whenever one problem was solved, two others took its place. Assisting these people in understanding and developing skills in handling these stresses could not be done as swiftly as one hoped; it is a long process but a necessary one if these people are to be helped.

The History

Initially, I discovered that there were two major opposing family-based groups, friends of each group, and a few who had little or nothing to do with either group. These two groups comprised half of the tenement population. I decided the focus initially should be to bring these two factions together, and later to bring in the others.

During the early weeks neither group would meet with members of the other. I would hold two meetings on the same day. At one o'clock I would meet with the Waters group, then at two o'clock I would go up and meet with the Wards. Then both sides agreed to get together. On the day of the scheduled meeting everyone was either out shopping or sick. I then decided to concentrate on the mother-leaders, and they agreed to meet even though their daughters refused. Both mothers found something else to do at the time of the scheduled meeting, but it was finally held that day on fairly neutral territory: Olympia's third-floor apartment. Mrs. Ward went down two floors, and Mrs. Waters went up two. Then another meeting was set, but no one was at home on the planned day.

During the following week, Mrs. Ward contacted her best friend, Mrs. Moore, and Mrs. Moore told me she wanted to be included. One must note that Olympia is Mrs. Waters' best friend. The next meeting would be composed of the two mother-leaders and their respective best friends. Something happened before this meeting was held, though.

For almost three weeks the tenants had been without heat. Installing the new heating system was supposed to take five days, but unfortunately was dragged out to fifteen. On Monday, I received an "emergency call" from Edna and went to the building to learn that everyone was now angry enough to forget differences and do something. Mr. Ward agreed to go around with a petition and got almost everyone to sign. We then took it to a Community Council Legal Unit [CCLU] lawyer; I met him there after again calling Mr. Tubb, who "guaranteed" it would be taken care of that day. After speaking with the lawyer, Mr. Ward and I returned to the building to await the man who was supposed to finally okay the installation. For several hours Mr. Ward and I waited together in the doorway, to keep out of the rain and cold. Finally, the heat and hot water were restored.

When Wednesday came, all four came to the meeting at Olympia's, and Mr. Ward also joined us. When we attempted to relate the action he'd taken Monday, Mrs. Moore cut him off and said she didn't care to hear; she was there for other reasons. Gradually an argument developed and Mr. Ward left, cursing at Mrs. Moore. At the conclusion of this meeting I explained that I had asked the lawyer to talk with us at a next meeting. Mrs. Moore offered the use of her apartment.

Throughout all this beginning effort to get together, there was constant complaining about the building and its agent. There was a stated goal to meet with the man, and he had already agreed to it, but I felt the group needed further development before such a meeting could take place. The CCLU lawyer was part of this development. I met with him a couple of times before the meeting and agreed to what he would talk about, the questions I would ask, and his fostering of a group spirit.

At that meeting Mr. and Mrs. Ward, Sally, Mrs. Moore, Mrs. Waters, Faith and Olympia attended. They left this meeting stating they had to get together and stick together; "there can be no loose ends." The next meeting was also scheduled to take place in Mrs. Moore's, but a couple of days later I learned the Waters subgroup refused to return there because of Mrs. Moore's intoxication and insulting of Olympia. An agreement was reached to switch the meeting place to Edna's; even Mrs. Moore agreed, though I did not fully explain why the others wanted to switch. In this conflict the Wards stated they'd meet anywhere and saw justification for the others' not wanting to meet in Mrs. Moore's. This was quite a change of attitude for them.

The next meeting was held with the new DSS [Department of Social Services] caseworker. I spent a few hours with him before the meeting, and he was very willing to help and understood what I hoped to accomplish. At the meeting he too fostered a group spirit and cohesion, but cautioned them about how to handle themselves with the building agent. He offered his support in their planned confrontation with the building agent, and he promoted good feeling between the tenants and himself.

Here I must restate one objective: to help the tenants negotiate the complex systems they are faced with. I tried to focus always on cooperation and communication. On one hand the meeting with the caseworker was intended to prepare them for the meeting with the building agent; but at the same time it was the big initial step in better communication and cooperation with the DSS.

The meeting with the building agent was one big "if"; no one even had a hint as to how it would turn out. In the two previous fairly formal meetings I felt secure about the outcome beforehand because of my contacts with the "guest speakers," but I had no lengthy discussion with the building agent beforehand. He was coming only because he felt "sorry" about the lack of heat in December. Neither the tenants nor I expected anyone other than Tubb, and they were even doubtful he would show his face.

Throughout this period of time I was developing relationships with the tenants. Since the day we waited in the cold and rain I had spent much more time with Mr. Ward; he had bluntly stated he wanted no responsibility, but would help me when he could. Primarily, I was trying to enhance his self-image and to "educate" him as to how we should deal with key persons. Previous to this he had usually cursed at me and treated me as part of the hated establishment.

Mrs. Moore was none too friendly from the beginning either, but we had a working relationship. Though she drank heavily, I responded to her as I would do to any other and would discuss the details of situations with her, though I was extremely doubtful that she could comprehend one word. I always had a sense that there was very strong racial feeling involved on the part of Mr. Ward and Mrs. Moore, but I believed I could not confront it until something was stated outright and a positive relationship of some kind had been developed.

Edna and Mrs. Waters were always friendly, but had long since learned "not to get too involved" if someone came to help. Be nice to him or her, get what you can, but don't stick your neck out. The most fearful of any risk or conflict, though, was Olympia. Only after constant reassurance did she permit the first meeting to be held in her place, and as soon as the group was growing and things were happening, she flatly told me she was afraid and didn't want her apartment used. She was almost terror-stricken whenever someone mentioned "taking on" the building agent. She and Faith were the only two participating members who paid December rent even though all had agreed to stick together and not pay. That risk was too much for her. Our relationship was rather well established and she had found some support in me, enough to finally enable her to disagree with her subgroup prior to this meeting.

I had met individually with Helen only once prior to this session, but that talk was enough to change the image I had had of her when she was in the company of her mother and sisters. I was struck with her intellectual ability, her ability to understand her situation, and her methods of coping with it.

Mrs. Taylor was almost an unknown to me. Previously she had been so intoxicated that she didn't understand anything I said. I had asked Mr. Ward and Olympia to speak with her and try to motivate her. They succeeded, for she did finally come to the meeting with the DSS caseworker. She came to that session thinking I was the lawyer others had told her about. I finally convinced her otherwise.

The Members

I will discuss only those who attended this session, but one must remember that there were other tenants and I did consider them as clients and, in a way, definitely part of the group.

Waters Subgroup.—*Mrs. Waters* lived in Apartment 1A, was the mother of Edna, Helen, and Faith, was a middle-aged Negro Methodist, was very religious. Her "adopted" children—Joe (12) and Vera (15)—lived with her. Her son, John, was the superintendent of the building, and the apartment actually belonged to him. She received DSS assistance for Joe and Vera. She declared a "Charleston divorce" from her husband years before, and he lived nearby with John. She could not read or write. Olympia was her best friend. Mrs. Waters had a bad heart and switched apartments with Helen (5C) because of this.

Our relationship was quite friendly, and she asked others to be as honest and truthful with me as she was. She found great comfort in her religion, did not promise and wanted to avoid conflict. She provided warm mothering to her daughters, and one by one they returned to her dwelling. Initially she was very much the sole leader of the group, but a sharing developed, especially with Edna.

Edna lived in Apartment 2A, was the twenty-nine-year-old mother of three small children, was a Methodist, was married but did not live with her husband, and received DSS assistance for the children. She recently had been hospitalized twice, yet she was the type who couldn't rest or relax. The diagnosis was yet to be made, but they thought she had heart trouble and she was taking medication. Her apartment, since her illness, was the hub of Waters activity.

Prior to her emergency call she was polite and cordial, but there was little strength to our relationship. After that call our relationship blossomed and she began to take more of a leadership role with the subgroup and the overall group as well. Of all of those in her subgroup, I felt she was the most interested in a group and wanted everyone to be friendly. She thought very much in terms of the group and influenced the others to think this way also.

Faith lived in Apartment 3B, was the mother of an eleven-year-old daughter, was in her mid-twenties, and was also a Methodist. Her husband lived with her, yet she received DSS assistance for the child. She just recently had moved into the building (four months before) to be closer to her mother, Mrs. Waters.

For the most part she was quite independent, spent most of her time in her own apartment cleaning, and appeared cool toward the others. She began to change, though. At the meeting with the lawyer, she came for herself; at this one she was more a part of the group. She had often said she wanted nothing to do with the group, but she was changing.

Helen lived in Apartment 5C, was the mother of one son, had just turned thirty, and also a Methodist. Though not as religious as her mother, she was the most religious of the daughters. Her male "cousin" was usually seen in the home and I became friendly with him after this session. She was very much attached to her mother and was rarely in her own apartment. She received DSS assistance for her child and had discussed a desire to return to work; she formerly had been a Youth Corps enrollee at the Alliance. Our relationship was good and I contacted the building through her [telephone]. She was willing to help and would participate, but was pessimistic about the outcome. As long as the group appeared together she would participate, but if conflict arose (which was the case) she retreated and said she would rejoin the group when the troubles were straightened out.

Olympia lived in Apartment 3C alone (her Egyptian husband had been deported four years before) and was a middle-aged, overweight black Catholic. Until her husband's deportation she worked as a domestic; she received DSS home relief assistance. We were trying to change her category, though, since she too had heart trouble.

She was highly dependent on others for everything, and avoided conflict for fear of losing friendship. She always kept her front door ajar for fear of dying and not being found for weeks. Any legal-looking paper threw her into a dither. Our relationship was good, but had been better in the past. I felt she was jealous because I had also developed a good relationship with others. She and Mrs. Moore had been the best of friends, but this turned into almost continual conflict, which was made up two days after. She seemed to get involved in these arguments because the Waterses didn't like Mrs. Moore and she felt she must oppose Mrs. Moore in order to be "in" with the Waterses.

Ward Subgroup.—*Mr. and Mrs. Ward* lived in Apartment 5A and had eight children and two grandchildren living with them. Two daughters, Sally and Bonnie, lived in separate apartments with their own children; two other children were institutionalized. They had been receiving DSS assistance for almost twenty years. Both were middle-aged Negroes. Mr. Ward worked (and probably still does, part time) as an electrical draftsman until he was laid off. Then his heart went bad. He had just about attacked every caseworker up until that time. The previous caseworker said she hated the family and would go out of her way to give them as little as possible.

The Wards disliked the Waters group because they were not New Yorkers, yet got things the Wards couldn't get. To them the Waters family were newcomers making out better than they were. They saw the Waterses as snobbish and pretending to be better than they, yet John Waters was responsible for Bonnie's child and also her new pregnancy. Mr. Ward had always been called upon in case of extreme emergency, by everyone, including the Waters group. He apparently had been able to put aside his feelings when a real crisis hit, and everyone realized this.

Sally lived in Apartment 5B, right next to her parents. She had two very young children and was about twenty years old. She received DSS assistance for the children and also was a Youth Corps enrollee at the Community House.

She was extremely aloof and hard, and until recently hadn't spoken with her father in many months. She considered herself better than all the others in the tenement, had a "cousin" who provided her with fine clothes, etc., and saw herself getting out of the tenement as soon as possible. She demonstrated no liking for anyone, even her mother, and was very cool to me. Our talks were formal and fairly sophisticated—at her desire.

Mrs. Moore lived in Apartment 4B, next door to Bonnie. She had three sons, but only one was at home and she was then arranging to have him institutionalized. The eldest son, twenty-seven, had raped her daughter (then nine), ten years before and the girl had died in the hospital. The middle son was in "boarding school" in South Carolina. Her youngest son she accused of stealing her welfare checks. She was twice married and divorced and spent most of her time with her boy friend, Jack. She continued to receive DSS assistance for the children. Except for Mr. Ward, she was the only high school graduate of the group. Only once did I see her when she was not intoxicated.

Our relationship was conditional on my willingness and ability to help her with personal complaints. Through what happened in group sessions, though, we were very honest and frank. Every other tenant had verbalized that she had an inferiority complex and they pitied her, but she was not well liked, even by some Wards. From the beginning she was desirous of a working relationship, yet definitely not a friendly one. She never brought up the subject of race, but I felt she had deep, strong negative feelings toward whites.

Mrs. Thomas lived in Apartment 1B with her three teenage sons and received DSS assistance for them, was almost deaf in one ear, and had had four operations on her leg, was a middle-aged Negro, and was considered by all to be the one who drank the heaviest. One could almost always find her in the company of four or five drinking companions.

She was generally liked by all, and they believed she had suffered so much that she broke under the strain. Her son had been imprisoned with the Ward boy about the time her leg was injured. Before that she had been a hard worker, energetic and kind to everyone. Mr. Ward was one of her drinking companions, and he and Olympia stated that they felt the group was a success, for at the very least it had gotten Mrs. Thomas on her feet again and active as part of the group.

Outsiders.—Mr. Tubb was the building agent for the building. He was unwilling at first even to talk to me. Then we talked a few times on the phone, but still he refused to meet with me. Eventually he came to this meeting, though reluctantly. He refused to discuss the meeting beforehand and said nothing about the fact that his superior was also coming.

Mr. Ryder was Mr. Tubb's superior, and I knew nothing of him until the meeting.

Rocky was one member of a two-man team which did the small repair jobs around the building. I did not know he would attend either.

Part 2: Group Meeting—January 16, 1968

This meeting was to be the climax of the group's movement toward unity; it was to be a show of strength and solidarity. I also hoped to have the group members to realize some of their potential and ability, see that they could assert some independence, and plan their next moves with as little intervention on my part as possible.

Though they had long asked to meet with the building agent, I doubted their stated actions once they would actually meet with him. All had said they would believe it only when it actually happened. On the one hand, they wanted to really let loose with him, and on the other, they feared the situation. It was an unknown and a risky one at that. Behind them lay the experience of a friendly outsider who met with them, then the DSS caseworker who represented that "machine" they hated and felt was always looking over their shoulders; and now they were to face the representative of the organization which aroused their most negative feelings.

Had they learned from these experiences? Had they fostered the feelings of security and competence that I intended they should? Were these enough to help them face today, realize their situation, and grow from it? I didn't know for sure, and my anxiety was showing. I went so far as to suggest an early lunch to my co-workers so I could get to the building early, urge a high attendance, check on their readiness, etc. At lunch I realized my own feelings and saw that such action would be contrary to what I hoped would result from the meeting. If the meeting was to stimulate greater independence, then that is what I would have to foster right from the start.

I arrived at Edna's apartment a few minutes before one o'clock, which was the time set for the meeting. She was well dressed and very anxious since no one else had come yet. If dress were any indication, I would say she felt the meeting was the most important to date. At earlier informal sessions she wore nightgowns, at the meeting with the lawyer a house dress, with the DSS caseworker a dress, and this time it looked more like evening wear or her Sunday best. As time went by her mother, Mrs. Waters, came with Vera, who took the children downstairs. (This pattern was now well established and working well.) Soon after, Olympia came, followed shortly thereafter by Faith. "Where is everyone else?" was the common question. I suggested that, if they were worried about it, one of them should check on the others. (This would no longer be my function but theirs.) No one moved. Mr. Ward came in, asked for his wife, then went to get her. They continued to verbalize their anxiety about the others not being there. I remained silent, but I think I was just as anxious as they were. Finally, Edna took it upon herself to check on the others.

Meanwhile, Mrs. Thomas arrived and was helped in by a middle-aged man who quickly left after she was seated. She began jokingly yelling at me because of the postcard I'd sent. "I can get upstairs by myself, it's the getting down I can't do," she remarked. We all laughed and I realized she was "just what the doctor ordered." She was slightly intoxicated, and her remarks were very humorous. This light touch was what was needed at that point, and everyone took the opportunity, including myself, to release some of the anxiety through laughter. Edna returned with Helen and they joined in the fun. Now present was Edna, Helen, Faith, Mrs. Waters, Olympia, Mrs. Thomas and myself.

Mr. Tubb arrived, paid no attention to the tenants, came over to me, and, after a brief exchange of names, asked, "Are you going to hold the meeting?" His manner was more than abrupt, and I suggested his eyes speak for themselves. "Is this all?" he quipped. "We expect some more . . . that's what we're waiting for," I retorted. He then said his superior was waiting outside in a car and he went to get him. The tenants were extremely anxious at this point and began to move about. They said they couldn't believe it; "His boss too?" they asked. Edna rubbed her hands in delight about her chance to really tell them off. I reminded them of last week's session and what they said they would say today. Mrs. Waters and Olympia wondered where Mr. Ward was: "What's keeping him anyway? He should be here," said Mrs. Waters. I then asked about the other tenants. Yes, they had contacted the Puerto Rican families but no one could come. Also Mrs. Roland was out looking for a new apartment in the Bronx. "What about Mrs. Moore?" asked Edna.

I tried to reassure them, but they remained very anxious. I couldn't even reassure myself. Laughter worked before so I tried it again; I talked about the room, and they joked about the difference between "Charleston people" and other Negroes. Mrs. Thomas's remarks were beautifully funny, but then again anything probably would have seemed funny at that point. We all needed a good laugh.

Mr. Tubb returned and introduced me to his supervisor, Mr. Ryder, and the handyman who usually did the work in the building, Rocky. I then introduced them to the others. Olympia was still muttering, "Where's Tom?" I suggested we wait a few minutes for the others; Ryder said he was a busy man and either we begin or he'd leave; the others knew what time the meeting began, and the Department of Real Estate men were punctual. I began by explaining my interest, agency affiliation, and why we were holding this meeting. Mr. Ryder seemed not to be listening and asked, "Where's the lawyer?" I explained that he wasn't here, nor was he supposed to be, and strongly reiterated my point that he was here to talk with the tenants, not a lawyer or myself. "All right, all right, what's your problem?" he asked as he pointed at Mrs. Thomas. She was numb. I interrupted and told him this is no interrogation. "I know it isn't," he retorted, and pointed at Olympia and asked, "You got a complaint?" She almost fainted. I pulled his arm down and told him he was acting like a Gestapo officer and that he was here "to talk with" these people and not to yell at them. He said he didn't realize he was acting like that, but if that's how it looked, he'd stop. Then he asked me to "watch that I don't do it again." Then he put his hands under his legs to demonstrate his change of approach.

Again the harsh questions, but this time without the pointing. No one answered; they seemed perched on the limb of a tree. Then he loudly said, "See, this is a waste of time. They know they're treated right, they've no complaints, see for yourself!" He stood to leave. I sat way back and told him he was a "load of bullshit" and again told him the stupidity of his actions. I also mentioned that the tenants were doing the right thing in not talking. "Not until you really show a willingness to talk should they speak out." Then he asked if I were blaming him, and I said I was.

He sat down again and asked how he should act. I explained the difficulty of the situation because he'd already acted the way he had, but possibly he had now convinced the tenants that he wished to talk. I asked if anyone cared to say something. Dead silence. I suggested, in an asking way, that I relate Mrs. Moore's complaint since I had received her request to do so if she weren't present. I told the story. "Where is she?" Ryder quickly asked. I told him that this was not the point and asked if he'd really come to talk. "If so, explain it, not ask where is she," I told him. He looked at Tubb, and Tubb now had a quantity of official-looking cards in his lap. He sorted through them, then said three times his men tried to correct the situation but she was never at home.

This irritated Edna and she said that was a lie. Olympia supported her; they were finally talking. I decided to restrict my intervention from this point on. Then they all began to yell at once about these "supposed calls" with no one at home. Ryder turned to me "Now who do I believe?" he asked, holding his hands over his ears. Rocky yelled out that the tenants were wrong, and he was almost assaulted. Ryder intervened and told Rocky to keep quiet. "Where do we go from here?" Ryder asked. I refused to answer, quite loudly, and suggested he pose this question to the tenants. At this they resumed order.

As he began to ask them, Mrs. Moore came in. They all tried to fill her in at once. Mr. Ryder introduced himself. She took the floor and began to go over her complaint time and time again. Mr. and Mrs. Ward came in during this talk. Ryder promised to take care of it by Friday, but this didn't end her talking.

The others were getting annoyed at her. Mr. Ward was asked to talk by the others. Still Mrs. Moore would not stop; she was very drunk. We all sat painfully through this; at times I was asked to intervene, at others, Mr. Ward; side talks started. I continued to look at Mr. Ward, asking with my eyes that he intervene.

I was being torn apart inside, but I couldn't intervene. This was Mr. Ward's chance and I wanted him to seize it. He tried, he yelled at her, but still she continued. Then he made a motion to leave. Mr. Ryder pulled him back when he realized how much the others were pleading with him to stop her and not to leave. I felt sick to my stomach.

Then Mrs. Waters screamed at Mrs. Moore and told her everyone wanted Mr. Ward to speak. Mrs. Moore became silent. Mr. Ward began by thanking Mrs. Waters, then Mrs. Moore started in again. The others were almost out of their seats by then, but Mr. Ward gave her a dressing-down that quieted her. Then he began to relate his feelings. Mrs. Moore started in again; this time Olympia put her hand over Mrs. Moore's mouth and Mr. Ward continued. When he finished he looked questioningly at me. I said he had stated the problem very well but it might help if he gave some examples that would refute Mr. Tubb's records. In a low voice, "Give me some help . . . get me started," he asked. (Or was he telling me what to do? I'd like to feel it was the latter.) Then after I said, "the exterminator bit," he gave example after example.

Ryder then turned to Tubb and said he was taking control of the building "until I get to the bottom of all this." Mr. Ward was proud, very proud, and everyone could see it. I was jumping inside. He had taken that big step. Totally unlike him, he didn't use one curse, even at Mrs. Moore. At times he stood there like a meek lamb, worried, scared, unsure of himself. But he finally came through and provided the strength the others needed. I felt that no amount of "talking" about his position could have done for him what today's meeting was doing. I'd assist as I saw fit, but I would at least hesitate in interventions; I felt even more certain they could really declare some independence. In short, I was relieved.

Then Mr. Ward and Mr. Ryder began to go over the details of repairs and equipment. The list grew so long that Mr. Ryder promised to have a team of his men go through the entire building and fix everything and write down anything needed that they couldn't do. This brought responses from Mrs. Thomas, Edna, Mrs. Moore, and Olympia. Olympia really let loose. She refused to let his men in her apartment because they only "make things worse." Then she said Rocky did sloppy work. All the others disagreed and said his partner was a jerk, not him. Olympia stuck to her guns, stood yelling, and grabbed at Rocky. Edna and Helen tried to restrain her, but she quickly put them down verbally. Each had had a say, now she was having hers and she really brought this point home. They retreated and Olympia concluded her complaints. I had seen her angry before, but her taking on the whole group was almost inconceivable. Three times during her excited statements she remarked about her "bad heart" and "high blood pressure," but these remarks only affected Mr. Ryder; the others were now used to them.

Mr. Ryder said he would stay with his team and they wouldn't leave until the work was done to the tenants' satisfaction. Olympia then accepted his proposal and the others quickly followed. Then they began to praise Mr. Ward and talk among themselves.

While this was going on, Mr. Ward leaned over and whispered, "Should I bring up the rent?" and I winked in response. Then he stood in the middle of the room and told the story of no heat and no hot water in December. He concluded by asking where they [the tenants] stood on the rent. Mr. Ryder looked to Tubb and Tubb explained about the 33 percent. Ryder said, "Well, where's the problem? You're getting a 33 percent cut . . . I see no problem about the rent." Mr. Ward briefly spoke about the hardship it caused and concluded by emphatically stating that he wouldn't pay one cent of December's rent and that he'd only accept a 100 percent cut and nothing else. This really irked Mr. Ryder, and he suggested a 10 percent cut instead. I could not believe my ears, nor could Mr. Ward. Mr. Ryder went on to say they couldn't have everything they asked for and began to tell how expensive it was to keep up a building. With this, Mr. Ward pushed his way out. As the others attempted to bring him back, I talked with Mr. Ryder. I said 33 percent was already offered and saw no reason for lowering it. Then his attitude got the best of me and I lost my cool. I literally blew my stack and let him know how Tubb strung us along and how only the tenants suffered, while everyone else made money on the deal. Regaining control, I asked Helen to try to clear the air. I asked her because of her abilities and the way I thought she'd react.

She began by explaining what a good paying tenant she was and that she had no major complaints, but she couldn't permit the rent situation to be left as it was. In a low but firm voice she told of illnesses and hardships of the tenants, and then she too placed much of the blame on Tubb's faulty handling of the situation. When she finished, I added a few facts about specific attempts to correct the situation. It now became apparent that Mr. Ryder had not been told all the details, as Tubb had said he would do earlier.

Ryder was moved by Helen's talk and looked angrily at Tubb, then he asked if 50 percent would be acceptable. I said that the tenants would have to decide, and, as I told Tubb, the decision would be made at our get-together after this meeting. I then asked the tenants if they wished a change in plans. They did not and felt we should stick to our original plan.

Then he told us this 50 percent figure was not assumed; he'd first have to get permission, but in light of the situation, he felt he would get that permission. Mr. Ryder rose to leave, but I stopped him and we summarized the agreements reached today for all to hear. The primary ones were: He'd have an answer on the 50 percent cut in a few days; he and his team would go through the building next week; no punitive action would be taken against any tenant; the building agent would meet with us once a month and would have to report to Mr. Ryder on each session; Mr. Ryder would also visit some apartments today at the request of those tenants who wanted it.

I reminded everyone to come back for the get-together and thanked Mr. Ryder for coming, and then he assured me of his cooperation. As Rocky passed us he commented, "Now they like me . . . now they like me." Ryder laughed.

Informal Session

I helped Mrs. Thomas downstairs and she said she could be told later about our get-together. She didn't want to go upstairs again after Mr. Ryder left. I rejoined the others in Edna's.

When I returned, I discovered that Sally had come down. This was the second time she had come after the meeting for the informal session. Edna, Helen, and Faith filled Sally in and seemed happy with the results. Then they began to discuss Mrs. Moore and verbalized their dislike of her coming intoxicated. Sally was laughing at their accounts; I was in the kitchen, but I could hear.

When I came back they asked me to talk about the meeting. I suggested we wait for the others before making any decisions, but we could begin to talk in the meantime. Helen asked if I felt things were really going to change. I said they already had and began to explain what it had been like in the building a few months before. Some interrupted with supportive statements and concluded with Edna's "Now we're really together . . . it's real . . . but we gotta stick together." Olympia started talking about the meeting.

I began to get back to Helen's question and explained our gains, but cautioned about what the actual results might be. We couldn't hope for too much, and a bumpy road lay ahead; but we had communicated, we had let them know we had a group that was concerned and willing to take action; we had gotten together. I reminded the Waters girls and Sally about their earlier feelings about each other, and how their mothers tried to get together because they possibly saw the merits of friendship. "You know, I don't hear any more remarks like that," I said, commenting on their previous refusals to see each other.

Then Mrs. Moore came back, listened a minute, then interrupted. She began by calling us all a bunch of nothings. "You're nobodies talking about nothing. You just talk; it doesn't mean nothing." I asked if she was angry with me and she said she wasn't. I said I was angry at her because I thought we'd reached a stage where we could talk frankly and I felt she was angry with me. She replied, "I'm not really angry with you. It's us. Why the hell do we need you? Who are you anyway, coming here? If we need you that only proves we're nothing, you're a white man. (The others cut her off and I asked her to continue.) I'm really mad at us. Why can't we hold a meeting without you?" she concluded.

I said that Mrs. Moore and I had talked about this before and that I whole-heartedly supported her views. "Why can't you hold meetings without me?" I asked. Olympia and Faith felt that they couldn't. Olympia said, "We're not strong enough yet, don't you see that?" Faith said I had the power to get things done and without me they were "lost." Mrs. Moore objected and began to repeat that I was white and she was a "Negro female." I began to respond when Olympia blew her top and said such remarks were out of order and called Mrs. Moore a drunkard. Mrs. Waters supported Olympia, but the others wanted to hear my reply. Olympia quickly left in a frustrated state. Only Mrs. Waters tried to stop her. I was tempted to also, but felt it best not to do so. Such action at the very least could be damaging to the group, particularly at this crucial point.

Then Mrs. Waters asked me to return to the earlier discussion about the meeting with Mr. Ryder. I said I felt it best to deal with Mrs. Moore's remarks instead and told them that just as we asked the white caseworker to spell out his philosophy, so too I should do the same today. "I'm white and you're all black. Now it's said out loud. Does it change anything? (Mrs. Waters pleaded for me to stop.) Maybe now that it's said we can talk more frankly. I don't know, sometimes I feel I don't belong here, and at others it's more like a second home. The thing is, you're a group now. I helped, but I, a white guy, shouldn't be in the front. You have to develop your own leadership. A black person should be your leader, not me. Let's face it, there's a hell of a lot happening these days, and if I stayed in the front, I'd be hurting you, all of you, and me too. I think you've got what it takes, you're ready. Just think about it a minute."

Edna broke the silence by yelling, "But Jack, you're our leader." Her mother, almost in tears now, said just about the same thing. Helen hit on another point I had hoped to get back to. She said this was a risky business and today they'd all stuck their necks way out. She wasn't prepared to do it again without me. She commented that I almost lost my cool a couple of times, but I'd gained control, something they couldn't do. She remarked, "I was watching you. I saw you struggling to keep calm. You warned him he was getting you hot under the collar. You realized what the risk was. I don't know if everyone here really knows even now."

I said a big part of this I'd failed to say; I wasn't going anywhere. I suggested I continue as I had been doing, but with a new twist. "From now on your leader will tell me what he wants from me. I'll help him or her all I can, and I'll remain available to all just as in the past."

Now Edna changed her view and began to praise Mr. Ward for both today's action and past ones. Helen played up the point that they also were crucial to today's success. Yes, I was needed, but they were gaining strength and should begin to realize this and do for themselves. She felt meetings should be held without me, so they could discuss things in their own way. I'd be told of the results, but not all that was said or how it was put.

Edna took the leadership and they began to formalize my future role as they saw it. Each had a say, even Sally, and gradually they defined specifically what I should do after they selected a leader. I would consult with "him." I'd continue to come to the more formal meetings, speak when I saw fit, but wouldn't lead it. After such meetings I'd tell them what was right and wrong and give them any information I thought they should have. I would also continue to see them individually and help in any way I could. I was pleased that they based many of these suggestions on their experiences with our group meetings. Edna, for instance, said it was a good idea to have me explain things after a meeting because it was working well. This was the third time we'd done this. I praised them on what they'd just done, explained what they'd done in moderately sophisticated language, and said I totally agreed with their decisions. Everyone was happy except Mrs. Moore.

She had more to say. She knew they were all talking in terms of Mr. Ward as the leader and she didn't like this. "Why him?" she asked. "I'm the one who got Jack—Mr. Benton—to come here. I'm the one who went around asking for help. You'd be no place without me. We wouldn't even be together here today if it weren't for me." Olympia came back as she was talking, and Olympia told Mrs. Moore to keep her mouth closed. The others giggled and Olympia looked at them sternly but proudly.

Helen asked how everything looked. I pointed out the great steps forward they'd taken, but again cautioned about bad days ahead. I'd be there to help, though, and they shouldn't feel too bad if I was asked to take a more active role. I hoped the situation would not arise, but if it did, they should remember it would only be temporary. They couldn't expect themselves to be a well-organized, sophisticated group overnight. They'd have to learn to deal with internal problems and conflicts, and if individuals had a fight, they'd have to stick with the group—even if with the persons in the room who had just fought with them. Faith and Olympia emphasized that either they would be a group or they would return to their "old ways" and live in their own separate "cat holes."

Then I asked Mrs. Moore if she had anything to say. She replied that she'd been told to be quiet. I said, "Well, if you think you should." She began to talk again about the leader. Edna interrupted and said they'd decide that later, not today, "since Tom ain't here now." Edna looked at me and explained that Mr. Ward was involved in "personal business" today, had come a long distance to be here for the meeting, and had had to get back. "That's why he left when he did, really." I acknowledged this.

Then Edna asked me about an earlier comment of mine concerning MacMahon Clinic; she wasn't sure what I'd said and felt we should discuss it before we ended the meeting. I said I would, but before I did, I just wanted them to be thinking about the rent decision. "This should be discussed too," I said.

Edna said she was concerned about her children's health. Helen felt the situation at the clinic was very poor, and Edna disagreed and related a recent incident. With that, Mrs. Moore jumped up and screamed that her daughter had been "murdered" there. This drew immediate silence. Edna broke it by first sympathizing with her and then explaining that things were changing now. Sally supported Edna, and Mrs. Waters asked that I speak.

I began by saying I felt the doctor who was used by most of them was unfit. I was amazed at their approval of this statement; I thought they liked him. I then went on to explain that someone from MacMahon Clinic was coming to talk with us and we should hear him out, even if we had strong feelings against MacMahon. Mrs. Waters pressed for my particular stand. I said, "If right now I was faced with only the two choices, I'd have to select MacMahon as the better one." This apparently satisfied them. Then they decided to hold off on the rent decision since Mr. Ward had a big voice in this and shouldn't be left out.

In concluding, Edna suggested that they adhere to the idea of moving the meeting place around. Mrs. Moore's offer was turned down since she'd already held one. Faith's offer was accepted and they remarked about gradually getting Mrs. Thomas to exercise more. Next time she'd have to make it up to the third floor.

Next, Edna suggested that from then on they have coffee and snacks at the meetings. "Coffee for Jack and snacks for me. How about it? Let's have some eats too. If they're really our meetings we should be able to do what we want at them—and have what we want at them too." Everyone agreed except Faith, who said she couldn't fix coffee. Edna said she'd take care of it. "Then it's fine with me," Faith concluded.

There would be no planned guest speaker at the next meeting; instead they would choose a leader, decide on what to do about rent, and plan following meetings. They began to leave one after the other, and I spoke to most individually before they departed. The general trend of each of the comments was how much of a success they felt the meeting had been.

Part 3: Early Contacts with Olympia—November 1, 1967

As I knocked on Mrs. Waters' door (receiving no answer) a short, very heavy black woman with very sharp and pleasant features walked down the hall and inquired, "Are you Joe?" I said I was and added, "But are you sure I'm the right Joe?" She smiled and asked if I was the one she was told to expect. "Aren't you going around meeting all the tenants?" She explained that Mrs. Waters had told her to expect me and expressed her desire to talk with me.

She explained that Mrs. Waters was around somewhere in the building and was about to help me find her when I suggested we talk. "Well, not out in the hall, I hope; that's not proper. Let's go up to my apartment," she said in response.

As we reached her apartment (3C) she stood rather motionless and seemed to be trying to catch her breath. I asked if she was feeling ill and she explained her poor health. "I just have to take my pill and then I'll be fine," she said as she opened the door. At her suggestion I went to the living room and waited for her to take her pill. The layout was the same as Mrs. Roland's apartment (the bathroom a few feet from the front door, then an open kitchen area, then the living room, and, at the far end, the corridor opening into the bedroom).

A few seconds later she joined me and had apparently undergone immediate transformation. Now she was alert and revitalized completely. (I thought this rather strange.) I complimented her on the appearance of the apartment and she thanked me, explaining that such cleanliness was proper. She added that possibly because others had children it was harder for them to keep things clean. I agreed but felt she meant me to think she was trying to be nice to the others but was really better than them. (At this point there was just an inkling, but I felt this definitely was the situation as our conversation continued.)

We then made the appropriate introductions and I explained my hopes of organizing a tenant group. Her name was Olympia. She said she should be glad to take part but doubted that many would participate. I explained who I had already seen and said they had reacted in a positive way for the most part. "Oh, Mrs. Thomas is interested?" she asked. I asked if there was a particular reason for her questioning tone, and she stated, "It's just that she's one of those I wouldn't think would want to, but I guess she can really use help. I'm glad to hear she's at least trying."

Then she changed the subject to her health and explained that she had an enlarged heart. She spoke of her Egyptian husband, who had been deported four years before (he had been deported four times), and said he had tuberculosis. When they discovered this about him they ("doctors") also made her take an X-ray and discovered no TB, but did discover an enlarged heart.

A number of times I attempted to get her to discuss any problems in the building but each time she changed the subject back to herself (her husband, her past life, her health, etc.). The talk was pleasant and rather frank, and I felt convinced she wanted me to like her and feel sorry for her and at the same time applaud her for what she had been able to do under difficult circumstances.

Under no circumstances would she tell me of other tenants, saying, "I can't speak for them. That wouldn't be right, would it?" Concerning her feelings she would only say, "I wouldn't want to give you a wrong notion. I think you should meet them and make up your own mind after you've talked to them." And when I asked who lived in a particular apartment (part of a stream of conversation), she said, "Oh, look at me, I never give out information and here I am talking to you this way. But I wouldn't want to give out any information like that, it wouldn't be right."

I felt that a rather positive relationship could be established without much difficulty and that she could very possibly be a great help to me and the others in a group. Though the conversation for the most part received its direction from Olympia, I was able to learn a great deal about her, her relationship with certain other tenants, facts about the building and its internal system. In a sense I felt as though we were playing a game. To any question, she would first have to maintain the privacy of others, then I'd rephrase it, then it would be permissible for her to answer (after I had first seen that she was a proper person and that it was customary for her not to talk about others).

November 3, 1967

For a while I didn't know which way to turn; Olympia wanted to control the conversation. At numerous points she revealed some of her needs; for instance, when we were talking about certain foods Mrs. Waters eats and makes, Olympia looked at me and said, "Now, you and I don't eat such stuff—do you?" They asked if I drank; I said I did. Olympia quickly added, "But not like they do around here; white people know how to hold their liquor. That's what you mean, ain't it?" I said that I had gotten plastered a few times, but she was right, it wasn't a habit with me (they howled with laughter). Olympia added, "The same with me. I don't drink no cheap wine, and I know how to hold it," and went into a long story about the many "fine restaurants" she drank in and didn't get drunk.

I had a constant feeling she was trying to play up to me. She wanted me to recognize her as being better than the others and a fitting person to socialize with "white folk."

November 8, 1967

We both came to the door (opposite sides) at the same time and I startled her. I explained about Mrs. Waters' absence and Olympia said she couldn't attend the meeting anyway. She was ill with "an extremely bad cold." On invitation I went into her apartment and she fixed a cup of coffee for me. As happened at our first meeting, she set up a TV table in front of her living room chair (she suggested I sit there), then came the cup of coffee, two spoons and a creamer. A second later she came with sugar. "You know, I'll bet I'm the only one here with this kind of sugar (cubes)." I thanked her, but said I took my coffee without sugar. She replied, "Oh, I do too, sometimes. You know some people just can't take it that way." When she came back she sat at the dinette table. I got up, moved everything over to the table, returned the creamer to the kitchen, came back, and sat at the table with her.

She began to discuss her cold and how she and Mrs. Waters had gone to the clinic the day before. I felt the conversation was strained and commented on this. She replied, "It's just what I told you; you can't help these people. Look, even Mrs. Waters—she couldn't have forgotten." I explained that quite a few days had passed since we had planned this meeting. She said I should have come by and reminded people. I explained my earlier intent and said that something had come up at the office. I said, "Well, I guess it is a bit more than just partly my fault." "That's not it, it's the people here."

As we continued to talk I learned some of her true feelings. She explained how she had been dispossessed from her apartment on City Street in Brooklyn. The people in that tenement were warm and friendly. "But over here it's cold." I asked what she meant. Instead of answering she asked, "Is it like this all around the neighborhood?" I said she probably knew more than I about that, and asked in a leading but empathetic manner, "Is it everyone that's cold?" She spoke of Mrs. Waters in particular. "Even though we're best of friends, there's still something there, a coldness. Do you know what I mean? In Brooklyn we all cared for each other. If something happened to one of us, it happened to all. We helped each other and really loved each other. It was family, real family, not like here. Everyone here only cares about himself. They'll be friendly, but not real friends. Do you really understand what I'm saying?"

I said I had experienced a similar situation, but that it was even harder for her because she couldn't get away as much as she might like. I offered, "Probably sometimes you even feel trapped. But I think you have done a good job of making the best of things." That, she then explained, is what keeps her going. "Everyone needs a purpose. These people have children and the kids give them a purpose for living. But me, sometimes I wonder. But I do the best I can. That's my purpose, and to me it's just as important. Everyone needs a purpose, right?" (She was deeply serious.) I said she was correct and added, "I think a big thing, though, is that we can all find much purpose if we just look around and maybe a little inside. It's there; I'm really glad you feel it, and I think you are being great. You know, I see you are one of the strong people here."

She then explained about some of the others and how even though they had children they didn't even try to help themselves or become better people. She asked very pointed questions, like "Whose fault do you really think it is?" and in a sense we argued. She felt most in the building were responsible for their own condition. "You can't blame the government or other people. Hell, it's them, it's their own damn fault." I explained that I couldn't find it in me to blame them. "It's just that some are stronger and able to take it, like you. And then some others are missing a little something, I don't know what. It's probably even different for each one. I can understand how you feel; after all, you live here and I don't. It's easy for me to say I'd rather understand than blame, but someone who lives here would really have to be a great person to be understanding and not get angry." Continuing after a pause, "You know, I think if I lived here I'd feel hurt—like the others are letting me down. I mean, they're human and so am I; they should care."

She then wanted to know if I felt hurt about the meeting's "falling to pieces." I said I'd be a damn liar if I said it hadn't bothered me; it had, but it "wasn't catastrophic." She asked, "What does that word mean?" I said, "In other words it's not the end of the world. It's a setback, but it's not a very bad setback. I didn't expect it, but I'm not going to give up. I'm like you. I'm going to keep on. You can't expect people to trust and like you right off the bat. They have to take their time, see what's happening first."

"But they should realize they have to do something too. The thing is that they don't even want help, some of them," she added.

The talk went on for some time and she revealed one great theme—her loneliness. She always spoke around the subject, and would probably not admit it if a direct question were put to her. I saw two major factors which I had to deal with: her health and her loneliness. It goes without saying that there were many tangentials to each area.

In discussing a meeting I suggested a change of strategy. I asked for her opinion about having only Mrs. Ward, Mrs. Waters, and herself meet with me the first time, instead of trying to get more tenants to the first meeting. She asked why I included her. She could understand about the other two, but not herself.

I explained that I felt she had much to bring to the group. As we continued she was hesitant about making any commitment. She realized Mrs. Ward's position without my saying anything and would permit her apartment to be used for the meeting. Other meetings including the other tenants would have to be held elsewhere. She didn't mind meeting with them, but she didn't want all of them in her apartment. She doubted that Mrs. Ward and Mrs. Waters would come to her place—"They never come in to see me, I always have to go to them"—but if I spoke to them and they agreed, it would be fine with her. We then went down to Edna's again.

I told them I'd come again next Wednesday, and went back upstairs with Olympia to get my coat. When we got upstairs we began to talk again. The discussion was serious and meaningful. The major point I wanted to make was to have her tell me she couldn't sleep at night. She said it wasn't that she was afraid of dying; it was that she is afraid of dying and not being found for weeks. She related a story from her past and explained that a friend had died and she had discovered it two weeks later. "I said goodnight to her and she must have just gone in and dropped dead." She screamed this last part and seemed to be in a trance. I tried to be sympathetic and reminded her of her friends. She said they really weren't friends and they wouldn't even bother coming up to her apartment. She then related a few instances when she was sick and no one had come to her aid. But she always kept her door ajar so she could "feel closer" to the others.

I said I wouldn't be by every day, but at least a couple of days a week, and I cared and would always stop in at least to say hello. She was apparently happy, but commented, "Why should I have to rely on you? They should care; they live here; people who live together should care about one another." She went on to say I must have a lot of things to do rather than be concerned about her—real important things. I said she was my concern and was one of those real important things she was speaking of. Her reply was a warm, friendly smile. I told her I'd be in again next Wednesday, collected all the data she had given me (her doctor, real estate agent, DW caseworker) as we talked, put on my coat, and let myself out.

November 10, 1967

After the meeting I went to Olympia's and she immediately asked about the meeting. I explained the "wait and see" situation. She quickly left that topic and began to talk about herself. Formerly she had been a maid and liked to work with rich people so she could have certain luxuries surrounding her. We discussed this at length, and our relationship became stronger with each talk.

At another point she explained that her doctor would not give her a note so that the Welfare Department would change her status from home relief to aid to the disabled. She told me of her "naughty" habit of using salt, though she was told not even to buy a shaker. As she put it, "Who can eat fried chicken without salt? That's just plain crazy." Also she confessed she should not be smoking—"doctor's orders."

We talked of her problem with the toilet and about her welfare check not coming—she had to go down on Mondays to pick it up in person. I explained my intention of contacting the caseworker and the building agent. She favored this, but impressed on me that they did their best and that both were liked by the tenants. "The last welfare person was just a horrible man. Don't do anything to get her [present worker] changed or mad at us," she commented. I reassured her and explained in detail of my intentions.

There were times during this talk when we laughed and joked. The feeling was friendly and I believe she saw me as an informal professional. I could relax and laugh, but the job of helping and organizing a group never left me and she realized this. I didn't come just to comfort and befriend her; I was there to get things moving on the path of organized self-help.

Part 4: Summary, February 1968–May 1968

1. Though no tenant left the building, there were two cases that were important in this respect:

Kathy Waters, daughter-in-law of Mrs. Waters, moved from the Bronx to stay with Mrs. Waters. With the help of Miss Tegran of the CCL Unit, Mr. James of the Martin Welfare Center, and Mr. Collins of the Southside Welfare Center, we were able to relocate her in a five-room apartment in Brooklyn. She then contacted her assigned welfare center in Brooklyn.

Delores Watson, a friend from Charleston, came to stay with Edna because of her family situation. She came with her four children. With the help of Mr. Collins and Mr. Curtis of the Southside Welfare Center, we were able to temporarily relocate her in a three-and-a-half-room apartment in the area.

Both parents and their children frequent the building and in this respect, the Waters subgroup had expanded to include Edna (or Gertie), Helen, Faith, Olympia, Delores, Kathy, John Waters, and Mrs. Waters. As you can see, it was now a rather sizable grouping.

2. The group's contact with Mr. Tubb and Mr. Ryder of the Department of Real Estate proved fruitful during this period. The halls were painted and patched, toilet facilities were repaired for many, holes in apartments were patched, radiators were fixed, and those who requested them received new stoves and refrigerators. Much remained undone, though. Windows still had to be fixed and apartments were in need of painting.

A very positive working relationship was developed between the group and Mr. Collins of the DSS. Also, Mr. Curtis, unit supervisor, had a positive feeling toward the 165 Howell Street group and was helpful and ready to extend himself.

The group went through a very trying period, and Mr. Ward's leadership was challenged. As housing and welfare problems diminished in scope and intensity, the group turned inward and conflict was apparent in almost every meeting. Mrs. Moore was seen by the group as a destructive element in their quest for progress. Though all agreed she could be acceptable and helpful when sober, no one wanted any part of her when she had been drinking.

The Waters grouping grew in strength and number, but did not seek formal leadership. They felt it was a man's job. Joe Thomas was able to demonstrate some of his ability in leadership and was to be looked to in this respect. Mr. Ward, though the formal leader, lost the esteem and respect of the group and angered the others to the point where they no longer really wanted him as a leader.

Olympia began to speak out much more and confronted Mr. Ward a few times. She went outdoors more often and generally opened up quite a bit. The group provided her with a vehicle to grow and become more active and involved with others.

Faith, because of a number of specific actions, gained much respect, and possibly even Mr. Ward feared her ability and its recognition by the others.

Mrs. Cole of 193 Howell Street, a friend of Mr. Ward and Mrs. Thomas, became involved in the group and was a very active participant. Her relationship with the group did not rest solely with Mr. Ward.

3. *Goals:* (a) Though there had been some improvement in their living conditions, improvement as a concrete goal was not yet fully realized. (b) The goal to involve all tenants never crossed the racial barrier. There still remained two Puerto Rican families to be involved and the Ross brothers in Apartment 2B. Their involvement was open to discussion. Perhaps it would be better to focus on individual family problems instead, including these three families, and view the present group as a secondary force; maintain the group, but focus on *all* families; possibly then, these others would join the group. Note: There was a problem of drug addiction in the Acevedo family. (c) Constant contact, even if not in person, was advisable. Other workers, too many others, came and went, with gaps between. I felt the worker should impart the sense that he was there all the time, even though he wasn't. Possibly, too, more attention could be given to the children and teenagers—or, if desired, they could be the new focus.

4. *Agencies and contacts:* Ed Collins of the Department of Social Services was helpful in regard to the group as a whole, as well as to its individual members. He was particularly helpful regarding Mrs. Moore and Kathy Waters. Because of work pressures, he often got bogged down. A call to him was all that was necessary for him to react positively and, if possible, quickly. At last contact there were two caseworkers assigned to the building, but Ed would probably be the real contact person for a while, even if he was no longer assigned there.

It goes without saying that Mr. Tubb and Mr. Ryder were involved with all tenants, but as leader, Mr. Ward had much more contact with them and was recognized by them as the leader of the building.

Though CCLU was involved for a period around the no-heat situation, Miss Tegran continued to help at a later date, specifically in the case of Kathy Waters.

Other contacts were not as intense or involving but of possible concern would be two parole officers: In the case of Nicholas Duke, the contact was Mr. Coshen; in the case of Mr. Ward, Jr., the contact was Mr. Femolo.

REFERENCES

Chapter 1

Bell, Winifred (1983). *Contemporary Social Welfare*. New York: Macmillan.

Dusky, Lorraine (1983). Detroit's sad voices. *The New York Times Magazine,* June 12, 1983, pp. 79ff.

Fitzgerald, Thomas (1983). Homosexuality: the myth of the composite portrait. In Ronald Federico and Janet Schwartz, *Sociology,* Third Edition. Reading, Mass.: Addison-Wesley, pp. 216–221.

Keith-Lucas, Alan (1972). *Giving and Taking Help*. Chapel Hill: University of North Carolina Press.

King, Wayne (1982). Texas trailer lots are bare as many job-hunters head home. *The New York Times,* December 10, 1982, p. A-16.

McPheeters, Harold, and Robert Ryan (1971). *A Core of Competence for Baccalaureate Social Welfare and Curricular Implications*. Atlanta: Southern Regional Education Board, p. 15.

Peterson, Iver (1982). Homeless crisscross U. S. until their cars and their dreams break down. *The New York Times,* December 15, 1982, p. A-15.

Prevention Report (1982). Family based service: relevance for prevention. *National Resource Center on Family Based Services*. Oakdale, Iowa: University of Iowa, pp. 1ff.

Robson, William (1976). *Welfare State and Welfare Society*. London: George Allen and Unwin, p. 174.

Towle, Charlotte (1952). *Common Human Needs*. New York: Family Service Association of New York.

Valle, Ray, and Lydia Mendoza (1978). *The Elderly Latino*. San Diego: Campanile Press.

Washington Social Legislation Bulletin (1983). Vol. 28, Issue 5, March 14, 1983: 19.

Zimbalist, Sidney (1977). *Historic Themes and Landmarks in Social Welfare Research*. New York: Harper and Row. The section on research in Chapter 1 of this book is broadly based on Zimbalist's book.

Chapter 2

Anderson, Susan Heller (1982). New York clergy fault government for failures in housing homeless. *The New York Times*, December 25, 1982, p. 1ff.

Becker, Howard S., et al. (1961). *Boys in White*. Chicago: University of Chicago Press.

Bell, Winifred (1983). *Contemporary Social Welfare*. New York: Macmillan.

———— (1969). Obstacles to shifting from the descriptive to the analytical approach in teaching social services. *Journal of Education for Social Work* 5 (Spring):5–13.

Dunbar, Ellen, and Howard Jackson (1972). Free clinics for young people. *Social Work* 17 (September):34.

Gailey, Phil (1982). Homosexual takes leave of a job and of an agony. *The New York Times*, March 31, 1982, p. A-12.

Greene, Wade (1976). A farewell to alms. *The New York Times Magazine*, May 23, 1976, pp. 36–46.

Hall, Richard (1968). Professionalization and bureaucratization. *American Sociological Review* 33 (February):92–104.

Johnson, Harriette C., and Gertrude S. Goldberg (1982). *Government Money for Everyday People*. Garden City, N. Y.: Adelphi University School of Social Work.

Kahn, Alfred J., and Sheila B. Kamerman (1977). *Social Services in International Perspective*. Washington, D. C.: U. S. Government Printing Office.

Kamerman, Sheila (1983). The new mixed economy of welfare: public and private. *Social Work*, Vol. 28, No. 1 (January–February), pp. 5–12.

Kerr, Peter (1982). Woman's work: rarely blue collar. *The New York Times*, July 23, 1982, p. A-12.

Kleiman, Dena (1982). Language barrier is thwarting young Vietnamese immigrants in Elmhurst. *The New York Times*, December 8, 1982, p. B-3.

Kramer, Ralph (1973). Future of the voluntary service organization. *Social Work* (November):61–62. Paraphrased by permission of the National Association of Social Workers.

Landy, David (1965). Problems of the person seeking help in our culture. In Mayer Zald, ed., *Social Welfare Institutions*, pp. 559–574. New York: John Wiley.

Mouzelis, Nicos (1968). *Organization and Bureaucracy: An Analysis of Modern Theories*. Chicago: Aldine Publishing Co.

Nelson, Bryce (1982). Demands of intense psychotherapy take their toll on patient's spouse. *The New York Times*, December 28, 1982, pp. C-1ff.

Rule, Sheila (1982). Black divorces soar; experts cite special strains. *The New York Times*, May 24, 1982, p. A-17.

Sidel, Ruth (1972). Social services in China. *Social Work* 17 (November):5.

Smothers, Ronald (1983). Medical groups aiding the uninsured jobless. *The New York Times*, May 13, 1983, p. A12.

Stanton, Esther (1970). *Clients Come Last*. Beverly Hills: Sage Publishers.

Teltsch, Kathleen (1983). Donations for poor quickly depleted in big cities. *The New York Times*, January 1, 1983, p. 17.

Washington Social Legislation Bulletin (1983). Vol. 28, No. 9, p. 1.

Wax, John (1968). Developing social work power in a medical organization. *Social Work* 13 (October):62–71.

Wilensky, Harold, and Charles Lebeaux (1958). *Industrial Society and Social Welfare*. New York: Free Press.

Windschild, Gunther (1978). Social policy—a comprehensive network. In *Meet Germany*, 17th ed. Hamburg: Atlantik-Bruche, pp. 82–88.

Chapter 3

Berger, Robert, and Ronald Federico (1982). *Human Behavior: A Social Work Perspective*. New York: Longman, Chap. 3.

Bremner, Richard H. (1960). *American Philanthropy*. Chicago: University of Chicago Press.

Bruno, Frank (1957). *Trends in Social Work*. New York: Columbia University Press, p. 108.

Civil Rights Update (1982). United States Commission on Civil Rights. November 1982.

Cohen, Nathan (1958). *Social Work in the American Tradition*. New York: Dryden Press, p. 49.

Coll, Blanche (1969). *Perspectives in Public Welfare*. Washington, D. C.: U. S. Government Printing Office.

Federico, Ronald, and Janet Schwartz (1983). *Sociology*. Reading, Mass.: Addison-Wesley Publisher, Chapters 3 and 4.

Hardcastle, David (1973). General revenue sharing and social work. *Social Work* 18 (September 1973), pp. 3–4.

Klein, Philip (1968). *From Philanthropy to Social Welfare*. San Francisco: Jossey-Bass.

Kurzman, Paul A. (1970). Poor relief in medieval England: The forgotten chapter in the history of social welfare. *Child Welfare* 49 (November), pp. 49–50. This article provides an excellent discussion of even earlier social legislation, including the Statute of Laborers of 1349, as well as also discussing the Industrial Revolution.

Leiby, James (1978). *A History of Social Welfare and Social Work in the United States*. New York: Columbia University Press, p. 111.

Leonard, E. M. (1965). *The Early History of the English Poor Relief*. New York: Barnes and Noble, p. 16.

Lubove, Roy (1969). *The Professional Altruist*. New York: Atheneum, Chap. II.

Mencher, Samuel (1967). *Poor Law to Poverty Program*. Pittsburgh: University of Pittsburgh Press, p. 27.

Miles, Arthur P. (1949). *An Introduction to Social Welfare*. Boston: D. C. Heath.

Miller, Judith (1983). Public mood tied to Mobile's hospital care woes. *The New York Times*, March 8, 1983, p. A10.

Notestein, Wallace (1954). *The English People on the Eve of Colonization*. New York: Harper and Row, p. 245.

The New York Times (1983). Social Security: The benefits, the history, the problems. February 4, 1983, p. A12.

O'Neill, John (1982). Bankrupted economic policies; inhumane social programs. *Newsletter,* Vol. 5, No. 3, Spring 1982. Eastern Washington University School of Social Work and Human Service, p. 1.

Pear, Robert (1983). U. S. would ask children to pay for parent care. *The New York Times*, March 30, 1983, pp. A1ff.

———— (1982). Study finds U. S. cuts harm the poor. *The New York Times*, March 19, 1982, p. A4.

Perspectives: The Civil Rights Quarterly (1982). Speaking out. Vol. 14, No. 2, Summer 1982, pp. 42–57.

Romanyshyn, John (1971). *Social Welfare: Charity to Justice*. New York: Random House.

Schenk, Quentin F., and Mary Lou Schenk (1981). *Welfare, Society, and the Helping Professions.* New York: Macmillan, pp. 45–47.

Shribman, David (1983). House, 243–102, passes legislation on Social Security. *The New York Times,* March 25, 1983, pp. 1ff.

Smith, Russell, and Dorothy Zeitz (1970). *American Social Welfare Institutions.* New York: John Wiley, p. 43.

Statistical Abstract of the United States (1981). Bureau of the Census. Washington, D. C.: U. S. Government Printing Office.

Steinberg, S. H., ed. (1963). *A Dictionary of British History.* New York: St. Martin's Press, p. 280.

Washington Social Legislation Bulletin (1983). Vol. 28, Issue 4, February 28, 1983.

———— (1983a). Vol. 28, Issue 3, February 14, 1983.

———— (1982). Vol. 27, Issue 30, March 22, 1982.

———— (1974). Monitoring revenue sharing. Vol. 23, Issue 42, September 23, 1974, p. 170.

Chapter 4

Brill, Naomi (1978). *Working with People.* Second Edition. Philadelphia: J. B. Lippincott, pp. 91–103.

Day, Peter R. (1977). *Methods of Learning Communication Skills.* New York: Pergamon Press, pp. 1–20.

Devore, Wynetta, and Elfriede Schlesinger (1981). *Ethnic-Sensitive Social Work Practice.* St. Louis: C. V. Mosby and Co., pp. 111–120.

Eriksen, Karin (1977). *Human Services Today.* Reston, Va.: Reston Publishing Co. Based on pp. 130–144.

Federico, Ronald (1980). *The Social Welfare Institution: An Introduction.* Third Edition. Lexington, Mass.: D. C. Heath, pp. 367–390.

Keith-Lucas, Alan (1972). *Giving and Taking Help.* Chapel Hill, N. C.: University of North Carolina Press, p. 108.

Konle, Carolyn (1982). *Social Work Day-to-Day.* New York: Longman.

Landy, David (1965). Problems of the person seeking help in our culture. In Mayer Zald, ed. *Social Welfare Institutions.* New York: John Wiley, pp. 559–574.

Loewenberg, Frank (1977). *Fundamentals of Social Intervention.* New York: Columbia University Press, pp. 24–28.

McQuail, Denis (1975). *Communication.* New York: Longman.

Piven, Frances, and Richard Cloward (1971). *Regulating the Poor*. New York: Pantheon.

Schoen, Elin (1983). Once again, hunger troubles America. *The New York Times Magazine*, January 2, 1983, pp. 21–23.

Sheehan, Susan (1978). *A Prison and a Prisoner*. Boston: Houghton-Mifflin.

Chapter 5

Anderson, Joseph (1981). *Social Work Methods and Processes*. Belmont, Cal.: Wadsworth, pp. 99–106.

Baer, Betty L. (1981). A conceptualization of generalist practice. Unpublished manuscript.

Bell, Alan P., and Martin S. Weinberg (1978). *Homosexualities*. New York: Simon and Schuster.

Brody, Jane (1982). How diet can affect mood and behavior. *The New York Times*, November 17, 1982, pp. C-1ff.

Clarke-Stewart, Alison (1978). *Child Care in the Family*. New York: Academic Press.

Davies, Martin (1981). *The Essential Social Worker*. London: Heinemann Educational Books, pp. 161–175.

Davis, James (1978). *Minority-Dominant Relations*. Arlington Heights, Ill.: AHM Publishing.

Federico, Ronald, and Janet Schwartz (1983). *Sociology*. Third Edition. Reading, Mass.: Addison-Wesley Publishers.

Good Tracks, Jim. Native American non-interference. *Social Work*, Vol. 18 (November), p. 33.

Herbers, John (1982). Census report shows gains in education and housing. *The New York Times*, April 26, 1982, pp. 1ff.

Hilgard, E., and G. Bower (1975). *Theories of Learning*. Fourth edition. Englewood Cliffs: Prentice-Hall.

Langer, Jonas (1969). *Theories of Personality Development*. New York: Holt, Rinehart and Winston.

Lidz, Theodore (1976). *The Person*. Revised edition. New York: Basic Books.

Marx, Jean (1983). Spread of AIDS sparks new health concern. *Science*, Vol. 219, January 7, 1983: 42–43.

Mazur, Allen, and Leon Robertson (1972). *Biology and Social Behavior*. New York: Free Press.

Miller, Judith, and Mark Miller (1982). Hands off! *Perspectives: The Civil Rights Quarterly*. Washington, D. C.: U. S. Commission on Civil Rights: 31–33.

Monat, Alan, and Richard S. Lazarus, eds. (1977). *Stress and Coping.* New York: Columbia University Press.

Montiel, Miguel, ed. (1978). *Hispanic Families.* Washington, D. C.: The National Coalition of Hispanic Mental Health and Human Services Organizations.

The New York Times (1982). Slave descendant fights race listing. September 15, 1982, p. A-16.

Norton, Dolores G., ed. (1978). *The Dual Perspective.* New York: Council on Social Work Education.

Pierce, Dean (1984). *Policy for the Social Work Practitioner.* New York: Longman.

Plummer, Kenneth (1975). *Sexual Stigma.* London: Routledge and Kegan Paul.

Reinhart, Charles (1981). *A History of Shadows.* New York: Vintage Books.

Roach, Marion (1983). Another name for madness. *The New York Times Magazine,* January 16, 1983: 22ff.

Siporin, Max (1975). *Introduction to Social Work Practice.* New York: Macmillan: 22.

Tischler, Henry, Phillip Whitten, and David Hunter (1983). *Introduction to Sociology.* New York: Holt, Rinehart and Winston: 103.

Towle, Charlotte (1952). *Common Human Needs.* New York: Family Service Association of America.

Underwood, Jane (1979). *Human Variation and Human Micro Evolution.* Englewood Cliffs: Prentice-Hall.

United States Commission on Civil Rights (1982). *Confronting Racial Isolation in Miami.* Washington, D. C.: U. S. Government Printing Office.

———— (1982a). *Minority Elderly Services: New Programs, Old Problems.* Washington, D. C.: U. S. Government Printing Office.

White, Edmund (1982). *A Boy's Own Story.* New York: E. P. Dutton.

Chapter 6

Alexander, Chauncey (1983). Belgian car manufacturer sports social work program. *NASW News,* Vol. 28, No. 1, January 1983, p. 13.

Brill, Naomi (1976). *Teamwork.* Philadelphia: J. B. Lippincott.

Brody, Jane (1982). Personal health. *The New York Times,* November 24, 1982, p. C3.

Kamerman, Sheila (1983). The new mixed economy of welfare: public and private. *Social Work,* Vol. 28, No. 1 (Janurary–February 1983), pp. 5–11.

Kim, Paul K., S. Zafar al-Hasan, and Dan Egli (1981). *Mental Health Professionals Perceive Knowledge and Skills Need.* Lexington, Ky.: University of Kentucky, p. 11. Based on data from J. J. Rosenstein and C. A. Taube (1978). *Staffing of Mental Health Facilities United States 1976.* NIMH Series B, No. 14. Washington, D. C.: U. S. Government Printing Office.

Konle, Carolyn (1982). *Social Work Day-to-Day.* New York: Longman.

NASW News (1983). Geriatric social work picked as growth area. Vol. 28, No. 1, January 1983, p. 3.

Prial, Frank (1982). More women work at traditional male jobs. *The New York Times,* November 15, 1982, pp. 1ff.

Smothers, Ronald (1981). Social work growth is reported slowed by cuts in spending. *The New York Times,* November 29, 1981, pp. 1ff.

Spingarn, Natalie Davis (1982). Primary nurses bring back one-to-one care. *The New York Times Magazine,* December 26, 1982, pp. 26ff.

Stetson, Damon (1982). Service work gains against production jobs. *The New York Times,* July 6, 1982, p. A11.

Chapter 7

Auletta, Ken (1982). The underclass—a down-to-earth mystery. *New York Daily News,* February 7, 1982, p. 44.

———— (1981). The underclass. *The New Yorker,* November 16, 1981, pp. 63ff.

Baer, Betty L., and Ronald Federico (1978). *Educating the Baccalaureate Social Worker.* Cambridge, Mass.: Ballinger Publishing.

Bell, Winifred (1983). *Contemporary Social Welfare.* New York: Macmillan.

Bernikow, Louise (1982). Alone. *The New York Times Magazine,* August 15, 1982, pp. 24ff.

Brownlee, Ann Templeton (1978). *Community, Culture, and Care.* St. Louis: Mosby.

Clymer, Adam (1983). Joblessness causing stress and gloom about nation. *The New York Times,* February 2, 1983, p. A19.

Collins, Glenn (1982). Some broken families retain many bonds. *The New York Times,* December 20, 1982, p. D12.

Colony, Joyce (1981). Diary of a glad housewife. *The New York Times Magazine,* December 6, 1981, pp. 44ff.

Coulton, Claudia J. (1982). Quality assurance for social service programs: lessons from health care. *Social Work,* September 1982, Vol. 27, No. 5, pp. 397–402.

Cummings, Judith (1982). New California homeless move from park to park. *The New York Times,* August 7, 1982, p. 6.

—— (1982a). Surge of homeless people in nation tests cities' will and ability to cope. *The New York Times,* May 3, 1982, p. B13.

Dullea, Georgia (1983). Wide changes in family life are altering the family law. *The New York Times,* February 7, 1983, pp. 1ff.

Galper, Jeffrey (1974). Social work as conservative politics. *Module 55.* New York: MSS Modular Publications, Inc., pp. 1–33, especially pp. 3–9.

Germain, Carel (1982). Teaching primary prevention in social work: an ecological perspective. *Journal of Education for Social Work,* Vol. 18, No. 1 (Winter), pp. 20–28.

Herbers, John (1982). Poverty rate on rise even before recession. *The New York Times,* February 20, 1982, pp. 1ff.

—— (1982a). Poverty rate, 14%, termed highest since '67. *The New York Times,* July 20, 1982, pp. 1ff.

—— (1982b). Census reports that growth of Hispanic population is largely in big cities. *The New York Times,* December 13, 1982, p. B18.

—— (1982c). In many ways, regions of U. S. grow more diverse. *The New York Times,* August 26, 1982, pp. 1ff.

Hornblower, Margaret (1980). Hmongtana: Laotian tribe starts over in bewildering new world. *Washington Post,* July 5, 1980, pp. 1ff.

Kahn, Alfred J., and Sheila B. Kamerman (1976). *Social Services in International Perspective.* Washington, D. C.: U. S. Government Printing Office.

King, Wayne (1982). Northerners who follow dream of jobs in Texas find work scarce and welfare skimpy in reality. *The New York Times,* June 14, 1982, p. A12.

Kleinfield, N. R. (1983). Operating for profit at hospital corp. *The New York Times,* May 29, 1983, pp. A1ff.

Lewin, Ellen, and Terrie A. Lyons (1982). Everything in its place: the co-existence of lesbianism and motherhood. In William Paul, James D. Weinrich, John C. Gonsiorek, and Mary E. Hotvedt, eds., *Homosexuality: Social, Psychological, and Biological Issues.* Beverly Hills, Ca.: Sage Publication, pp. 249–274.

Lindsey, Robert (1982). The new Asian immigrants. *The New York Times Magazine,* May 9, 1982, pp. 22ff.

MacNair, Ray, John S. Wodarski, and Jeffrey Giordano (1982). Social assessment instrumentation: the implications for delivery of human services. *Arete,* Winter 1982, Vol. 7, No. 2, pp. 11–24.

The New York Times (1982). Birth rate highest for Latins in U. S. May 26, 1982, p. C4.

—— (1982a). Average U. S. pay put at $15,691 last year. December 13, 1982, p. B18.

O'Connor, John J. (1982). TV and civil rights. *Perspectives: The Civil Rights Quarterly.* Summer 1982, Vol. 14, No. 2, pp. 39–41.

Pear, Robert (1983). By 1989, Medicare will use up fund, 2 U. S. reports say. *The New York Times,* February 21, 1983, pp. 1ff.

——— (1983a). U. S. plans to ease rules for hiring women and blacks. *The New York Times,* April 3, 1983, pp. A1ff.

Piven, Frances Fox, and Richard Cloward (1971). *Regulating the Poor.* New York: Pantheon.

Reid, P. Nelson (1972). Reforming the social services monopoly. *Social Work,* Vol. 17 (November).

Rule, Sheila (1983). 17,000 families in public housing double up illegally, city believes. *The New York Times,* April 21, 1983, pp. A1ff.

Schmeck, Harold, Jr. (1983). U. S. panel calls for patients' right to end life. *The New York Times,* March 22, 1983.

Schwamm, Jeffrey, Karen Greenstone, and Harriett Hoffman (1982). Resettling newcomers: the case of Soviet Jewish immigration. *Arete.* Winter 1982, Vol. 7, No. 2, pp. 25–36.

Severo, Richard (1983). Elderly increasingly seek legal help in dealing with financial labyrinth. *The New York Times,* May 3, 1983, p. B2.

Statistical Abstract of the United States (1981). Washington, D. C.: Bureau of the Census, U. S. Government Printing Office.

Stevens, William K. (1982). Sun belt finds it is having increasing problems living up to all its promises. *The New York Times,* July 5, 1982, pp. 1ff.

Toffler, Alvin (1982). Civil rights in the Third Wave. *Perspectives: The Civil Rights Quarterly,* Vol. 14, No. 2, Summer 1982, p. 36.

Washington Social Legislation Bulletin (1983). January 24, 1983, Vol. 28, No. 2.

——— (1983a). April 25, 1983, Vol. 28, No. 8.

——— (1982). April 26, 1982, Vol. 27, No. 32, p. 128.

——— (1982a). August 9, 1982, Vol. 27, No. 39.

Wiseman, Jacqueline (1970). *Stations of the Lost.* Englewood Cliffs, N. J.: Prentice-Hall.

GLOSSARY

Accountability Demonstrating that social welfare programs are effective in meeting needs. This usually requires that program objectives are clearly specified.

Adequacy The effectiveness of a program in meeting the needs of the target population (that is, the people the program is intended to serve).

Administration The effective management of professional resources and responsibilities in social welfare agencies and structures.

Advocate role Part of an interventive strategy, advocacy involves helping users obtain needed services. This may require the implementation of new services.

Aid to Families with Dependent Children (AFDC) A federal-state grant-in-aid income maintenance program to help support needy families with young children.

Almshouses Facilities developed in England in the 1600s to house those considered legitimately needy in which basic life-sustaining needs were met.

Behavior-changer role Part of an interventive strategy, behavior change involves modifying specific parts of a user's behavior.

Behavioral psychology The branch of psychological theory that asserts that all behavior is learned in separate units (acts), that the units are related to each other, and that the units become established in the individual's behavior repertoire by means of external reinforcement.

Binuclear families   Family units linked together through divorced and remarried spouses.

Biopsychosocial whole   Helen Harris Perlman's concept, which suggests that helping professions must understand the total person in that person's social environment. The helping relationship must include an awareness of the person's biological, psychological, and social characteristics and functioning.

Bread scale   A subsistence level, used in the Speenhamland Act of 1796, calculated according to food costs and family size, with welfare aid given if a family's income fell below that level. Public assistance budgets used today are a kind of bread scale.

Broker role   Part of an interventive strategy, brokerage involves knowing services that are available and making sure those in need reach the appropriate services.

Bureaucracy   A type of formal organization of people, tasks, and materials characterized by clearly specified goals and means, and impersonal relations between those working in the bureaucracy.

Capitalist-Puritan value system   The belief that people are responsible for themselves and that those who become dependent on others should be required to find ways to become self-sufficient.

Care-giver role   Part of an interventive strategy, care-giving involves providing supportive services for those who cannot fully solve their own problems and meet their own needs.

Casework   An interventive method that seeks to improve social functioning by concentrating on one person in depth, examining the individual's biological-psychological-social behavior within that person's social context.

Charisma   The personal qualities of an individual that enable that person to win the trust and loyalty of others.

Charity Organization Society   Begun in England in 1869 and established in America in 1877, its purpose was to improve the organization of private helping efforts and to reduce the abuse of charity by those who were not needy.

Children's allowances   The payment of a cash allowance to parents of children who are still minors.

Civil rights movement   An ongoing attempt to achieve equal rights for all minority groups in American society. Most often, this term refers to the attempts during the 1950s and 1960s to achieve racial equality for black people.

Collective bargaining   The negotiation between a union and a business (or an entire industry) to establish mutually agreeable work contracts.

Common human needs   The framework used by Charlotte Towle to identify the basic needs shared by all people, including food, shelter, affection, and productive activity.

Community   A spatially defined social unit within which there are identifiable patterns of social interdependence.

Community organization   An interventive method that seeks to improve social functioning by using organizational and community groups to develop skills in identifying needs and organizing to meet these needs.

Confidentiality   Ensuring that information obtained from and relating to users is only shared professionally and with the permission of the users.

Curative social welfare services   Services provided to solve an already existing problem.

Coverage   The number of people actually participating in a social welfare program.

Countervailing power structures   Structures that arise to check or balance a lopsided distribution of power.

Decentralization of services   Dispersing social welfare services throughout a community so that they are more readily accessible to persons who may need them. Decentralized services are usually operated by a centralized administrative, bureaucratic structure.

Diagnosis   Interpreting information from and about users to understand their situations and the problems involved in them.

Disposable income   The amount of money available to be spent by an individual, household, group, or organization.

Dividing the client   Dividing a person's problems into specialized subparts and assigning different professional persons or agencies to deal with each subpart.

Economic institution   The major social structure for managing the resources needed to produce, distribute, and consume goods and services.

Ego psychology   An adaptation of psychoanalytic theory that focuses on the present, and uses the personality's rational processes to understand the problems of the present.

Eligibility requirements   The criteria used to determine who is eligible to receive services in a social welfare program. Eligibility requirements may include such factors as age, income, employment status, parental status, and so on.

Elizabethan Poor Law   Passed in 1601 in England to help preserve the existing social order, it categorized the needy as helpless, involuntarily unemployed, or vagrant. It also established the practice of indenturing children from destitute families.

Empathy   The ability to comprehend and sense another person's situation and feelings from that person's point of view.

Equity   The degree to which a program is actually available to the people in the target population. Although in theory a program may specify a certain target population, in practice various characteristics may serve to exclude certain members of that population (lack of transportation to reach an agency to apply for service, for example).

Extended family   The form of the family comprised of three or more generations. It commonly also includes other blood-related persons.

Fee programs   Programs that charge users fees that cover some or all of the actual cost of the service.

Fiscal policy   The government's intervention in the market to establish and implement economic policy.

Formal helping structures   Bureaucratically organized structures whose services are provided by professional helping people.

Gaps in service   When a social welfare agency or service network offers only part of the services needed by a person.

Grant-in-aid programs   Making direct financial grants to people to help meet their needs (Supplemental Security Income, for example).

Great Depression   Starting with the Stock Market Crash of 1929, the Great Depression created massive unemployment, bank failures, and unprecedented need in the society.

Great Society   President Lyndon Johnson's concept that society could be improved through the enacting of various pieces of social welfare legislation aimed at reducing poverty and inequality.

Group dynamics   Social behavior in small groups, including such factors as group composition, leadership, goal setting, and cooperation or competition in group interaction.

Group work   An interventive method that seeks to improve social functioning by using the small group as the context and process of change.

Guaranteed income   Guaranteeing that the income of all persons or families reaches a predetermined level though a system of income supplements paid by the government to those whose income falls below this level.

Health Maintenance Organization (HMO)   A medical organization that contracts with persons to provide comprehensive health services for a flat fee. It is a type of health insurance.

Helper   A person providing help, who may be a professional, a paraprofessional, a volunteer, or simply a friend or other concerned person.

Helping relationship   The mutually desired interaction between a person seeking help and a professional helping person that is based on trust, respect, sharing, and mutual involvement in the problem-solving process.

Holistic perspective Understanding human behavior in terms of the range of factors involved and the way these factors interact and fit into patterns of actions and beliefs.

Host social welfare agency An agency in which there is a high degree of sharing between several professions that participate in decision making and the provision of services.

Human diversity The ways in which people are different because of biological, social, and cultural characteristics.

Humanist-Positivist-Utopian value system The belief that it is society's responsibility to meet the needs of its members, and that most human breakdown is caused by societal malfunctioning.

Income maintenance services Services that provide or increase the income available to a person or family.

Indenture The archaic practice of removing children from their own homes if their parents sought welfare help, and placing the children in more affluent families in return for the child's labor.

Indoor relief Providing welfare services to persons who reside in a facility for that purpose (originally almshouses, workhouses, and the like; today prisons, mental hospitals, rest homes, and so on).

Industrial Revolution Basic changes in the system of production in Western societies caused by the use of mechanical power in the production process in place of predominantly human or animal power. The roots of the Industrial Revolution go back to economic and social changes in the seventeenth century, with the main impact occurring in the eighteenth and nineteenth centuries. The revolutionary new use of mechanical power had far-reaching effects throughout the social structures affected.

Informal helping structures Those that help people to meet their needs without using professional helping people.

In-kind grant Providing people with a needed item (such as furniture) rather than the money to buy that item.

Institutional inequality The comprehensive disadvantage created for members of particular groups by systematic and cumulative discriminatory actions carried out within all of the major social institutions. Members of racial, ethnic, gender, age, physical-ability, and sexual-orientation minority groups are especially affected.

Interviewing Purposeful communication, including both verbal and nonverbal communication.

Judeo-Christian value system The belief that people have the right to make their own choices but that society has the obligation to provide resources to help them do so and to aid them when the results of their choices create problems for themselves or others.

Latent functions of social welfare   Functions that are less visible and that serve the special needs of powerful groups who influence societal decision making.

Laissez-faire capitalism   First formalized by Adam Smith in 1776, the idea that minimal government regulation of the economic system promotes healthy competition and maximum efficiency. Most capitalistic societies of today have considerably more governmental economic control than that suggested by a pure laissez-faire system.

Legal credentialing   Legal regulation of members of a profession. Licensing may be of two kinds: (1) title licensing—legal regulation specifying the qualifications necessary to use a professional title (who can call themselves social workers, for example); (2) practice licensing—legal regulation specifying that certain professional activities may only be performed by members of a particular profession. Practice licensing usually includes title licensing.

Life cycle   The progression from birth to death through socially structured experiences related to chronological age. At each point in the life cycle, the individual draws upon physical and social resources to solve problems and achieve gratification.

Lobbyist   A person paid to represent the interests of a person, group, or organization in the political and legislative processes.

Market   The economic mechanism that relates consumer demand to producer supply.

Manifest functions of social welfare   Functions that are highly visible and intended by most people in society.

Means test   A test of eligibility for aid in which applicants must demonstrate that their financial resources are below the level specified by the program from which help is being sought.

Medicaid   A federal-state grant-in-aid medical-care program for the needy.

Medicare   A federal social insurance medical-care program for the elderly.

Mobilizer role   Part of an interventive strategy, mobilization involves helping users to employ existing services more effectively.

Monopolistic social welfare services   The lack of choice in social welfare programs. Often only one program exists to meet a need, leaving the user no choice about where to turn for help.

Negative income tax   A tax system in which those whose income falls above a predetermined level pay an income tax, while those with incomes below this level receive a supplement.

New Deal   Legislative actions aimed at restoring the nation's economic health enacted during the presidency of Franklin D. Roosevelt.

New Federalism   Transferring as much decision making as possible from the federal government to the states. This concept was developed by Richard Nixon and implemented during his presidency, and involved transferring funds from the federal to the state governments through a process called revenue sharing.

New Frontier   President John F. Kennedy's concept that the future development of society lay in the area of social justice and improved social welfare programs.

Nonjudgmental attitude   Separating attitudes about a person from attitudes about that person's behavior. Although the behavior may be unacceptable, the person continues to be accepted as a worthwhile, autonomous individual.

Nuclear family   The form of the family comprised of two generations, parents and their children. Under special circumstances, other blood-related or nonblood-related persons may be regular members of a nuclear family.

Objective research approach   Research that uses systematically collected data as the basis for decision making.

Obstacles   Whatever makes it more difficult for people to function, meet their needs, or solve problems.

Old Age, Survivors, Disability, and Health Insurance (OASDHI)   A federal social insurance income maintenance program for retired and disabled persons and their families.

Ombudsman   A person or agency that reaches out into the community to identify need and help people in need make use of appropriate social welfare resources (or develop such resources if they don't already exist).

Outdoor relief   The provision of welfare services to persons who are living in their own homes. This is the major form of welfare services provided in this country today.

Outreach role   Part of an interventive strategy, outreach involves reaching out into the community to identify need and to follow up referrals to service contexts.

Paraprofessional   Helping people whose training develops technical skill focused on particular types of problems. Home health aides and mental-health technicians are examples.

Parish   In Tudor England, the local governmental unit providing for public welfare services and payments. Roughly equivalent to our modern-day counties.

Participation of the poor   The belief incorporated in the Economic Opportunity Act that the poor should be involved in planning the programs that will affect them.

Passing on   The practice, common in Colonial America, of transporting people to their legal residence if they became dependent.

Personal social services   See social services.

Personality   The individual's distinctive and regular manner of confronting and dealing with persons, problems, and situations.

Pluralism   The expectation that major groups in American society will define and protect their own interests. It is assumed that coalitions will be formed among groups, based on compromises that allow each group to have its major interests represented in the political process.

Policy   The decision making that uses the political and administrative processes to identify and plan economic and social objectives.

Political institution   The major social structure for allocating power through a system of government.

Position   A named collection of persons performing similar functional behaviors.

Poverty   A condition in which economic resources are inadequate to provide the basic necessities of life as defined by a society. Poverty is both the objective reality that basic necessities are lacking and the subjective reality that one lives on the fringe of society.

Power   The ability of one person to influence others regardless of the wishes of the person being influenced. Bases of power include expertise, legitimacy, the ability to reward or punish, and identification (the ability to win the affection of the person being influenced).

Practice wisdom   The understanding resulting from accumulated practice experience.

Preventive social welfare services   Services provided before a problem exists, in an attempt to prevent the problem from arising.

Private income-transfer program   Using monies voluntarily donated by one group for the benefit of other groups.

Private practice   Professional helping in which the helpers work out of their own private offices to provide services to users.

Private social welfare services   Those that are funded from private monies, exist by mandate from an agency's policy-making body, and are administered in an agency supported mostly by privately earned or donated funds.

Problem solving   The part of the helping process that involves the gathering of information, defining problem situations, assessing helping resources and obstacles, formulating a plan of action to solve the problems identified, and evaluating the success of the plan after it is carried out.

Problem-solving process   The part of the helping process that involves communicating effectively with others, relating effectively to others, assessing situations holistically, planning with others, carrying out plans, and evaluating the results of the helping effort.

Process goal   Using the helping process to enable users to learn how to meet their needs in the future.

Profession   An organization of specialists that emphasizes (1) using specialized knowledge and skills to serve the public and (2) close colleague relationships to ensure competence in professional training and performance.

Professional   Helping people whose training combines knowledge, values, and technical skills useful for managing the professional helping process in specified problem areas.

Professional credentialing   Standards established by a profession that indicate that practitioners have met criteria established by that group's professional association.

Professional objectivity   The ability to systematically evaluate people and their situations in an unbiased and factual but caring way.

Progressive tax   One that taxes a larger percentage of the income of high-income people than of those with low income.

Psychoanalytic theory   A theory of personality development formulated by Sigmund Freud. It asserts that the three major personality structures—the id, ego, and superego—result from the competition between the demands of society and the attempts of the physical organism to find gratification.

Public social utilities   Alternative term for universal social welfare services.

Public social welfare services   Those that are funded from public monies, exist by public mandate, and are administered by publicly funded agencies.

Referral   Sending a user to another social welfare resource when an agency is not able to provide the help needed. In some cases, users may be referred to a more appropriate helping person within one agency. Referral involves the identification of a more appropriate resource and follow-through to ensure that the user actually receives service as intended.

Regressive tax   One that taxes a larger percentage of the income of low-income people than of those with high incomes.

Rehabilitative social welfare services   Services that are provided to solve an already-existing problem and to prevent its recurrence in the future.

Research The collection and analysis of data in order to assess the effectiveness of interventive efforts and the operation of any part of the social welfare institution.

Residence requirement Making the receipt of welfare benefits contingent upon residence in a specified geographic area for a specified period of time.

Residual social welfare services Social welfare services that are provided only to those who can prove need and who qualify by meeting restrictive eligibility requirements.

Resources Whatever helps people function, meet their needs, or solve problems.

Revenue sharing A program that provides local communities with federal funds and allows them to decide how the money should be spent. Revenue sharing was developed as part of President Nixon's New Federalism.

Role Norms associated with a position.

Rural community A community characterized by small population size, low population density, a relatively homogeneous population, and relative isolation from other communities.

Separate but equal The provision of separate facilities, supposedly of equal quality, for members of different (usually racial) groups; most often used in maintaining racial segregation, and struck down as unconstitutional by the Supreme Court in 1954.

Separation of powers The organizing principle, underlying the federal political structure, that provides a system of checks and balances to prevent one branch of the government from controlling the whole structure of government.

Settlement house A community facility for helping residents meet their social, recreational, educational, and collective-action needs.

Sliding scale of fees The setting of fees for services according to the ability of users to pay.

Social change Change within a part of the social structure that occurs without destroying the structure's identity.

Social Darwinism An extension of Charles Darwin's biological concept of survival of the fittest to social life. Social Darwinism maintained that those who were needy were less fit than those who were not and therefore should not be helped because the society would only be preserving defective individuals who could never be self-sufficient.

Social differentiation Socially defined distinctions between groups on the basis of ascriptive criteria (age, sex, race, and the like), or achieved criteria (income, occupation, education, and so on).

Social dividend A cash payment to all members of society regardless of income.

Social history Obtaining background information about a client that forms the basis of diagnosis and problem solving.

Social institution Structured behaviors and norms organized so as to meet a significant societal objective.

Social insurance Programs for meeting people's needs that are funded by contributions these people have made during periods when they are not in need (unemployment insurance, for example).

Social Security Act Legislation, enacted in 1935 and modified numerous times since then, that established the basic structure of our existing federal social insurance and grant-in-aid programs.

Social services Those that help people meet their nonfinancial needs.

Social welfare Improving social functioning and minimizing suffering through a system of socially approved financial and social services at all levels in the social structure.

Social work A socially legitimated profession that seeks to help people singly and in groups to meet their needs and achieve satisfaction in their daily lives.

Socialization Learning the norms and accepted behavior patterns of the culture in which one lives.

Speenhamland Act Legislation, passed in 1796 in England to help eradicate poverty, that provided a guaranteed income based on the concept of the bread scale.

Subjective research approach Research that uses the systematically collected views of those being studied as the basis for decision making.

Supplemental Security Income (SSI) A federal income-maintenance grant-in-aid program for the needy blind, disabled, and elderly.

Supply-side economics President Ronald Reagan's belief that stimulating business would reduce inflation, decrease unemployment, and reduce poverty.

Supportive social welfare services Services that aid people by helping them to achieve their life goals within the unchangeable limitations they face.

System An organized interrelated group of activities, each of which affects the others. In its broadest sense, the social system is the organization of the parts of the structure of a society in such a way that the functional interdependence that results enables the society to survive. Within the social system are a number of subsystems that are internally cohesive but also affect each other.

Task goal A specific task that is the focus of a helping effort.

Tax allowance Allowing an individual, group, or organization to exclude certain income from the total income on which tax is calculated.

Teamwork The collaboration of helping persons from several professions in order to address problems in a holistic way.

Third party payments Payment for social welfare services made from a source outside of the helper-user combination. An example would be Medicare paying a hospital bill.

Total institution An agency with total control over the users who live within it and that is somewhat isolated from the community in which it exists.

Underclass People cut off from society because of inappropriate education, skills, and socialization.

Unemployment Insurance A federal-state social insurance program for the involuntarily unemployed.

Universal social welfare services Services that are considered the rights of members of a society and provided as a regular part of societal life.

Urban community A community characterized by large population size, high population density, a heterogeneous population, and extensive ties with other communities.

Users of services People seeking help.

User participation The degree to which the people who need and use social welfare programs have the opportunity to participate in program planning and evaluation.

Volunteers Nonprofessionals who voluntarily contribute their time to help formal structures operate more effectively.

War on Poverty A major legislative thrust to eradicate poverty during the presidency of Lyndon B. Johnson, the keystone of which was the Economic Opportunity Act of 1964.

Warning out The practice of refusing residence to people judged by the community as likely to become dependent on welfare in the future.

Workfare The belief that people receiving financial aid should be required to work in return for this aid. Because the majority of financial aid recipients cannot work, for a variety of social and physical reasons, this concept contains an inherent contradiction.

Workhouse or house of correction An archaic facility that housed those considered shiftless (the illegitimately needy), in which the basic life-sustaining needs were met in return for forced work.

Workmen's Compensation A social insurance program to cover work-connected injury.

INDEX

4 5 6 7 8 9 0

29.50

361.973
F317

122119

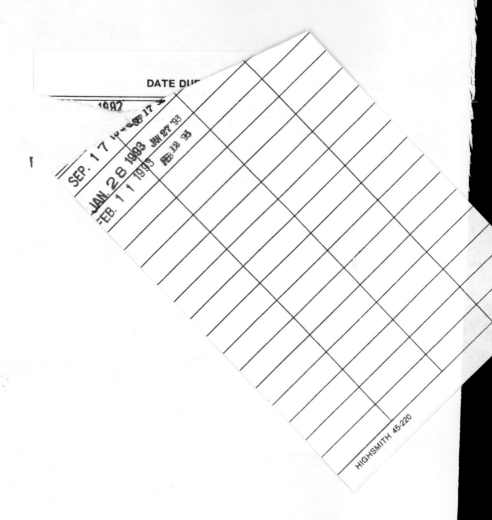

DATE DUE

1982

SEP. 1 7 1992   SEP 17

JAN. 2 8 1993   JAN 27 '93

FEB. 1 1 1993   FEB 12 '93

HIGHSMITH 45-220